THE MORAL MANAGER

CONSULTING EDITOR
EDWIN M. EPSTEIN
University of California, Berkeley

THE MORAL MANAGER

CLARENCE C. WALTON
Lamont Post Distinguished Professor
The American College
Bryn Mawr, Pennsylvania

HarperBusiness
A Division of HarperCollins*Publishers*

To my family

International Standard Book Number: 0–88730–309–9 (cloth)
0–88730–447–8 (paper)

Library of Congress Catalog Card Number: 88-11966

Printed in the United States of America

Library of Congress Cataloging-in-Publication Data

Walton, Clarence Cyril, 1915-
   The moral manager / Clarence C. Walton.
      p.   cm.
   Includes index.
   ISBN 0–88730–309–9 (cloth)
   ISBN 0–88730–447–8 (paper)
   1. Business ethics—United States.   2. Executives—Professional ethics—United States.   3. Corporations—United States—Corrupt practices.   I. Title.
HF5387.W324   1988
174'.4—dc19   88-11966
   91 92 93 HC 9 8 7 6 5 4 3 2

CONTENTS

v

PART III: THE "ETHIC" OF CHARACTER

PREFACE

Completion of a book brings a Proustian "remembrance of things past": days of frustration and exhilaration, support denied and help volunteered, colleagues' benign neglect and colleagues' enthusiastic support. Above all, the most remembered thing is the emotion of gratitude and the need to express it. My debts are many. Among my "creditors," however, are a few whose support has been extraordinary— people like Dr. Ronald Ziegler who performed invaluable research during the first stages of this book, as well as colleagues like Professors Edwin Epstein of the University of California at Berkeley, James Glenn of San Francisco State University, and Manuel Velasquez of Santa Clara University who critically read the manuscript. Above all, however, is Helen Schmidt of the American College in Bryn Mawr, Pennsylvania. Typist *extraordinaire* and superb critic, Ms. Schmidt pushed and prodded until the manuscript was complete. Working with me taxed her editorial ingenuity and, even more, her patience.

Finally, there is need to acknowledge the support of the American College as well as the Richard D. and Marie Irwin Foundation for providing generous support to the author. Beyond the foundation grant, in a rare expression of confidence and interest, Mr. Irwin made several welcomed suggestions that improved the work. To the few named and the many unnamed goes my total gratitude.

INTRODUCTION

John F. Budd, Jr., senior vice president, Emhart Corporation: "Business is beginning to recognize, the hard way, as usual, that there is a need to manage the factors that influence a reputation (of which ethics is a basic) just as carefully as they manage production, corporate finance and other basic functions . . . and to communicate this stewardship."[1]

DePaul University professor *Paul Camenisch*: "It is impossible and undesirable to speak of moral leadership *within* business without also speaking of moral leadership *by* business in the larger society."[2]

The Honorable Abdul-Latif, deputy governor of the Saudi Arabian Monetary Agency: "It is time for world leaders to forego expediency and return to those 'age-old moral values' of civilized conduct that have stood the test of time."[3]

Victoria Sackett, deputy manager for *Public Opinion*: "Ann Landers, described as the 'closest thing to a shrine the secular world has to offer' (she knew right from wrong and labeled our behavior as one or the other without flinching), confessed in October of 1986 that she was just 'as befuddled as everyone else' over what are basic values."[4]

Author and corporate lawyer *Louis Auchincloss*: "I wonder if there are any rules now? Do people care about anything else beyond being caught? Not from where I sit."[5]

THE DILEMMA

Comments from a quintet composed of a corporate executive, university-based philosopher, civil servant, media celebrity, and business lawyer are like tracer bullets forming bewitching trajectories in a night

1

sky. From the first three come calls for action; from the last two, cries of anguish. Why summon and cry characterize this small chorus may be explained by various factors, one of which is clear evidence of misbehavior. Less noted, but important, is the current state of management theory. Contrast illumines the point. Chester Barnard, the philosopher-king of New Jersey Bell Telephone, more than anyone else, won support for the idea that one very important role of an executive was to serve as a moral teacher for the company's employees. It was the executive who provided the incentives and conditions that induced employees to adopt attitudes and values supportive of the organization's goal and supportive, as well, of their own needs.[6] Barnard's ideas were accepted and refined in a series of brilliant essays by Nobel Laureate Herbert Simon of Carnegie-Mellon. Although skeptical of attempts to prove or disprove values, Simon recognized that decision making in organizational settings "always had ethical as well as factual content."[7]

Implicit in this strand of management theory was the idea that managers who "taught" values were themselves well schooled in values; knowing what was right and living by what was right, they could teach others what was moral and immoral behavior in the work environment. Today, however, concerns are expressed that too many managers have retained Barnard's rhetoric and lost his premise. To critics, teaching has become manipulation and the high ground of morality has collapsed into a pit of "me-first management";[8] it seems indeed that affairs have become so bad that contemporary management style and theory are "light years away from the [Barnard] vision [of moral leadership] and [have] taken a direction that does not represent progress."[9]

While the latest rash of misconduct in business's ranks does indeed support a gloomy assessment, it should be noted that miscreants have always been found in the ranks. So, too, have heroes. Perspective suggests, therefore, that many current portraits are too darkly drawn. Significant advances have come: child labor is proscribed; collective bargaining is accepted; *caveat emptor* (let the buyer beware) no longer reigns supreme; the arbitrariness of the employment-at-will doctrine is under attack. Because, however, business has historically been reactive, these advances have come from externs who presumably had a keener sense of ethics. But today's business leaders cannot wait for others to lead. Greater concern for social justice in the United States and throughout many parts of the globe drives key players in the corporate community toward a more proactive role. Instead of waiting

—often sullenly—for others to tell them what is morally right, managers seek to learn what is right. This means repeated forays into the world of ideas because, for good or evil, ideas shake the world and leaders shape it. In the long term, values count even more than money. To speak of values, however, is to take a number of calculated risks, and four deserve specific mention:

1. This kind of analysis, conceptual in nature and deductive in approach, runs contrary to contemporary scholarly trends that stress empirical investigations and quantification of results. Consequently, some may dismiss it as "soft" knowledge.
2. The sweep of the inquiry carries with it the vulnerability of serious misinterpretations. To speak of Athenian philosophers, English political theorists, American judges, and organizational analysts in short compass is risky business.
3. Value inquiry, if not related to specific recommendations for "quick fix" organizational improvements, often becomes unpalatable, if not downright indigestible, to pragmatic minds. The only reply, too flavorless for some tastes, is that synthesis provides the vision—the architectural design—according to which (and from which) specific applications can be made to specific needs.
4. Related to the preceding point is another problem of relevance. Values are rated differently in diverse cultures, mirrored differently in particular industries, and prioritized differently by individual managers. Values important to some are irrelevant to others.

AUTHORS AS INTERLOPERS

Theorists speak mainly through books, and when a book enters a home or falls into a hand, its covers enclose something more than text. For with messages come message makers, authors who can never fully escape the prisons of their own experiences. It follows, therefore, that interactions between readers and writers are something more than relationships of pages to persons. Readers rarely ask what they have every right to know: By what warrant does a particular author presume to speak? What experiences justify the presumption? What do writers expect to accomplish? As the reader am I ready for them? More importantly, are they ready for me?

The questions, all legitimate, raise the danger of encouraging writers to unveil, albeit unintentionally, a plethora of details that transform serious inquiry into frivolous memoir. With parsimony as disciplinarian, let it be noted only that this author has had a long scholarly interest in the field of organizational values, long administrative experience as a Columbia University dean during the troubled 1960s and as president of the Catholic University of America during the troubled 1970s, substantial involvement on corporate and college boards, and services as chair of a presidential panel on education and a state commission on fair housing. The assignments brought contacts with powerful people, and the odyssey raised numerous questions, all of which ultimately dissolved into one: why did some individuals have the staying power of the authentic leader while others lacked it? The question led to others—and still others—until a suspicion became a conviction. Leadership, an ill-defined word, comes from understanding and respecting four crucial ideals: equality, justice, truth, and freedom. Understanding them is what moral education is all about. Such education comes first from families and friends, schools and churches.

Further inputs influencing managers are co-workers and other managers. Such influences, however, tend to come in stops and spurts, and their rearrangements into a new synthesis require reflection. At the reflective level, moral philosophers claim a special competence, even when they talk loosely about "admirable immoralities."[10] Some even argue that people who believe this would be the best possible world if morality were universally practiced should "rethink their position since there are good reasons to be grateful that such a world does not, in fact, exist."[11] The "good reasons" often turn out to be lame rationalizations: refuges for the confused or sanctuaries for the wicked. Reason, on the other hand, seeks clarity—and that is what moral inquiry aims to provide.

THE INTENDED AUDIENCE

Borrowing from the grammarian's vocabulary, one might speak of "exclamation point" and "question mark" (QM) people, respectively. The first accept orders and propositions rather uncritically: a stay-off-the-grass sign in a public park means exactly what it says. QM people, more pesky, ask whether lovely lawns are more important than happy children. Just as sentences need both types of punctuation, so do societies need both types of people. But only QM types induce change.

They have asked: Why should every Ford car be black? Why should women not vote? Why should blacks sit in the back of buses? Why should workers not unionize? Why should business schools be established? In the light of history, such questions seem childish. But pain and suffering were endured before answers were given. To oversimplify, progress starts with people asking questions that lead to new answers and, invariably, new problems.

What, then, are the QM people now saying? The following are illustrative: Are antitrust laws, as currently interpreted and administered, helpful to American corporations facing stiff competition from the state monopolies of other countries? Is tort law going in the right direction? Will there be international unions? Should megamergers continue? Will the computer spawn a cottage industry? How will robots change the work rules? Do managers need sabbaticals? Is the comparable-worth doctrine a "cockamamy" (President Reagan's word) idea? Should the one-stock, one-vote rule be discarded by the New York Stock Exchange? Is community involvement in plant-relocation decisions a sensible idea? Does worker privacy impede organizational effectiveness? Is the breakdown of distinctions among insurance companies, commercial banks, and investment houses good for America? Should libel law change? In restructuring, what compensation should be given to those who pay the highest price? What impact will the April 1987 Supreme Court ruling (which allowed minorities to receive preferential treatment) have on the work force? Is it right for corporations to secure patents for inventing new forms of life?

Specific questions beg for specific answers. Managers expecting moral "quick fixes" will be disappointed. Managers, as well as others, seeking to locate moral microscopes to examine the social organism should be helped. One thing is clear: answers will involve moral components. So this book's natural affinity toward the "QMers" quickly becomes apparent. Constituting the QM genus are specific species, each of whom may find this text more useful for some purposes than for others. The intended reading audience falls therefore into five types:

1. Senior managers who have the inclination and time to reexamine their intellectual and moral roots. By so doing they can respond positively to former Du Pont chairman Irving Shapiro's message that the United States is experiencing a revolution for social justice where business leaders should play a part.
2. Midmanagers who want to become senior executives.

3. Human resource personnel who seek to provide background material for participants asked to discuss ethical issues in their executive development programs.
4. Professors responsible for preparing students for management.
5. Students of two types: (1) business majors who have substantial gaps in their liberal arts preparation and (2) liberal arts students who seek to link their knowledge to the practical world of business.

So far as professors and students are concerned, a special comment is required. In planning this book, an assumption was made that undergraduate education has lost focus with respect to its moral component. This assumption has been reinforced by three commentaries that appeared after the manuscript had been completed but before it had been received by the publisher. Three excerpts are illustrative:

• Allan Bloom's indictment of higher education for its capitulation to a moral relativism "which has extinguished the real motive of education: the search for a good life."[12]
• A report on students entering college that showed how, between 1967 and 1987, the number of freshmen who felt it important to develop a philosophy of life had dropped dramatically from 83 to 43 percent.[13]
• Harvard's 350th anniversary or, more accurately, a review of a book commemorating the event by a Harvard College graduate, John Wauck. Noting how Charles W. Eliot's long tenure as president (1869–1909) was a turning point in Harvard's history (because the institution introduced the elective system in liberal education and adopted Germany's model of a research center populated by professional scholars), Wauck wrote:

> For a brief period, the two ideals—of liberal education and professional scholarship—coexisted. This was Harvard's "Golden Age." . . . Professors of the "Golden Age" were not simply expounding upon their fields of expertise, they were selling philosophies of life and trying to shape the young men they faced. . . . [But] the ultimate consequence of the freedom of the purely elective system was an abdication of Harvard's responsibility to give a thorough liberal education to undergraduates . . .
>
> Harvard's diversity has one other consequence: it cultivates a spirit of jaded indifference to the spectacle of people and events. Having grown up in the circus, the Harvard student refused to be impressed

or surprised by anything. Not that he could do better; it's just that he's seen every trick before. Combined with a manner assimilated from wealthy classmates, this indifference often passes for snobbery, but it is usually simple ignorance: an inability to recognize what is distinctive and important. This approach to people and ideas ensures a bland, unbiased tolerance, but it guarantees no wisdom; it produces intellectuals rather than intelligent men and women.[14]

The conclusion may be too harsh. But even if a less astringent criticism is made of the flagship of American universities, it is important to take seriously Professor Bloom's charge that higher education has failed democracy and impoverished the soul of today's student. It is therefore essential for authors to try, in modest and diverse ways, to compensate for such omissions.

Making more explicit this writer's intent requires clarity on certain specifics, among which are the following:

1. The text takes into account the caveat raised by Stanford's Kirk Hanson, ethical consultant to more than twenty corporations, who said, "Executives need no one telling them what is right and wrong; they need someone to ask questions they can't ask of themselves."[15] This comment tends to promote a method of inquiry called quandary ethics, which focuses on situations in which it is difficult to know what to do—the famous gray areas of morality. The quandary ethics approach is too important to be ignored. It would be a mistake, however, to stop with quandary ethics because it can become quite ad hoc, much as the common law was ad hoc, but lacking the common law's capacity to grow into a rather consistent body of principles.[16]

2. The study acknowledges the value of certain strands in contemporary philosophy that focus on principles to define what is permissible and what is prohibited—the approach popularized by the great eighteenth-century German philosopher Immanuel Kant. But it seeks to add to this dimension the fruits of an older tradition that goes back to Plato and Aristotle, who emphasized moral character—what it is, how it grows, and who shapes it. Philosophers are shy about entering this domain because the effort can quickly wander from education to indoctrination. But their fear is no excuse for inattention to the importance of moral character. Teachers cannot ignore what leaders cannot do without.

3. Respected is the dividing line between philosophy and theology.[17] Ethical inquiry is based, quite properly, on reason and not on faith; it is the arena where skeptics and believers can commingle in relative harmony. To stay scrupulously within the field of ethics, however, risks neglecting the importance of a Judeo-Christian tradition that has molded the civilization of which America is a part. The stern Calvinists of New England may have been buried, but their ideas have not been completely banished. No one can speak meaningfully of the "civil religion" without knowing something about those other religions from which it draws some of its substance and from which it often departs. Few can understand the "work ethic" without knowing something of its religious source.

4. Caught up in analysis of principles, ethicians may ignore the "lived ethic," that is, those fundamental values which hold the community together. If Camenisch (whose comment was noted briefly at the beginning of this introduction) is right, then everyone must deal with the lived ethic because it influences both individual and organizational decision-making.

SPECIAL FEATURES

The circle may now be closed by a final reference to the question-mark readers: To encourage them to reexamine themselves even as they reappraise moral issues, two features have been used in somewhat novel ways. The first is a values quiz that appears at the beginning of each chapter. Readers are invited to record their instinctive reactions to the statements and then review them after the chapter has been read. If the return produces few changes, some may believe that the reading is love's labor lost. But this misses the point. The real issue is whether answers can be more logically defended. And where changes are made to original responses, the reader knows that the critical checkpoint, having been reached, provides opportunities for further competence in managerial decision-making.

The second feature is the interspersing of "scenarios." What gives scenario analysis its value is not the minicase itself but, rather, the way it raises different sets of values that decision makers have to weigh: values of the culture, tenets of the ideology, the power of the ideologues, the principles of ethics, the decision makers' own character, and the values of their organizations. Attempts at reconciliation of conflicting values can lead to moral schizophrenia. To avoid the danger, it is necessary to ask more questions: Which values are morally more compelling? How is the choice logically defended? When does the high road impact the bottom line? Am I prepared to pay the price? These indeed constitute the moral dimension of a manager's development.

One final note: in approaching this book, readers may draw positive reasons for doing so from the penultimate paragraph of a November 1987 report on America's declining competitiveness issued by the American Assembly, a prestigious association connected with Columbia University:

> On the important subject of values, we discern a marked deterioration in traditional values essential to competitiveness. A lack of both individual and institutional leadership has eroded respect for community and nationhood. We conclude that values of integrity, social justice, and moral leadership are not only necessary in themselves, but lead directly to competitive advantage. *Our standard of living and our standard of values are inseparable.*[18]

Note: Since the primary purpose of this book is to stimulate thoughtful consideration of questions as much as logical analysis of proposed solutions, each chapter is introduced by a values quiz. No protocol is provided to judge the correctness of an answer. Once intellectual appetites have been whetted, however, the reader is urged to return to the quiz *after* the chapter has been completed to see if answers to certain statements might be given differently. In this way, differences between "instinctive" first answers and more considered second answers can be noted—and weighed.

1

GATEWAY TO THE MANAGERIAL WORLD

THE VALUES QUIZ *(Mark True or False)*

1. _____ People with great power in an organization who violate the law should be punished more severely than people with little power who commit the same illegal act.
2. _____ Leaders should be treated more generously than followers for moral lapses in their private lives because they carry burdens heavier than those borne by followers.
3. _____ Reaching the company parking lot after work, you notice that adjacent to your car is your friend's car with a flat tire. You are ethically obligated to help in some way.
4. _____ Managers are not morally responsible for those acts performed by subordinates which, unknown to the manager, violate written company policies or public laws.
5. _____ If management contributes money for an employee Christmas party at which an employee gets drunk and later, while driving home, kills a bystander, management is morally responsible.
6. _____ The best way to judge whether CEOs have behaved morally is to see whether they acted in ways that their peers would have acted under similar circumstances.
7. _____ Law sets the moral responsibilities for business. Going beyond the law in the belief that more is required to be ethical is really irresponsible.
8. _____ When a manager's personal value system collides with the organization's value system, the latter takes precedence so long as the manager continues to be employed by the enterprise.

11

Whether genetic endowment, formal education, good luck, or acquired skills—or a combination —determines who heads organizations, the fact is that the top dogs constitute a breed apart. They respond to a variety of pressures and oversee various kinds of people. Often they develop a particular "style" that allows subordinates to anticipate their superiors' expectations and guard against their foibles. The common denominator in management's repertoire of skills is the "human skill," that is, the capacity to teach others what is important and what is incidental to the organization, what is moral and what is not. Not infrequently, however, managers are driven to ask the same question that Kaiser Wilhelm asked when confronted by a diplomatic crisis involving Germany's interest abroad: "Morality is all right, but what about the dividends?" The quick answer, of course, is responsible action, but what constitutes responsible action is often a matter of debate.

There are differences between responsibility as seen through the legal prism and responsibility as viewed from moral perspectives. Managers have been held accountable when they are not responsible. The first step in identifying the differences is to examine court decisions and ask, Does the verdict agree with my own and society's view of moral responsibility? Often honest people differ in their responses. The "difference factor" suggests the need to look in greater depth at those variables which make for such divergences. One such variable is level of responsibility. Drawing on his rich resources as chief executive of New Jersey Bell Telephone, Chester Barnard wrote compellingly of managerial functions:

> *In executive ranks . . . the tendency of activity to increase with scope of position is often controllable. The increase in complexity of moral conditions, however, is not controllable by the person affected, so that despite control of activities, the burden increases from conflicts of morals as the scope of the executive position broadens. . . . The important distinctions of rank lie in the fact that the higher the grade the more complex the moralities involved, and the more necessary higher abilities to discharge the responsibilities, that is, to resolve the moral conflicts implicit in the positions.[1]*

Especially noteworthy is Barnard's stress on the moral aspects of managerial responsibility, which arise from a role that makes the actor accountable to a higher authority. But when the law looks at the idea, it tends to define responsibility in such negative terms as negligence or culpability. When speaking of responsibility, it is important to remember that obligations exist to the self as well as to others—the organization (role) and society. In the following treatment, responsibility is viewed more from moral than from legal perspectives, but both culpability and obligation inhere in its meaning.

12

PERCEPTIONS

Management's importance to human progress has been traced rather simply in clocks and guns. Technologically speaking, the industrial age began in Milan during the early fourteenth century with the gear-driven time clock. All the mechanical hardware and engineering knowledge associated with the machinery of the industrial revolution were available during that century in small shops. But it was not until 1798 that Eli Whitney put technology into the more productive hands of organized unskilled labor by creating large-scale factories to replace one-worker rooms. It took more than four hundred years to go from Milan's clock to the marvel of organization represented by Whitney's musket factory. Managers organize people to do more effectively what individuals, working alone, cannot do. Moving and motivating people provide moral opportunities—and moral hazards.

If there is a unifying thread in what managers do, there is wide diversity in the way they actually perform. At their best, managers are like conductors of symphony orchestras—minor gods with an uncanny knack for performing miracles so convincing that people feel that what they are witnessing is, in its ultimate satisfaction, comparable to the quiet excitement gemologists feel when they view a perfect jewel under the microscope. IBM's Thomas Watson, Jr., Sears's Robert E. Wood, Hewlett-Packard's David Packard, General Motors's Alfred Sloan, NASA's James Webb, and General Electric's Owen D. Young illustrate this kind of virtuosity. Such executives reinforce the observation of anthropologist A.M. Hocart, who, fifty years ago, said that the "invention of a man who did not work with his hands, but merely existed and acted on his environment at a distance, like the sun, was one of the most momentous in the history of man; it was nothing less than the invention of government."[2] All organizations, public and private, require managers who resonate to John Ruskin's comment that bureaucracy without ethics is brutality and power without principle is corruption. Since ethical and nonethical executives coexist, sometimes even in relative harmony, and since both types can significantly shape a society, others have as much a vested interest in watching them as they have in observing themselves. Executives are seen through two kinds of glass: mirrors in which they see themselves and windows in which others see them.

The Mirror: Time Traps and Moral Pits

A mirror view reveals the caricature drawn by an unknown author, who wrote:

> As nearly everyone knows, an executive has practically nothing to do except to decide what is to be done; to tell somebody to do it; to listen to reasons why it should not be done, why it should be done by someone else, or why it should be done in a different way; to follow up to see if the thing has been done; to discover that it has not; to inquire why; to listen to excuses from the person who should have done it; to follow it up again to see if the thing has been done, only to discover that it has been done incorrectly; to point out how it should have been done; to conclude that as long as it has to be done, it may as well be left where it is; to wonder if it is not time to get rid of a person who cannot do anything right; to reflect that he probably has a wife and a large family, and that certainly any successor would be just as bad, and maybe worse; to consider how much simpler and better the thing would have been done if one had done it oneself in the first place; to reflect sadly that one could have done it right in twenty minutes, and, as things turned out, one has had to spend two days to find out why it has taken three weeks for somebody else to do it wrong.[3]

Like all caricatures, the description has an element of truth, and the ethical inferences to be drawn therefrom are important because they profile some of the more serious moral entrapments managers face. Time in one such trap. It has been estimated that 80 percent of the executive's work goes to trivia while major issues occupy only 20 percent of the time.[4] This "tyranny of trivia" often spawns such indifference to value issues that ethical concerns are discussed infrequently in executive suites until crisis strikes.[5] Time entrapments, therefore, often mean moral entrapments, and multiplicity of rushed interpersonal contacts dulls sensitivities. Reviewing his years as chairman and CEO of Baxter Travenoll Laboratories, William Graham asked, "How can anyone possibly keep up with all the people you want to see?" But Warren Bennis, a former university president, thought the reverse: too many people wanted to see him. He reported conversations with many new presidents of widely different enterprises during which

> each one told me the biggest mistake he made was to take on too much, as if proving oneself depended on providing instant solutions, and success was dependent on immediate achievements. . . . People were following

the old army game. They did not want to take the responsibility or bear the consequences of decisions they properly should make. The motto was "Let's push up the tough ones." The consequence was that everybody and anybody was dumping his "wet babies" (as the old State Department hands call them) on my desk, when I had neither the diapers nor the information to take care of them.[6]

Life in executive suites is a pressure cooker with recurring temptations to move in, take over, and move out. Henry Mintzberg's acclaimed study of the manager's hectic workday may have intrigued scholars but only confirmed what they already knew: time for reflection was overwhelmed by time for reaction.[7] Short-term priorities have been institutionalized—in political life (four years for the American president, six for a senator, a meager two years for a congressperson), in academic life (five-year contracts for university presidents), in business life by the annual report (now supplemented by quarterly reports requested by the Securities and Exchange Commission), by investor sensitivity to daily company performance, and by a brutal disciplinarian called Wall Street.

Dealing with things judged chiefly by the near term leads to other complications. For one thing, the line between an employer's use and abuse of workers becomes blurred. Walter E. Elliott, an industrial psychologist from Cincinnati, found from his study of senior managers that they often grow more self-centered and selfish and that, when they do, they increasingly rationalize their unethical behavior. A California psychologist, Charles Ansell, spoke of the "loss of conscience" not only in businesspersons but among everyone who does not see the victims. To rip off a bank, a telephone company, or an insurance company is to hurt no one because the company passes on added costs to so many customers that no single individual feels the pain. Depersonalization and distance dull moral vision. If the slowly grinding mills of the gods bring retribution, administrators are often the last to see any relation between cause and effect. By virtue of their position, however, managers are not like others. They cannot follow the advice tendered to journalists by one of the profession's most trusted and revered members, Walter Cronkite: "I don't think it is any of our business what the moral, political, social or economic effect of our reporting is. I say, 'Let's get on with the job of reporting the news —and let the chips fall where they may.' "[8] The stakes for large organizations are simply too high for such advice to be useful. Managers constitute a breed different from journalists and, for that matter, different from lawyers, accountants, doctors, and professors.

The Window View

From a window view, outsiders have a quite different impression. They see managers as people who earn a living by pressuring others to earn theirs; in a sense, managers are primarily nonproducers who alternately persuade and cajole, command and coerce, and praise and condemn to suit their need. Since all elements are part of administration, it is easy to focus on the less attractive activities and conclude that managers are primarily tyrants or manipulators. Further, since managers must assess society's needs to determine which ones their organization will attempt to satisfy, probability of error in forecasting is relatively high. Mistakes are more remembered than accuracies, and the luxury of Monday-morning quarterbacking is one leisure pursuit that nonparticipants in the game do not readily surrender. To be effective, therefore, managers need three kinds of skills: technical, conceptual, and human. Technical expertise reflects the ability to use methods, techniques, and equipment to get the job done; conceptual skills enable managers to see their organizations as systems of interacting and interdependent subsystems that must be linked; and human skill is the one that most directly touches the moral dimension of managerial activity because it involves the capacity to get the best from others by having others get the best from themselves. Of the three, the last is the most difficult to acquire because its competence rests on dealing with the physical, psychological, and moral needs of those persons the manager cannot do without: consumers, workers, and stockholders.

Even when acquired, the human skill can be jettisoned by managers who come, perhaps slowly, to prefer fast returns—for themselves and their organizations—over slow but enduring rewards. That the preference, which leads to a Gresham's law of morality, is becoming quite common was suggested by journalist Anne Crittenden, who wrote:

> *Fortune* may soon have to publish a 500 Most Wanted List. During the past few months the news has been filled with tales of business schemes and scandals, of corporate intrigues and downright crime. The offenses make up a catalog of chicanery: cheating on government defense contracts, check-writing fraud, bogus-securities dealing, tax dodges, insider trading and money laundering.[9]

From the crop of future managers come disquieting signs suggesting that reformation is not around the mythical corner. A young business school graduate wrote that "in all America you will not find a group more openly, unashamedly, exuberantly interested in money than the MBAs of our major business schools."[10] Alarmed by what he has seen, the vice chairman of Berkshire Hathaway, Charles Munger, testified before a congressional subcommittee that today's business was a great stew: "Look at those hostile takeover-related activities, and all this related money-making with no risk by the Jay Gould types which are increasingly predominating in the capital scene, and look at them as salt. In the old days we had a minor amount of salt in the stew; and all of a sudden, somebody's pouring a hell of a lot more salt in the stew."[11]

In the long run, image without substance is too fragile a reed on which to build an organization legitimized by public acceptance of its role. More than most people, managers walk on terrains laced with moral land mines. The position and influence they have, the goods and services they provide, the changing demands they must satisfy, and the tension between role expectations and personal goals—all combine to make their work especially vulnerable to criticism. To speak, however, of a need to restore values is to raise hackles. Some managers fear another muckraker crusade that will make them the source of all evil. In ways reminiscent of Tennyson's attacks on literary critics as "lice on the locks of literature," businesspersons fear they will be made the louse on the locks of society. While some criticism represents a festival of stupidity, literate executives are sensitive to the power of dramatists and novelists. Before their minds flash memories of Arthur Miller's *Death of a Salesman*, F. Scott Fitzgerald's *The Last Tycoon*, Sinclair Lewis's *Babbitt*, and many other works of this genre. Rarely popular among the people, corporate executives simply cannot afford to fuel the discontent by their own misdeeds.

New Breed? Or Breed Apart?

Some elder statesmen of business (retired CEOs like Irving Shapiro of Du Pont, Donald MacNaughton of Prudential, and Reginald Jones of General Electric) have suggested that changing times require a new breed of business leaders. Different revolutions produce different casts of characters. Shapiro noted that the first to confront dramatic new sociopolitical problems in the United States were the country's political leaders and their product was America's first major innovation, a constitutional government established to ensure individual liberty. The second revolution occurred in the mid-nineteenth century when industrialization swept Western society; while the responses of both political and business leaders met with mixed success, the overall result was a mighty industrial and financial machine that brought American economic superiority into the world. The third revolution, still unnamed, is powered by societal ambitions to bring social justice and equality to all; since this last revolt involves all organizations, leaders live under new ground rules that, in turn, will shape the new managerial type. [12]

Framed in the foregoing way, the question of a managerial breed is really the question of environmental impact on an executive's training, outlook, and performance. There is, however, another way of asking the question: Are managers like the Merrill Lynch advertisement—a breed apart? Are their modes of reasoning and their perceptions of time really "distinctive"? Data from both physical and psychological research suggest that managers do indeed constitute a special breed. It has been found, for example, that serotonin, the chemical that carries messages from the brain to other parts of the nervous system, is at a higher level in leaders than among followers. It is speculated that the chemistry of managers differs from that of followers because of the need to be ever alert to dangers and problems. Psychiatrists have suggested that the environment induces changes far more pronounced than previously imagined and that different environments create different psychological states. [13] While the psychological is not the philosophical, their intersections are many and subtle.

In addition, managers are said to possess a kind of intelligence not effectively measured by IQ tests that have predictive value for academic, but little for administrative, success;[14] they welcome complexity and move instinctively to find relationships between the parts and the whole; they have a great capacity for acquiring adequate information without being overwhelmed by it; they do not overplan; they think multidimensionally; they spot hidden patterns in a vast array of facts; they express themselves with a certain spontaneity;[15] they speak of a job well-done rather than of hours painstakingly spent; and despite the trivia they face, they conserve time by following the maxim that "if it ain't broke, don't fix it."[16] Such abilities stand them in good stead when they confront challenges. Perhaps what they need and what the more successful ones among them exhibit most are what Keats (whose achievements in poetry obscured his great skills as a philosopher) called the *negative capability*, the capacity to live amidst "uncertainties, mysteries, doubts, without any irritable reaching after fact."[17] In large organizations and in a complex world, this negative ability is particularly valuable since there rarely is complete command of facts and certainty on the consequences of actions taken. Adding to the complexity of managers' roles is the tension that arises when family and friends experience neglect and yet are fearful to express their feelings.

Public Roles and Private Lives

Managers are society's "commanders" who feel the temptation sometimes to ask for judgments on criteria different from those governing ordinary mortals. Swiss historian Jacob Burckhardt, for example, insisted that because powerful people are subject to powerful temptations, they are exempt from ordinary moral codes.[18] Americans, on the other hand, refuse to grant such exemptions and indeed apply a more stringent criterion: people with power are presumed to have had the intelligence and character to achieve such power and consequently should have the intelligence and character to behave more decently than ordinary folk. Since representative democracy and free markets depend on trust, those to whom much has been entrusted are those of whom more is demanded. In the American value system, public figures are public targets—as the Gary Hart/Joseph Biden episodes revealed—and even relatively small falls from grace can result in big falls from power.

What managers at all levels face is the recurring tension between organizational commitments and personal obligations. Long hours, frequent business trips, and regular transfers segregate managers from the outside world. Managers are also separated from their families and both from whole neighborhoods and other persons. Possibly the most insidious evil is take-home work because it makes managers unavailable to spouses and children. A subtle ruthlessness takes place, and the consequences are plain to see. Managers own their own homes but act like tenants, live in middle-class suburbs but have no neighbors, and enjoy large incomes but possess small wealth.[19] Critics ask whether managers work for a good life or live for good work. A common defense of workaholics is that they "do it for the family," yet spouse and children may have needs that have been consistently ignored. The saddest executives are those who lull themselves into the belief that zeal for and satisfaction in the job justify any burden they foist on others—without stopping to examine the hurt caused by such insensitivity. Whatever circumstances surround an individual's career, certainty exists that the way to the top is begun by many and made by few. Along the way are heartbreaks and hair-raisers, unexpected obstacles and unanticipated assists, old friends lost and new ones found. And, of course, there are the uncommon challenges and the uncommon temptations that come to uncommon people—the small number who have the competencies, character, commitment, and luck to go all the way. The going-all-the-way syndrome can be reduced to one quality: the capacity to take responsibility and exercise it wisely.

ROLE AND RESPONSIBILITY

The Paradox

To consider responsibility is to confront paradox. Responsibility means burdens that must be carried if life itself is to be lightened and enlivened. It means taking the heat when strangers have applied the torch. It affords opportunities of taking credit instead of giving credit. It is shared often with people who do not want it. It can be precisely allocated but imprecisely fulfilled. It always seeks to clarify but often winds up in confusion. Yet without understanding—and accepting —responsibility, bad situations get worse. Relevant is the fable of Everybody, Somebody, Anybody, and Nobody:

> There was an important job to be done.
> And Everybody was sure that Somebody would do it.
> Anybody could have done it but Nobody did it.
> Somebody got angry because it was Everybody's job.
> Everybody thought that Somebody would do it.
> But Nobody asked Anybody.
> It ended up that the job was not done.
> So Everybody blamed Somebody when actually Nobody asked Anybody.

What is fable is often fact in the workaday world, and contrasts between American and non-American executives provide interesting insights into the operational meaning of responsibility. Pulitzer prize winner David Broder commented on the tragedy that killed 520 persons when a Japan Air Lines plane crashed in September 1985. JAL

President Yasumoto Takagi announced immediately that he would resign as soon as the situation had settled down. Such resignations are common in the Japanese business and political worlds, where leaders are held to have ultimate responsibility for all acts of their subordinates. Broder then wrote: "I wonder whether there is not a lesson for us in the way that the Japanese airline executive responded and the contrast to our way of handling such matters . . . I wonder if we have not lost the whole concept of accountability at the top—and with it, a sense of self-discipline and organizational discipline that is essential in a competitive world."[20]

Responsibility consists of knowing what is due to whom and for what, as well as knowing when and how such responses should be made. Timidity in a subordinate's discharging of responsibility has frustrated many senior managers. Such timidity once prompted President Lincoln to write General McClellan: "My dear McClellan, if you do not want to use the army, I should like to borrow it for a while." Ducking responsibility can become a technique for survival in large corporations, for, as Plato observed in the *Republic*, if individuals knew in advance what is expected of leaders, they would run *from* rather than *to* positions of responsibility. One very hard decision is to determine who accepts responsibility.

"No-Duck" Responsibilities

Some situations require direct action by the CEO simply because the responsibility can be neither ducked nor delegated. Such cases occur when need arises to:

- *Field the repercussions of sudden changes.* In the summer of 1985, when Monarch Capital Corporation, a Massachusetts-based life insurance holding company, took action unprecedented among life insurance companies to eliminate the dividends on its common stock, the company's chairman, Benjamin F. Jones, noted: "Because of the potential reaction of the financial community, I decided that every phone call that came to us on this subject would be answered personally by me, by Gordon Oaks, our president, or by our chief financial officer. It was a duty that we absolutely could not delegate."
- *Perform rituals when power and prestige are critical factors.* Jay E. Helme, president of North Ferry Company (which operates car-

and-passenger ferryboats), found his company's application for a fare increase strongly opposed. When he learned that a hearing would be held, he said, "I could have sent our attorney and accountant to take the flak but I wanted everyone to know my personal concern about increasing the riders' costs of travel."

- *Reprimand and discharge.* "A job that should never be delegated is firing a subordinate," said George S. Jenks, chief executive of Sunwest Financial Services of Albuquerque, New Mexico.
- *Make policy decisions.* A critical credit decision on whether to ship and bill or require payment in advance had been given to billing clerks at Technical Insights Inc., a New Jersey publisher of high-tech reports. Some of the company's largest customers were annoyed by the ad hoc decisions of accounting clerks. Kenneth A. Kovaly, company president, said: "I then set up a procedure for our marketing people to set the guidelines for billing. That put the credit-policy decisions where they belonged."
- *Make final win-or-lose decisions.* Boston Celtics president Red Auerbach said: "I've never kidded myself that I had all the answers. But when the game was on the line, when we only had time for the last play, I'd *always* make the decision of who should take the shot, who should put the ball in play, who should set the pick, who should stand in such and such a spot, and what to do if the play didn't work. When winning or losing is on the line, the job can't be delegated."[21]

Inherent and Acquired Responsibilities

The preceding examples demonstrate that responsibility is a response to needs, and the nature of the need largely defines what ethics is all about. It is well, therefore, to make distinctions. Responsibilities fall into one of two broad categories: *inherent* and *acquired*. Inherent responsibilities arise by virtue of the individual's:

- religious beliefs (the theological ethic)
- existence, which demands duties toward the self (an egoistic ethic)
- being part of a particular family, which brings obligations toward relatives (a familial ethic)
- membership in the human community, which results in a necessary concern for others (the good samaritan or "brother's keeper" ethic)

- linkage in the chain of social evolution, which requires respect for past and future generations (the generational ethic)
- occupancy in a physical world, which imposes duties toward resource use (the environmental ethic)
- standing in a political community, which requires obedience to the law (the civic ethic)

Acquired responsibilities arise because of the voluntary actions of individuals themselves. They develop through:

- friendships (an affection/esteem ethic)
- marriage (the love ethic)
- business contacts (the commercial ethic)
- organizational and professional roles (a fiduciary/agent ethic)

Since some responsibilities are willed by the individual and some are, in a sense, "inherited" or "natural," it might be inferred that the latter logically precede the former. This is not necessarily so. A man who marries assumes responsibilities toward his wife and children that supersede those due even to parents and governments; a friend in need comes ahead of a stranger in need; and an organizational role may sometimes require subordination of duties toward brothers and sisters.

Resolution of conflicts of responsibilities is at least as difficult— probably more so—than resolution of conflicts of interest. The fact that an individual becomes the chief executive of an organization does not mean that other responsibilities disappear. Since people are more consumed with their own needs (Adam Smith's point), more aware of a rival's power (Machiavelli's point), more sensitive to clamorous employees (Samuel Gompers's point), and more responsive to friends (Aristotle's point), there is always needed the prodding of those who speak on behalf of others who are weak, silent, and unknown. Business managers often recoil against do-gooders—and often with reason— but a society without them is an impoverished society. Prioritizing and balancing responsibilities fall on everyone and fall most heavily on managers.

Max Weber long ago insisted that the ethic of responsibility is not the same as the ethic of conscience. The latter requires executives to act according to their own inner lights, sometimes without sufficient emphasis on the quality of the light itself. The ethic of responsibility, on the other hand, demands total commitment to the search for facts, courage to act in conformity with such knowledge, and constant awareness that inadequacies of that knowledge impose limited possibilities for action. Within such constraints, the manager acts only after measuring the costs and benefits of action or inaction. Superimposed on the old maxim "Let your conscience be your guide" is another: "Let your responsibility guide your conscience." Instead of conscience determining responsibility, it is nearer the mark to say that in management (and in the professions) responsibility defines the conscience. This was the distinction John F. Kennedy made during his presidential campaign when he appeared before southern Protestant ministers who worried whether his personal religious values would inhibit his performance in the country's highest political office. The distinction is one of great subtlety and not without its own problems of logic.

Defining responsibility and determining who has it are never easy; their complexities are best revealed through looking at several dilemmas.

ILLUSTRATIVE DILEMMAS

The Professions

Accountants.   Accountants had their historic encounter in 1976 when Ernst and Ernst allegedly mishandled its audit of a small brokerage firm named First Securities of Chicago, whose account it had reviewed over a long period. The facts are clear. Leston B. Nay, the firm's president (who owned 92 percent of its stock), induced clients to invest funds between 1942 and 1966 in "escrow" accounts that he said would yield a very high return. No escrow accounts existed, however, and the transactions were clearly outside the customary form of handling relationships between First Securities and its customers. Nay had directed clients to make personal checks payable to him or to a designated bank for his account. The escrow accounts were not reflected on the books or records of First Securities, and none were shown on its regular accounting to customers in connection with their other investments. Neither the Securities and Exchange Commission nor the New York Stock Exchange was informed. The fraud was discovered in 1968 when Nay's suicide note revealed that First Securities was bankrupt and that the escrow accounts were spurious. The case reached the Supreme Court, which ruled in favor of the accounting firm. Justice Blackmun, in dissent, said that the public had a right to rely on the auditors because they, as experts, carried *prime responsibility* to unearth frauds.

Who was morally right—the Court's majority or the dissenters?

Lawyers.   One of the most intriguing examples of the lawyer's responsibility involves the concept of confidentiality and its application in ways that adversely affect the rights of others. All law students take a required course in "evidence," the guru of which is the famous Professor Wigmore, whose definition of the attorney-client privilege states that: where legal advice is sought from a legal adviser in his or her professional capacity, the communications made in confidence by the client are at the client's instance permanently protected from disclosure by the client or by the legal adviser, except when the protection is waived. This definition, incorporated into the American Bar Association's code, provides that lawyers cannot breach client confidentiality unless necessary to prevent a client from committing a criminal act that, in the lawyer's judgment, might likely result in imminent death or substantial bodily harm. Are these, however, the only valid criteria?

A dramatic story became public toward the end of 1982 when the New York law firm of Singer, Hutner, Levine and Seeman (Singer-Hutner) discovered that its most important corporate client was in deep trouble—and that the firm was, too.[22] Holding center stage in the drama were boyhood friends Mordecai Weissman and Myron Goodman, who founded and ran a computer-leasing company called O.P.M. (Other People's Money). The firm borrowed money to buy computers and other business equipment and then leased them to corporate customers at fees that allowed O.P.M. to meet its loan obligations with enough to spare for handsome profits.

Growth was spectacular. By the late 1970s, O.P.M. ranked among the nation's five largest computer-leasing companies. It bought multimillion-dollar computers from companies like IBM and leased them to Rockwell International, AT&T, Revlon, Polaroid, and others. Prestigious banks, insurance companies, and other financial institutions gladly lent money. Almost from the start, however, the company survived through fraud and bribery. A single computer would be used as collateral for two or three loans with different banks and the value of equipment inflated to obtain larger amounts. Weissman bribed employees of potential customers, and Goodman pushed the company toward ever bigger loans. When IBM announced in 1977 a new line of computers that would revolutionize the business, customers started to cancel their leases. Bankruptcy loomed. Although Weissman's role in illegal actions diminished, Goodman continued to forge signatures, falsify documents to overstate the value of leases and computers, and obtain loans for nonexistent equipment to stave off disaster. Between 1978 and 1981, O.P.M. obtained from nineteen banks, pension funds, and other lenders more than $196 million in loans secured by phony Rockwell Corporation leases. These new loans went to meet payments on old loans until the company finally came crashing down.

All through the decade of fraud at O.P.M., Singer-Hutner handled the company's legal work as well as the personal legal affairs of "Myron and Mordy," as the owners of O.P.M. were called. As the computer-leasing company grew, so did Singer-Hutner. By 1980, more than $3 million in fees and expenses—about 60 percent of the law firm's total income—came from O.P.M.-related work. Relationships between Singer-Hutner and O.P.M., however, took a dramatic turn on June 12, 1980, when Joseph L. Hutner, a senior partner in the law firm, received an extraordinary visit from Goodman, who indicated he might have done something wrong—something he could not set right because it involved millions more than he could raise. Goodman told Hutner he had no intention of revealing details unless the attorney pledged not to tell them to anyone else, a pledge Hutner refused to give since his firm also represented O.P.M. itself and thus might have to inform Weissman.

Recognizing it was deeply involved in a huge, ongoing fraud, Singer-Hutner sought outside legal advice and stressed two points to its lawyers: (1) Singer-Hutner wanted to behave ethically, and (2) it wanted to keep the O.P.M. business unless obliged ethically and legally to quit. Counsel offered welcome advice: the firm could continue to represent O.P.M. (giving the benefit of the doubt to Goodman's assurances that there was no ongoing fraud), could continue to close new loans for the company, and need not check the authenticity of the computer-leasing documents with third parties before closing such new loans. As to the possibly false opinion letters and documents the firm had unwittingly provided to banks to facilitate loans for O.P.M., Singer-Hutner received another welcome opinion: it had no legal duty to withdraw them. The law firm's job was to stop new frauds.

When, however, Goodman continued to refuse to reveal any wrongdoing, the law firm sought to have him come clean in a way that would wrap the evidence in the code of silence sanctioned by the attorney-client privilege. Yet Singer-Hutner also accepted O.P.M.'s explanations for some strange new happenings—bills of sale for computers that the company apparently did not have the money to buy, a signature on a document that looked like a forgery, and the sudden resignation of an outside accounting firm because of its suspicion that Goodman and Weissman had been looting O.P.M. even when it was insolvent. Singer-Hutner voted formally to resign as O.P.M.'s general counsel on September 23, 1980; however, it planned to complete the process gradually, over the following three months, because the lawyers felt that any abrupt withdrawal would cause O.P.M. to collapse. The law firm demanded and received $250,000 for the withdrawal period and a like sum for services already performed. Once the decision was made to quit O.P.M., Singer-Hutner next had to decide what to do with the knowledge that it had been part of a giant fraud. On counsel's advice (that Goodman's secrets were still protected by the attorney-client privilege) the firm kept the facts to itself. Silence was maintained even after Goodman acknowledged on September 29 that the outstanding fraudulent loans totaled $80–$90 million, about three times the amount he had confessed to earlier in the month.

When word got out that Singer-Hutner and O.P.M. were going their separate ways, inquiries came from lenders and other interested parties. They were told by the lawyers only that Singer-Hutner and O.P.M. had agreed to part ways. Peter M. Fishbein, partner of Goodman's new law firm and an old friend of Hutner's, later phoned Hutner to ask "if there was anything we should be aware of" before accepting Goodman's account. Hutner told him only that the decision to terminate was mutual. The result of Singer-Hutner's close mouthed policy was that Goodman was able to use his unwitting new law firm during December 1980 to close more than $15 million in loans for O.P.M., all secured by fraudulent Rockwell leases.

After O.P.M. tumbled down, Singer-Hutner and four codefendants (including Rockwell and Lehman Brothers) became targets of multimillion-dollar lawsuits on grounds that the law firm was an accomplice in O.P.M.'s crimes. Singer-Hutner's lawyers, in a written brief, held nevertheless that under the adversary system of justice, "a lawyer's primary obligation, loyalty and responsibility must be to his client, rich or poor, likable or despicable, honest or crooked. Lawyers are not ordinary people; they sometimes are duty-bound to stand up for and protect liars and thieves." Lawyers see themselves as performing an extraordinary role in the United States.

How "extraordinary" are lawyers?
How ethical is a professional code that results in others being grievously harmed?
Does the responsibility of lawyers, as agents of the court, begin and end with clients?
If so, do lawyers follow a public-be-damned concept of responsibility?

Corporate Managers

Legal reasoning has thus far suggested that role responsibilities of professionals like accountants and lawyers are tending to be defined rather generously. Because of exceptions, it is unsafe to generalize. Clearly, however, in certain higher realms of business, a tighter noose is being drawn, as the following examples suggest.

Sam Goody.   On August 6, 1984, the New Jersey Appeals Court handed down a decision that seems to enlarge management's responsibilities.[23] A number of employees at a Sam Goody audio store held a Christmas party at which liquor was served; one employee was Charles C. Hiers, who, while driving home from the party, swerved across the center line of a bridge and struck another car head-on. Hiers was killed, and the driver of the other car, Frank Davis, died from his injuries three weeks later. When tissue samples taken from Hiers's body showed an alcohol level above the legal limit, Davis's son and daughter sued Sam Goody and the Hiers's estate for negligence, contending that the company sponsored the party and should therefore shoulder some of the blame for Hiers's purported drunkenness, even though the company did not directly serve the liquor. The company replied that, while it had lent stereo equipment for the party and donated $75 to defray other costs, it did not sponsor the party. The three-judge appeals panel wrote: "It is abundantly clear to us that liability in this state depends not on the nature or character of the supplier of alcoholic beverage" but on the more common question of whether the harm could have been foreseen. The company was held responsible.

Would laypeople agree with the judge? If so, on what basis?

Owens-Illinois.   What responsibilities should fall on the managers of Owens-Illinois when, on January 21, 1981, two of their employees at the company's bottle-cap plant in Brookville, Pennsylvania, were apprehended by state environmental authorities for dumping toxic waste chemicals at an abandoned site near the plant? The workers were participating in a plantwide cleanup in preparation for a visit by corporate officials later that same day. Owens-Illinois officials in Toledo insisted that the men were acting without the authority or knowledge of company management and in violation of plant procedures for handling waste chemicals. State regulators were unimpressed. In addition to substantial fines, the company was required to (1) perform tests of ground and surface waters near the dump site to determine if they had been contaminated, (2) submit detailed information concerning its management of hazardous wastes, (3) provide data on how it planned to react to emergencies, and (4) specify which corporate officers were responsible for each of the foregoing assignments. Lack of knowledge and lack of intent did not relieve the company of its responsibility.

Dotterweich.   Today's managers, disturbed by what they feel is a tightening legal noose, might profit by probes into the past that reveal when the law's larger rope becomes evident. Retrospect would lead them directly to what is known as the Dotterweich doctrine, promulgated in 1943 by the Supreme Court in a 5-4 decision. Dotterweich, a company president, was held criminally liable under the federal Food, Drug, and Cosmetic Act when his Buffalo pharmaceutical firm introduced adulterated and misbranded drugs into interstate commerce. The company purchased drugs from a wholesaler and repackaged them for shipment to out-of-state physicians. Dotterweich was not aware of the wrongdoing, participated in no fraud, committed no violative act, and neither knew nor authorized acts that constituted the violation. The court held, however, that an offense is committed by all who have a responsible share in the furtherance of the transaction that the statute outlaws. There is, therefore, no need for the Food, Drug, and Cosmetic Act to abide by the conventional requirement for criminal conduct, namely, awareness of some wrongdoing.

In this instance, would a concept of legal responsibility meet the standard of moral responsibility? The renowned medievalist Thomas Aquinas once taught that if "an act is not deliberate . . . it is not, properly speaking, a human or moral act."[24] In his dissent, Justice Murphy seemed to echo Aquinas when he wrote:

> There is no evidence in this case of any personal guilt on the part of the respondent. There is no proof or claim that he ever knew of the introduction into commerce of the adulterated drugs in question, much less that he actively participated in their introduction. Guilt is imputed to the respondent solely on the basis of his authority and responsibility as president and general manager of the corporation.[25]

Legal, as distinct from moral, definitions of responsibility are therefore important to remember. Corporate officials can be convicted legally even though they did not commit, know of, or authorize a violation of company policy or law. Jail sentences and criminal fines have been imposed—without necessity of proof, knowledge, or intent. Executives have been hauled into court so often that "CEO" has come to mean "cross-examined often." Even lawyers themselves have noted that while executives should not be totally excused from the deposition process, they should usually be excused because ninety-nine times out of a hundred they lack firsthand knowledge of the facts. The sad truth is that the party seeking the CEO's deposition is not trying to acquire probative evidence or narrow the issues but is trying to harass the manager to coerce a settlement. The task of CEOs is to manage their organization, and in so doing they derive detailed knowledge of their business from others. It follows that information sought from CEOs through depositions in a typical commercial case can almost always be obtained elsewhere more easily and less expensively. Fortunately, under the recently amended federal discovery rules, litigants are required to go elsewhere first.[26] Responsibility, however, remains.

PRACTICAL STEPS

Trend Lines

There are situations in which ignorance of the facts (unavailable or hidden from executives) provides a moral defense. Where there is no knowledge, there is no motive. In product liability cases, the CEO typically knows nothing about the design, manufacture, or sale of the product that allegedly injured the plaintiff. In breach of contract cases, the CEO usually knows nothing about the negotiation, execution, or performance of the contract that the company allegedly breached. In antitrust price-fixing cases, the CEO ordinarily knows nothing about any of the meetings in which company employees allegedly met with competitors to fix prices. Since jail sentences for violations of the law have been rare and fines rather small, it could be inferred that the courts are either soft on white-collar crime or unsure of their logic. Whose moral compass points toward the right direction—those who hold that individuals having any share in furthering a prohibited transaction are responsible, or those who insist that vicarious liability is a concept repugnant to every canon of morality?[27]

Even within the legal realm itself, trends indicate important differences in various judicial definitions of role responsibility. Lawyers engaged in commerce-related work tend to enlarge their obligations to clients and restrict their duties to society; shop stewards, understandably concerned with protecting workers' rights, seem at times to get away with a fair degree of irresponsibility toward their employers; managers who in the past literally did get away with murder in the commission of white-collar crimes are discovering that some judges have moved their definitions of responsibility to the old navy maxim "the captain is accountable for the ship. From society's perspectives, the tightened noose makes sense because the power center is the responsibility center. Yet from ethical perspectives, the "tightened noose" concept of responsibility often creates problems. The relevant point is that legal concepts of responsibility do not coincide consistently with ethical definitions and that, paradoxically, good ethics in America is not always good business. Ethically defensible behavior can lead to jail sentences. The paradox bears watching.

In the past, limited liability for economic failure has been paralleled by limited liability for role failure, so long as managers followed the prudent-man rule, namely, do what seems reasonable under the circumstances. Even this earlier and more restricted meaning of executive responsibility creates problems. Executives know that responsibility for actual control of everyone in large multiplant enterprises is impossible and that no foolproof system can be created. To protect themselves, businesspersons not only seek high insurance coverage but are also adopting an "if in doubt, don't" managerial philosophy. This philosophy can seep into other aspects of decision making, and when the seepage is accelerated, the manager's entrepreneurial function is jeopardized. Managers then tend to become interested only in structures, often bureaucratic, that protect them from risk and legal liability.

Reviewing the legal definition of role responsibility in America suggests three important trends:

1. In the business world—and especially where organizations provide goods coming under the purview of the Food and Drug Administration—managers are being held to an ever tightening set of responsibilities under the Dotterweich doctrine. It is not necessary to establish that the executive approved the prohibited action or even knew of it; it is sufficient only to establish satisfactorily that the CEO was less than scrupulous in carrying out his or her oversight responsibilities. The reason for this restricted view is obviously the public's expectation that responsibility should be tied closely to those having real power.

2. The trend is not without dangers. Overseeing organizations whose thousands of employees operate in different countries is inordinately difficult since the leader often lacks necessary basic information to control the situations. More and more, one can expect tighter organizational codes of ethics and, indeed, even surveillance methods that workers have long disdained. Some chief executives now insist that senior colleagues reveal their calendar of meetings with clearly stated explanations of reasons that led to travel outside the home base. Seasoned individuals with long periods of loyal service instinctively resent this seeming lack of complete trust in them; the fact is, however, that the chief executive may have little alternative because exposure to legal risk has become so substantial.

3. Like it or not, organizations could become more Orwellian Big Brother than either executives or workers want. Tighter codes of ethics, stricter monitoring for compliance, and stiffer sanctions for violations may become the rule. While the net effect may be for the better, the prized individualism and autonomy that Americans have cherished will undoubtedly be measurably curtailed. Moral dilemmas are the name of the game.

Stepping-stones

Peter Drucker, paraphrasing Julius Rosenwald of Sears, Roebuck fame, put the broad concept of responsibility quite simply when he wrote that managers "have to do good to do well."[28] Doing good usually flows from knowing good, not the other way around. A necessary first step is to get the philosophy straight, make it known, and insist on compliance to it. If managers are indeed a breed apart, it is a breed endowed with enormous power though sometimes hobbled by ambiguities on how that power should be used. There are, nonetheless, four guidelines managers should follow:

1. *Read the culture.* To know what is good requires managers and professionals to be semioticians, that is, adept signal watchers who then become effective signal callers because they understand the collective conscience or ethos of their own society. Culture is society's quarterback whose signals administrators must hear, understand, and act on. Interest is on such values as individualism, property rights, privacy, and freedom.
2. *Analyze the culture's values.* Is the ethos, or lived ethic, ethically defensible? Is the ideology that legitimizes the culture logical? If the culture transmits different meanings of the good, which should be heeded? To answer the questions requires examinations of what a human being is and what "being human" involves. It is important to note what the questions are not. They are not concerned with what is American or Russian, Christian or Jewish; rather, they address the core of our common humanity—the *Everyman* of medieval plays and the *Everyperson* of modern life.
3. *Do something with what has been learned.* That "something" is the development of a moral character, because it is in character that the values of the culture and the logic of the concepts come together.
4. *Shape the organization's values to harmonize with the dominant culture and with their own developed moral character.* People of integrity produce organizations with integrity. When they do, they become moral managers—those special people who make organizations and societies better.

To sum up: moral managers are those who understand, reconcile, and apply what might loosely be called the three ethics:

1. *The "ethic" of the culture.* This is the way common values hold both organizations and societies together and how they are explained through ideologies shaped by *particular* experiences and traditions. Emphasis is on the American.

2. *The "ethic" of concept.* This refers to the criteria established mainly by philosophers for *universal* application. Emphasis is on the person.
3. *The "ethic" of character.* This is the way values from the culture and values from the theorist are internalized to produce a manager of integrity.

Together they form a triangle within which they and their organizations are judged:

Figure 1-1.   Persons and Organizations

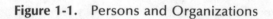

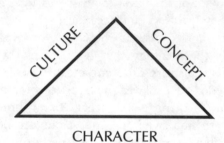

THE "ETHIC" OF CULTURE

2
THE NATURE AND POWER OF THE CULTURE

THE VALUES QUIZ   *(Mark True or False)*

1. _____ There is a widening gap in the United States between those values held by the elite and those values cherished by the common people.

2. _____ Ignorance of their own culture is morally indefensible for managers in today's world.

3. _____ When a conflict develops between liberty and justice, liberty should come first.

4. _____ Religious leaders should not pronounce publicly on court decisions or government policies relating to abortion, divorce, nuclear arms, foreign policy, business investments abroad, and the like.

5. _____ The characteristically American belief that "big is better" is the best organizational philosophy. Not to grow is to shrink.

6. _____ Religious values have lost their influence over American life.

7. _____ Our Founding Fathers established the Constitution on the belief that human nature could always be trusted.

8. _____ Because the United States has been one of the greatest success stories in world history, intellectuals in other lands have urged their leaders to adopt American values.

Administrators making critical decisions on behalf of their organizations do so within a social milieu that has criteria for determining whether such decisions are deemed good or bad, acceptable or unacceptable. These criteria represent a "collective conscience," respect for which is essential to the legitimacy of basic organizations as well as to the roles assigned to those who manage them. Since cultures vary, managers of large corporations also have a vital interest in knowing how people in other lands think and behave. That misunderstandings occur is often due to misperceptions of the impact of one culture on another. Two examples suffice to illustrate the point: the Foreign Corrupt Practices Act of 1977 (which prohibited payments to foreign government officials to secure business) and the behavior of multinationals abroad are both seen by other countries as examples of America's "moral imperialism." Nothing more aggravates non-Americans than the seemingly smug "we are better" syndrome.

On the other hand, Americans react negatively when they see cultures in which grease money and payoffs are commonplace, in which nepotism is honored as a family obligation, in which economic stability is preferred to economic growth, in which church and state act as one, and, finally, in which class distinctions are sharp and unchallenged. In such cultures Americans are the aliens who simply do not understand how things work. Do Americans, for example, understand their nearest southern neighbor? Mexico's distinguished poet Octavio Paz answered negatively: "To cross the border between the two countries is to change civilization. Americans are the children of the Reformation. . . . {Whereas} Americans overvalue the future and venerate change, Mexicans cling to the image of our pyramids and cathedrals, to values we suppose are immutable."[1]

Different cultures, of course, had in the past incorporated certain common features that proved to be unpalatable to contemporary thought. Two illustrations come to mind. The first relates to women, who were seen as sensitive, nurturing creatures, too weak and timid for the rough-and-tumble world of politics and business.[2] The second was the employer attitude in industrialized countries toward accidents that were assumed to be endemic to the system: factory workers could lose limbs and miners could lose lives, and the presumption was that, in most cases, it was their own fault.[3] But cultures change, dramatic examples of which are the ways legal and medical systems are used in the United States. America's new legal culture is built on two expectations: (1) the individual's sense of fair treatment, everywhere and in every situation, and (2) the belief that somebody will pay for all calamities that happen to a person so long as they are not that individual's own fault. No such expectations existed as recently as twenty-five years ago.[4]

Perhaps the word expectation *captures as well as any one word can what it means to be an American. The bicentennial of the Constitution prompted many Americans to reconsider the meaning and purpose of their homeland. Few did it with more elegance and grace than William Broyles, Jr. In prose stitched together with poetry, he wrote:*

"Who is the American, this new man?" asked essayist Michel Crèvecoeur in 1784. Two hundred years later, his question is still as provocative and the answer just as elusive. We are a nation without a nationality, a people without a race. We are an idea. We are Americans because we believe we are.

"Once I thought to write a history of the immigrants in America. Then I discovered that the immigrants were American history." So Oscar Handlin began The Uprooted, *his masterly work on immigration, in words that could have been engraved on the Statue of Liberty. Consider America as a play in three acts. First Act: The great immigration. Some 50 million people—the vast majority of them Europeans—abandon their traditional cultures and brave the Atlantic Ocean to begin a new life. Act Two: The great frontier. The vast continent they encounter transforms the immigrants into a new people—Americans. Both acts transpire in the same time frame—from the early seventeenth century to the beginning of the twentieth. Act Three: The new people find their destiny—a tale as yet without end. And at the curtain other immigrants appear from entirely new quarters to begin the drama again.*

Every man who turned his back on the Old World and went to America was, in a way, defeated. If he had been successful where he was, why leave? And every pioneer who left the settled life of the East and went west was recreating that original immigrant experience. The frontier was where a man could start over— implying that he needed to.[5]

MEANING AND INFLUENCES

According to the *British Institute of Management:*

The key to business success in the [years ahead] will lie in the ability of managers to foresee, relate and respond to the changing perspectives of society: changes which question the economic results of business performance, the basis of managerial authority and the very purpose of business itself; and changes in the values and expectations of people—individually, as customers and employees, and collectively, both as the market for goods and services and as the society to which business belongs.

The practical problems facing organisations and the people who run them are not only to recognise the many dynamic changes taking place around them, but to ensure that the outlook and performance of their managers and employees are in tune with the times. This is no easy task.[6]

Managers as Semioticians

The importance of good communications to managerial effectiveness is a staple in management folklore. IBM, General Foods, Hewlett-Packard, and General Motors are frequently cited as examples of companies that have long recognized the role that effective communications plays in their destinies.[7] Emphasis here is on the manager as superb quarterback whose voice barks the right signals for the right plays. Less stressed, however, is the manager's role as a signal receiver—the semiotician par excellence who knows not only how to call but how to receive signals. Two developments impel managers to search for changes: (1) the vast political transformations that came swiftly after World War II and (2) the internationalization of the world economy that, paradoxically, brought economic interdependence and political independence into an uneasy partnership.

Organizations whose leaders do not monitor the implications of relatively fixed—as well as shifting—values are doomed. Missed signals are missed opportunities, and both are classic elements in stories of management failures.[8] One of the world's greatest managers, Caesar Augustus, provides a convenient illustration of a leader who lost control because he lost touch. For a half-century he ran an empire of more than 5 million square kilometers and a population of nearly 100 million people. He brought beauty to Rome, peace to Europe, highways to merchants, and prosperity to people. In the latter years of his life, he so neglected warning signs that revolutions brought the empire to near disaster.[9] Caesar has counterparts in the United States. On the eve of World War II, Baldwin Locomotive executives could not bring themselves to believe that diesel power would replace the steam engine. After the war, Detroit carmakers ignored the small-car phenomenon, central city merchants missed the message of early suburban shopping malls, and political and business figures ignored cues regarding racial equality and women's rights.

Signal watching today goes under various guises in well-managed organizations—environmental scanning, futuristics, social auditing, megatrend analysis, and the like. This kind of endeavor, however, is essentially reactive, a role to which business has been habituated for centuries: Elites (clerics, philosophers, rulers) wrote the script, and business actors dutifully read their allotted lines. The irony was that people, bold and innovative in their economic systems, were cautious and staid in others. Historian Miriam Beard once called businessmen moral eunuchs who, like Alfred Nobel, drifted like purposeless wrecks "with no lovely memories of the past and no false illusions of the future."[10]

If Beard is correct in her interpretation, it means that business leaders—certainly in Europe—comported themselves with a form of irresponsibility bordering on the unethical; nevertheless, what is past is not prologue. The days of the eunuch are over, and corporate managers are accepting as part of their function an obligation to share in redefining society's values. This means greater involvement in the political process, greater interaction with the media, more frequent encounters with clergy, and more direct contacts with academic and other opinion makers. Dropping their reactive role for a proactive one invites a future of intense and possibly dangerous encounters. The net result is that receiving as well as calling signals is an essential part of the manager's portfolio of competence.

Culture as Veneer

Expected to conform to high ethical standards and stung by criticisms over departures therefrom, managers may wonder why the search for values must begin with an examination of the culture when the word itself seems so ambiguous. This confusion arises, in part, because culture has meant many things to many people. As veneer, culture relates to such things as manners of dress, of eating, of thinking, and of talking. It may mean what the masses practice—as in England, where the black cap became standard working-class apparel and fish-and-chips a staple of working-class food, where reliance was not on doctors but on patent medicines, and where the local pub was a center of social solidarity. It can also mean a neighborhood value system such as is found in a south Brooklyn neighborhood called Canarsie. There, Jewish and Catholic residents earn barely enough to support a middle-class existence, yet they feel that their ascent from poverty into middle-class status is due to their own hard work and sacrifice. Beneficiaries of no affirmative action programs, they resent those who seem unwilling to pay their dues; their political philosophy is simple: "We made it, so why can't they?"

Culture has also been used to describe the values of different social classes. There is, for example, a blue-collar culture revealed in a vocabulary of double negatives: "I can't get no money from the kids";

there is a middle-class culture whose vocabulary is, grammatically, very proper and rather uniform; and finally, there is an upper-class culture composed of the Harriman/Rockefeller types whose descendants, born to wealth, feel obligations to serve as ambassadors, preferably to large countries, or as unpaid directors for universities and prestigious organizations like the American Assembly and the Council for Foreign Relations. This is culture at an easily seen level. Better approaches toward understanding its subsurface dimension require larger perspectives.

From Civilization to Culture

During the late eighteenth century, when England's domestic problems were compounded from afar by its upstart colonials in America, people of influence in Britain began to ask, What holds us together? The question, old even in antiquity, has always surfaced when societies experience major difficulties. To his troubled countrymen Edmund Burke sought to provide an answer:

> Society is a partnership between those who are living, those who are dead, and those who are to be born. Each contract of each particular state is but a clause in the great primeval contract of eternal society, linking the lower with the higher natures, connecting the visible and invisible world according to a fixed compact sanctioned by the inviolable oath which holds together all physical and all moral natures, each in its appointed place.[11]

The stunning imagery of the prose promised more than it really delivered because Burke never defined the nature of the contract. He nonetheless recognized that, since human societies are characterized by recurring forms of behavior (nurturing the young, earning a living, providing the common defense, and the like), approval for certain kinds of activities and disapproval of others were essential to the survival of both individuals and groups. Public approbation and sanctification became, in certain respects, standardized or ritualized. Medieval serfs accepted automatically their obligations to the manor lord; apprentices acknowledged their duties to master craftsmen of the guilds; Frenchmen willingly joined Napoleon's citizen army when previous generations had relied on professional soldiers; and women overwhelmingly accepted domestic roles.

As a term, *culture* first became widely used in France during the late nineteenth century as an antonym to the word *civilization*, which itself first appeared there in print in 1776. People initially thought of civilization as the most convenient way to distinguish themselves from barbarians. When an obscure French monk named Emeric Cruce stepped forward in 1623 with what was probably the first League of Nations idea, he popularized the idea of civilization by saying that all peoples could join the league when they became civilized, that is, when they had given up violence and conquest. [12] The old monk probably had in mind the lesson implicit in the feudal period when chivalry, despite its affectations and extravagances, rose to tame barbarian warriors. Savage soldiers began to civilize themselves by acquiring more polished and humane modes of conduct toward the weak as well as toward one another; later, the increased circulation of material goods (and the skills entailed in producing them) represented another major step in the direction of a commercial and polite society and the civilizing characteristics that went with it. [13]

Definition

In time, however, civilization came to mean industrial and technological communities inhabited by new "barbarians" whose overriding concerns for material progress allowed them to be swallowed by a money lust and by the machine. [14] At this juncture, civilization began to mean the disintegration of all that humanity itself implied. Culture was the new coin used to prescribe the ideals that defined proper habits for thinking and feeling. Tocqueville gave greater precision to Burke's definition when he said that society was held together by its mores, that is, "the habits of the heart . . . and the sum of ideas that shape mental habits." [15] In this sense, culture differed from its earlier and more common usage (separating the illiterate from the educated, the masses from the elite) to become a barrier against an industrial civilization that allegedly debased humankind. Needed was a new term that, incorporating the best of traditional values, would describe a social order where the machine would be tamed and human experience again made meaningful. [16] Culture now meant, from a generic perspective, that element which:

- responds to all people's needs for an ordered universe marked by frameworks, categories, and rules

- uses traditions (which change slowly and selectively) to provide such frameworks
- legitimizes institutions that turn abstractions of the culture into realities for individuals
- produces ideologies that explain and defend the group's values and basic institutions

When needs change, traditions are modified; when traditions are challenged, the legitimacy of existing institutions is questioned. Since the variables multiply geometrically, the resultant complexity makes it harder to preserve stability. So many values suddenly appear that viewing them is like gazing at the mad geometry of a large city whose buildings clash violently in purpose, shape, color, style, and age. A further point should be made: while the power of a culture is profound, its visibility is negligible in the sense that its norms are so ingrained that they are accepted, almost universally and instinctively, as the ultimate source of all value. Culture is thus a two-edged sword: it liberates people from life's uncertainties and enslaves them by legitimizing baneful institutions. But critics have produced no better word to describe the process whereby a group not only acquires, defines, and reinforces specific actions, thoughts, and feelings but also limits the way they may be legitimately experienced.

Since culture represents those embedded and uncritically accepted values which must be first understood before formal ethical analysis begins, they are the "lived ethic" that embraces images of both ideal behavior and actual behavior.[17] The lived ethic defines virtue and vice and thereby sets the general moral tone and direction for the community. Culture becomes:

[the] property of an independently defined stable social unit. If one can demonstrate that a given set of people have shared a significant number of important experiences in the process of solving external and internal problems, one can assume that such common experiences have led them, over time, to a shared view of the world around them and their place in it. There has to have been enough shared experience to have led to a shared view, and this shared view has to have worked for long enough to have come to be taken for granted and to have dropped out of awareness. Culture, in this sense, is a *learned product of group experience* and is, therefore, to be found only where there is a definable group with a significant history.[18]

There is a big difference between the lived ethic of the people and the theoretical ethic of the philosophers, and the "fit" between them is neither a total misfit nor a perfect fit but, rather, an incomplete and partial fit. Philosophers' versions of morality have not passed the practical test of being transmitted from parents to children when the moral conscience is formed; in important ways, concepts are less thoroughly tested than those unintellectual, uncritical tenets of the culture that some philosophers derisively call unreflective.[19] Yet these so-called unreflective values have evolved over long periods of time, have adapted to geographic location and natural resources, and have been influenced by victory or defeat in war. It is these factors, leading to different results for different people, that make understandings of culture a necessity for leaders.

To sum up: *Culture consists of the distinctive way different societies standardize and ritualize approved behavior and the methods used to condemn disapproved conduct in order to preserve the social group and make living meaningful for the individual.* The preservation of individuals and their society goes beyond meeting the sheer physiological needs for food, clothing, shelter, and production; culture itself is a central ingredient in personal and group growth, and its changes induce changes in the way individuals perceive their fulfillment. How cultures are formed —and re-formed—is an enormously intricate process involving multiple groups in any given society. Of these groups, certain elites recruited from education and the professions tend to exercise a paramount influence.

Elites and Culture

Because culture relies for survival on communications, communicators enjoy a special status. Today's emphasis on the written word makes contemporaries forget that Homer could not write and that Plato felt speech came before writing much as fingers came before forks. Because oral cultures tend to be quite different from literate cultures, representatives from the latter often tend to look down on the former: storytellers and balladeers should be taken joyously but not seriously.[20] In nineteenth-century America, the influence makers were those who had the leisure to follow their vocational preferences because they were the sons of successful fathers. Often their clubs (the Tuesday Club of Philadelphia, the Calliopean Society in New York, and the Anthology

Club of Boston) exercised great influence; in such associations were men of commerce who, as patrons, shared indirectly in shaping the culture, a point Beard missed in calling businessmen moral eunuchs.

Whether it is an oral or a literate culture, elites play central roles in fashioning it—and with mixed results. The point is important. Since university and media elites generally espouse liberal causes and common folk hold more conservative values, a widening gap between the two usually means trouble. Significant splits between the elites and the "masses" have occurred recently over such issues as divorce, abortion, premarital sex, homosexuality, and family composition. According to a Connecticut Mutual Life Insurance Company study, these differences threaten to rip the American culture in two;[21] perhaps the fundamental conflict of twentieth-century America is between two cultures, an older one loosely labeled Puritan-republican and a newly emerging culture of abundance and hedonism. The older culture demanded something it called character (moral qualities of self-discipline), whereas the newer one insists on a personality cult that emphasizes being liked and admired.[22]

When severe strains in the culture show, important questions surface: What happens to respect for authority? to parent-child obligations? to relationships between the sexes? to corporate legitimacy? If questions go unanswered, distrust grows, and with it, healthy differences between classes degenerate into unhealthy conflict. Ideological dogmatism replaces rational debate; special interest groups ignore the common good; judges move from being interpreters of law to remakers of it; media pundits don the garb of moral arbiters; and professors write for one another or venture gleefully into nonelected government posts. In every instance, organizations are affected and managers are called upon to be smart semioticians who effect internal organizational changes because they are sensitive to external societal changes.

That Western industrialized societies are experiencing "culture crises" is rather widely accepted as a fact of life. The results are disturbing as politicians lose the ability to develop efficient consensus-forming mechanisms, educators squabble over curricula, secular humanists collide with religious fundamentalists, and in-depth reporting becomes shallow special pleading. Cohesiveness slips slowly from society.[23] When governments cannot govern—or when they govern ineffectively—people edge toward mob rule. Like drivers at unsynchronized traffic lights, people are never sure when to start and when to stop. Tempers flare, accidents multiply, frustrations deepen. Needless to say, when signals emitted by the culture are erratic, unclear, or even contradictory, the organization's leaders must assume a heavier burden if for no more practical reason than to preserve legitimacy for their enterprises and for their roles.

Culture's Impact on Organizations

The extent to which the national culture affects management practices and organizational development has stimulated animated debate. Some investigators contend that management functions are substantially independent of the culture because they are influenced primarily by technological factors;[24] against this is the view that culture establishes the primary constraints over management. One person associated with this latter view is Geert Hofstede, a well-respected Dutch psychologist and management theorist.[25] Hofstede administered a psychological inventory to 116,000 employees of the IBM Corporation in forty countries around the world. On the basis of these data he identified four criteria to describe how national cultures influence organizational structure:

1. *Power Distance* (PD) is the degree to which hierarchical power places people at a psychological distance from one another and, more importantly, the willingness of people to accept the unequal distribution of prestige, wealth, and power. Where PD is high, employees tend to accept inequality, bureaucracy, and social pecking orders.
2. *Uncertainty Avoidance* (UA) refers to the different ways people experience anxiety and stress and their attempts to avoid such situations. Open societies encourage individuals to tolerate ambiguities and differences of opinion, whereas unstable societies encourage people to demand precision in the law and in job specifications as well as in defining the nature of organizational structures.
3. *Individualism-Collectivism* (IC) suggests that when people feel they are masters of their own destinies they should be expected to take care of themselves. Opposite to individualism is collectivism, seen in cultures in which people expect to be cared for.
4. *Masculinity* (MAS) means the degree to which a society cherishes aggressiveness, independence, and achievement—values pre-

sumed to stand in stark contrast to such "feminine" virtues as nurturance, empathy, and security. This index is built on the premise that men seek advancement, higher earnings, and competition, whereas women prize interpersonal relationships, service, quality of life, and stability.

Applying the four indices, Hofstede ranked America first of the forty countries in individualism (confirming the point made over a century ago by Tocqueville), thirteenth on the masculinity scale (reinforcing the belief that America is an aggressive and assertive society), twenty-sixth in power distance (reflecting the egalitarianism first made politically visible during Jacksonian democracy), and among the very lowest in uncertainty avoidance, which suggests that Americans, feeling psychologically secure and safe in their own society, are willing to tolerate ambiguity. Hofstede made the added point that America is inclining toward a "counterculture" that is essentially "feminine" and is reflected in such things as sensitivity training, encounter groups, youth culture, transactional analysis movements, group dynamics, and the like.

The magnitude of Hofstede's sample and the boldness that characterized his conclusions have stirred both support and criticism. It has been suggested, for example, that by restricting his sample to one corporation Hofstede unduly limited the reliability of his findings.[26] Critics have also pointed out that one noteworthy feature of Hofstede's conclusions—namely, the similiarity of cultures in the United States, England, Canada, Australia, New Zealand, and Ireland —runs against some significant facts in both Western and oriental societies.

The Critical Epoch

Despite criticisms, Hofstede's model has served to stimulate further investigations into the nexus between national and organizational cultures. A growing conviction regarding managerial career patterns is that selection processes and reward systems are the most significant variables in all good organizations. That one result justifies the attention given to comparative analyses; it may be a prelude to increased knowledge about how to make people more efficient, organizations more stable, and society more rewarding. The point is especially true at this juncture in American history, when, for the first time, executives of large and established corporations worry that global competition threatens the very survival of their firm. In the "new order," loyalty to workers, to host communities, and even to the country itself is an imperiled virtue; concern for job creation, much less than commitment to it, is fast eroding; interest in the long term is another casualty; and the idea of single corporate ownership of a large plant is being replaced by joint organizational ownership of many small plants in a confederation of corporate property holders—the "floating factory" idea.[27] Everyone has a stake in wondering what else will float away when loyalty, employment growth, long-term vision, and ownership responsibilities seem possible candidates for extinction.[28]

Increased union militancy, greater government intervention, and more aggressive moves by public interest groups loom. The famous TGW (things gone wrong) index for the automotive industry in the Rogers poll may soon measure things gone wrong in a moral order as well; it is, indeed, an irony that as American work goes abroad, foreign investments come in. Understanding other cultures and, above all, understanding his or her own culture are part of the moral manager's development.

ELEMENTS OF THE AMERICAN CULTURE

It is impossible to speak definitively of a single and homogenous American culture. There are urban, suburban, and agrarian cultures, genteel and punk-rock cultures, liberal and conservative cultures—each with its own protagonists and its own expressive forms.[29] Because of the existence of so many subcultures, defining and redefining the country is as American as apple pie. That the United States does not explain itself is a proposition many have consistently stressed, and while that may be true of every nation, it is especially true of this one.[30] The nation is an experiment, and to forget it is to forget everything. Reproposing the "American proposition" is essential to the nation's survival. Lincoln understood this need when he reproposed America as "a new nation, coinceived in liberty, and dedicated to the proposition that all men are created equal." Slogans like New Deal and Fair Deal, New Frontier and Great Society, reveal efforts by other American presidents to define and redefine the country.

Woven into the texture of American society are psychosocial, religious, political, technological, and economic threads, each of which has its own distinct coloration and texture. Together they loosely tie Americans into a community in a dizzying kaleidoscope that caught the keen eye and ear of Tocqueville in the early nineteenth century and Dos Passos in the early twentieth. The first wrote the great sociopolitical tract and the second the great novel of America.[31] Yet despite the genius of each, the country continues to defy precise definition—a defiance that, to repeat for emphasis' sake, makes signal watching as necessary as it is difficult. Admired and reviled, open yet mysterious, materialistic and generous, spiritual and secularistic, America is paradox personified. The fact side on the contemporary United States is straightforward enough.

In land area and in population, the United States is the fourth largest country in the world. Once the fastest growing in numbers, it is now one of the slowest; once a country of the young, it is now a domicile for the old; once its Northeast and the Midwest bulged with new births, but for the past decade those areas have had zero population growth; once economically unchallenged, it now faces stern competition in many industries; once isolationist, it is now in the eye of every diplomatic storm. The country is growing middle-aged and more solitary. Men and women are delaying marriage, delaying childbirth, and having few or no children at all. Real income, once expected to rise as naturally as a hot-air balloon, has leveled off. For many, home ownership, once deemed nearly a constitutional right, has become a dream denied. Demography is destiny, and Americans of today, in ways both obvious and subtle, are inventing the America of tomorrow.[32] So a question arises: what held—and what will hold—these people together? What follows is an attempt to answer.

Psychosocial Elements

The face that the North American continent presented to Europeans in the seventeenth century was the newest, largest, wildest visage they had ever seen. Without yielding to historical determinism, it can be said that certain things would inevitably appear in the American character: diversity, individualism, a penchant for growth expressed in the "bigger is better" maxim, and above all, optimism wedded to braggadocio.

Few disagreed with historian Max Lerner, who, shortly after completing *America as a Civilization*, was hosted by a group of writers, editors, and teachers in Warsaw. When asked to express in one word what he considered the essence of American civilization he pondered the question carefully and, after rejecting freedom, justice, tolerance, decency, equality, and enterprise, said: "*Access*—access is the key to America's culture."[33] There was little fear in taking a chance because there would always be other choices. Access has come to mean equal opportunity, and managements that missed the expanding meaning of *access* found themselves engaged in prolonged and costly litigation.

A feature of the American landscape that incorporated contradiction was the country's alleged uniformity: towns looked alike and malls were alike. Behind stale uniformities, however, were remarkable differences: Poles in Detroit, Germans in Milwaukee, Swedes in Minneapolis, Chicanos in Los Angeles, Cajuns in Louisiana's bayou country —all had distinct cultures.[34] The mixture proved too great for the melting pot to melt. Regions also had a particular flavor. New England differed from the mid-Atlantic region, and both differed from the agrarian culture of the South.[35] Unlike Paris, which influenced all of France, American provinces resisted direction from any single center. To easterners, anything west of the Ohio River meant illiterate mountaineers and country yokels; to westerners, Boston meant Brahmin snobs, New York financial sharpsters, and Philadelphia shyster lawyers. Westerners were convinced they were the authentic Americans because they had built the heartland of liberty—freedom of mind, muscle, movement, spirit, and, above all, freedom to be oneself.

Special mention should be made of America's brand of individualism. So valuable was this perceived virtue that in 1951 the editors of *Fortune*, in what was then accepted as a major statement on "the American condition," intimated that any institution that subordinated the individual to the group was evil.[36] Whereas the brilliant Frenchman Joseph de Maistre saw in individualism a "frightening division of minds" and compatriot Emile Durkheim saw it as the cause of the greatest moral crisis in a hundred years,[37] Emerson perceived in it "the one major doctrine, the infinitude of the private man," who can carve his own secure niche in the material world.[38] Characteristically, Americans adjusted its meaning to fit a new environment. During the eighteenth century, individualism (the self-sufficient person) harmonized with the realities of an agrarian society; a century later, when the industrial revolution brought in its wake large organizations, scientific management, and heavy concentrations of wealth, individualism survived in the ideology as the "self-made man"; in the twentieth century, it came to mean personal fulfillment through organizations that encouraged participation.

Growth was another American belief, and growth was everybody's business. Towns would grow. States would grow. Firms would grow. People would grow. Since economic growth meant borrowing and lending, trust had to be cultivated. Debtors defaulted only after struggling to make repayments, and bankruptcy was seen as a moral failure. "Hanging in there" was a trait that transformed trust from abstraction to reality. Here again, however, a contradiction appeared in that Americans never fully trusted their politicians or their businesspeople: rascals were in state houses and thieves in counting houses.

Movies revealed a good deal about changes in American culture. Developed initially by immigrants (Goldwyn, Lasky, Cohn, Zukor, Warner, Mayer, and Zanuck) who more than anything else wanted to assimilate American values and make them known to others, early motion pictures reinforced the cult of optimism and individualism. The plots had a certain purity: "good guys" and "bad guys" were instantly recognized, and the former would always win. Tom Mix and Hoot Gibson were the cinematic heroes—strong, laconic, chaste, and 100 percent American. The heroes and the thieves were quite unlike today's popular figures, antiheroes who make a specialty of being "bad guys" and "losers."[39]

If Americans saw themselves as complex but essentially decent, foreigners often saw them as single-minded and ugly. Earlier criticisms had reflected a love/hate syndrome—as when Georg Friedrich Hegel, one of Europe's most influential eighteenth-century philosophers, glowingly praised the new world but ended his work by stressing Americans' acquisitiveness, self-aggrandizement, and obsession with commercial profit.[40] It seems today that the intellectuals' love has totally disappeared. Fairly representative of the European view—and certainly most quoted because of his preeminence—is England's George Orwell. In an essay entitled "Boy's Weeklies," Orwell used a typical bookshelf to enlarge on the more important theme of how the boyhood weeklies of his day (play-the-game-fairly and never-hit-below-the-belt) have changed. The new breed of English magazines featured stories about bombs, death rays, Martians, robots, and the like. But, in Orwell's view, English publications were nothing compared to the "Yank mags" in which "you get real blood lust, real gory descriptions of the all-in, jump-on-his-testicles style of fighting written in the jargon that has been perfected by people who brood endlessly on violence."[41] To Orwell's many admirers in America, the new hero was the thug who put everything right by socking everybody else on the jaw. American democracy was like the British monarchy—"the gold filling in a mouth full of decay," to use John Osborne's vivid metaphor. Orwell's views were echoed by Jack Lang, France's minister of culture in the Mitterrand government, who repeatedly warned not only his own countrymen but all Europeans that American culture was a plague engulfing the world. The warning was somewhat muted when outraged critics accused Lang of monstrous distortion.[42]

For a variety of reasons, some good and others puerile, European intellectuals have therefore, been, quick to fault America, conveniently ignoring the violence of their soccer fans, the antics of the teddy boys, and the self-indulgences of the Riviera types. What is new and disturbing is that anti-Americanism has become well-nigh universal. Part of the antipathy is due to America's power and part to a distaste for some of its values. The Arabic world wants American technology but not American values; the Chinese have recently turned toward the market system yet decry the "decadent" capitalist ideology. While Americans become understandably upset by foreigners' criticisms, history reminds them that homegrown critics have been equally severe. Over a century ago Walt Whitman saw American culture as "a sort of dry and flat Sahara, crowned with petty grotesques, malformations, phantoms, playing meaningless antics;" he summoned his countrymen to confess that "in shop, street, church, theatre, barroom, official chair . . . are pervasive flippancy and vulgarity, low cunning, infidelity; everywhere the youth puny, impudent, foppish, prematurely ripe; everywhere an abnormal libidinousness, everywhere shallow notions of beauty, with a range of manners—or rather lack of manners— probably the meanest to be seen in the world."[43]

Since the drumbeat of criticism has not slowed, a question arises: Is the American culture as deformed and as craven as depicted? A nonanswer is too feeble a response. The truth, however, is that the country simply has so much of everything that friends and foes can easily document their respective positions. In important ways, Americans have never been able to resolve two fundamental contradictions in the way they see themselves. The first was the view of the Founding Fathers who felt that Americans were like others and that the establishment of the Constitution represented an experiment. Engaged in experimentation, Americans obviously could not presume to guide others when their own design had not been tested. Against this view was the self-perception of a people not conducting an experiment but fulfilling a divine mission in the world. Americans could tutor others on righteousness because they were God's elect or could chastise others because their innocence was unsullied by European corruptions. The result was a people at once humble and overbearing, sinful and saintly, self-appointed and God-anointed.

The second contradiction related to the clash between moral absolutism and hardheaded pragmatism. Few countries were better at pursuing their own self-interest while proclaiming total uninterestedness—a posture that in foreign policy irritated America's friends and enraged its enemies. Since this contradiction continues, the drumbeat of criticism will obviously continue.[44]

To some Americans, Whitman is unerringly on target. Committed to excessive self-interest whereby they take what they can and when they can, the country is mired in a "Silicon Valley" bog of vulgar materialism;[45] enchanted by individualism and pluralism, Americans are left without any sense of moral community and national purpose;[46] their addictive use of guns makes the large American city a prison, especially for the elderly; traditional authority is being eroded; and the declining influence of the legal system, the church, the family, local communities, the schools, and universities is pushing American culture to a breaking point.

Finally, there has been in the American story a deep strain of ethnic prejudices. Irish were "micks," Italians were "wops" or "dagos," Slavs were "honkies," Jews were "kikes" or "hymies," blacks were "niggers" or "coons," and Orientals were "chinks." Reflecting this seamy side was the 1890 incident in New Orleans in which eleven Sicilians were lynched even after they were found not guilty of murdering a police detective. The *New York Times*, the *Washington Post*, and many other influential newspapers praised the citizens of New Orleans for "teaching the dagos" a lesson. Teddy Roosevelt called the lynchings "a rather good thing" and offered this gem on the killing of American Indians: "The most ultimately righteous of all wars is a war with savages. The fierce settler who drives the savage from the land lays all civilized mankind under a debt to him."[47]

Walter Goodman, writing in the *New York Times* on May 20, 1984, noted how bias continues to infect American humor, radio talk shows, situation comedies, and the like:

The principle at work here is: Give us the wretched refuse of your teeming shores and we will mock them. Jews are affluent and ostentatious; blacks are shiftless; the Irish drink and fight; Poles, of course, are stupid; Italians are stupid, too, and also crooked; the crippled are, well, crippled. It is a democratic melting pot, where stereotypes leak into each other and many of the jokes do service in more than one category. There is something for everybody to be offended at.

However, at the point when evil threatens to bury America's virtues forever, new evidence appears. Relevant is a Japanese-sponsored poll that found young Americans took more pride in national achievements and characteristics than young people in eight other countries surveyed did. Young adults were asked: "Do you think that [name of country] has something to be proud of or not?" Of the eleven categories, American respondents put their country first in six, second in three, and third in one; only in their evaluation of the country's provisions for social welfare did the United States rank a poor fourth.[48] If these results are reasonably accurate, not only do the nation's youth not share the gloomy outlook of some of their more vocal elders but they, like their forebears, grab at the brass ring of success; they tolerate diversity in race, religion, and politics; and they feel that theirs is not the ideal country—only the best of the imperfects on an imperfect planet. Yuppies, not hippies, are the "real" Americans. Whether this is a passing phase—as distinguished sociologist Seymour Lipset believes—or whether it is a rebirth of traditional optimism remains to be seen.[49] It is, however, comforting to learn that between 1981 and 1985, polls showed a threefold increase in confidence levels of Americans in their institutions. It is the function of leadership to sustain such trust by performance.

In the welter of contradiction and ambiguity, are there any reasonably consistent themes in the American culture? Perhaps the closest approximation of an ideal response was penned by James Bryce (1838–1922), the brilliant English political theorist who visited this country and concluded that America was based on five things: a desire to rival the best thought and work of other countries, a love of bold effects and comprehensive generalizations, a respect for brilliance over delicacy, a disrespect for traditions, and a desire for quick and obvious results.[50] Bigness and greatness coalesced. While the implications for management are still being sorted out, it is worth noting that successful organizations continue to stress many features Bryce discovered in the nation itself—a desire for innovation, excellence, growth, and quick results.

Religious Elements

The Judeo-Christian tradition, the screen through which Americans filter their psychosocial attributes, means that synagogues and churches fill important institutional roles. Because of its famous "wall of separation" between church and state, however, Americans have created special problems for their religious institutions that, in turn, pose problems for the state. To some elites, religion is "piety in the sky" —an afterthought glossed on a secular culture already fully formed and in no need of the supernatural. Why, then, are churches so prevalent in American society? Part of the answer was given by John Stuart Mill, himself an unbeliever, who felt that religion was useful because, like poetry, it supplied a common need for those grandiose and more beautiful ideals found lacking in the ordinary prose of human life. In Mill's view, religion gave to the common morality a certain seriousness; it justified heroism, sacrifice, dedication, and service— all necessary to a meaningful society.[51]

One lesson, however, that Americans never forgot was that the religious wars that rent Europe in the seventeenth century and the intolerance that prevailed during the eighteenth would not be tolerated on American shores. No established church built along patterns found in England, Spain, Greece, Finland, and other European countries was supported. This does not mean, of course, that religion's influence will vanish. The plain fact is that the famous wall of separation can deny public funds to religious institutions but it cannot eliminate the church's influence. It has been too long a force in Western civilization, has been too interconnected with America's colonial culture, and is too important today to millions. The work ethic, the role of the family, the moral implication of economic competition, the shape of foreign policy, the right to life, and the right to choose are but a few examples of the diverse ways a religious ethic has influenced the culture. Indeed, the great question of politics is to know how we ought to live together, and that, inescapably, is a moral and a spiritual question.

In all discussions regarding church-state relations, a factor that has received insufficient attention is the role of what has been called the civil religion, reflecting Mill's stress on religion's utilitarian value.[52]

Its substance has tended to be defined in Fourth of July oratory and in presidential addresses, 90 percent of which have made reference to a deity in some form. Originally, the petitions were to "the Almighty Being," "the Great Author," "Parent of the Human Race," and the like, but later commentaries included references to a personal god interested in the welfare of humankind. Because politicians have been among its most prominent expositors, a certain cynicism exists toward the civil religion; remembered is Franklin Delano Roosevelt's alleged request to a staff writer: "Get some of that God stuff for my inaugural." Less remembered are his frequent mentions of God in speeches to Congress and in fireside chats.

Whatever cynicism persists toward it, civil religion had certain positive strengths in a pluralistic culture: it provided a framework in which individuals could understand and interpret their own experiences in ways that helped unify the community; it muted the idea that America had an inherent moral superiority over others; it vigorously supported the separation of church and state; and it emphasized personal freedom and voluntarism. Reassertions of the nation's dependence on God at a particular point in the national experience often occurred when Americans had experienced a widespread loss of confidence in themselves.[53]

The problem with civil religion was that its advocates often used it as a strategy to establish their own monopoly over the nation's value systems. Examples included regulations over the Amish schools, sex education programs, books that offended the cherished belief of religious fundamentalists regarding creation, secularistic indoctrination, and the like. The success of the civil religion has meant the transfer of the socializing function of children from family, church, and community to an all-encompassing educational structure that can then produce individuals free of allegiances to their basic institutions. Unattached individuals then act as mobile and morally interchangeable parts in a technologic society.[54]

To restate the thesis: the relationship among church, state, and business, like all triangles, creates tensions that must be faced and managed. The church's drive to influence corporate investment and hiring policies, public welfare programs, foreign aid, and tax/fiscal strategems is a sharp reminder that theological vision without realism is romanticism and business realism without vision is tragedy. Spiritual elements are a reality whose impact, in one way or another, will be felt by every segment of society, including business. It is self deception for managers to think, for example, of policies toward South Africa without taking into account Reverend Leon Sullivan and Archbishop Tutu; it is unrealistic for multinational corporations to devise strategies for the Third World without taking note of the World Council of Churches; and it is, finally, an inadequate conception of wage (and other employment) policies that ignores the position on the economy taken by the American Catholic bishops or the early writings of John Ryan of Catholic University. As good semioticians, managers look beyond demographics and global competition—or any other single variable—to do an effective job for their enterprises.

Political Elements

America's distinctive political tradition was forged through selective use of theological elements in Lutheranism and Calvinism, as well as philosophical elements from the Enlightenment. Whereas Luther felt governments should instill in people the New Testament emphasis on charity, Calvin asked governments to inculcate the Old Testament respect for justice. Choosing Calvin over Luther had important political consequences. By their choice, the framers of the Constitution assumed that the natural state of humanity was evil and that very tight reins were needed to prevent turbulent and selfish masses from creating public mischief.[55] On the other hand, the founders hoped that concern for the general welfare would show appropriate deference to Luther's stress on benevolence.

More important than either Calvin or Luther were the Enlightenment thinkers who believed in the individual's innate goodness, a view that directly clashed with the Calvinist emphasis on humankind's mischief-making capacity. Reconciling the two contradictory views was achieved eventually through representative government based on a system of checks and balances.[56] Absurdities, inefficiencies, and controversies resulted. Delaware, for example, provided corporate charters on such generous terms that public needs often seemed to be subordinated to organizational desires; Nevada granted quick divorces and sold silver at exorbitant prices; midwestern farmers worked to defeat market forces by government subsidies; and Wall Street got control of the financial markets. Asked why they accepted such anomalies, Americans answered that these were small prices to pay for a society that draws unity and strength from "reason, morality and the Christian religion"—what John Adams called "the divine science of politics."[57]

Part of the present problem is traceable to a popular tendency to assert Enlightenment rights and repudiate Calvinist duties. There are disquieting signs that this is happening at all age levels. An American Council on Education survey, for example, showed a fifteen-year decline in students'expectation of participation in political life, in any form of altruism, and in concern for the interests of others. Over the same period, there was a steady rise in students' interest in values associated with money, status, and power. Values showing the greatest increases since 1972 were (1) being very well-off financially, (2) being an authority, (3) having administrative responsibility for others, and (4) obtaining recognition. Values showing the largest decline were (1) developing a philosophy of life, (2) participating in community affairs, (3) cleaning the environment, and (4) promoting racial understanding. The reported trend is hard to reconcile to the renewed interest among the young and the elite in religion. Perhaps resolution of the conflict is due to a belief that one can have "all this and heaven, too," a comforting but disquieting form of reasoning.[58]

Technologic Elements

A first impact of machine technology was on industry and plant location, which, in turn, created cultural ripples by drawing large numbers of people to the city to work for large organizations. Max Weber's son Alfred (1868–1958) was one of the first to point out that technology, by changing the nature and location of work, had brought to the world such mixed blessings that understanding its impact on culture was necessary to the management of society's great organizational monoliths.

A second effect of technology on culture—namely, its impact on religion—was less discernible but no less important. In a famous poem, Matthew Arnold (1822–88) told how, on Dover Beach, he had listened to the "melancholy, long, withdrawing roar" of the outgoing tide, and in it sensed the ebb tide of religious faith. But what was there to take its place? Arnold's answer was literature, and especially poetry; people would have to turn to poetry to interpret life, to console it and sustain it. Without poetry, moderns are left dangling between imagination and faith, and it is unlikely that they have enough of the former to replace the latter.

A third impact of technology was on government. By reducing uncertainty, technology stimulated the belief that contingencies can be controlled. Science protects against disasters, eliminates disease, solves world problems, and increases prosperity. From physical control the mind moves slowly toward social control, seen as a response to higher expectations for justice in all its guises. Governments are expected to do more for more, and the expectation runs counter to the laissez-faire ideology. Private enterprise apologists dislike Big Brother because he exacts more from them in taxes and takes more control over them through myriad regulations. Further, the old tension between science and religion has been intensified by technology, and, depending on the wisdom brought to the use of technological processes, humans may use it to attain new glories or to plummet to new depths.[59]

At the core of contemporary technology are computers and robots, symbols of a postindustrial culture. A secular dogma teaches that computers breed winners and losers; technology-rich nations will outgrow technology-poor ones; companies with well-managed technical resources will outperform computational laggards; and children with personal computers will outdistance children who lack them. The computer, of course, made possible the robot. Unlike the steam engine, the spinning mule, and the power loom, robots were conceived long before they were invented; however, what writers and inventors of the past had in mind was what today would be considered automation.

The impact on the work force will be staggering. Welders, painters, machinists, toolmakers, machine operators, inspectors, and industrial assemblers—in short, most of the industrial working class—will soon face the end of the road.[60] For them, the robot's golden arm can become a squeeze of death, and this, too, will transform the culture. For unlike an industrial society based on machine technology, the postindustrial society is based on intellectual technology; unlike industrial commodities that are produced in discrete units that are exchanged, sold, and consumed (such as a loaf of bread or an automobile), the information society produces nonconsumable products that, even when sold, remain with the producer and become collective goods. The main characteristics of the new postindustrial culture include:

• supremacy of theoretical knowledge

- creation of a new intellectual technology through mathematical and economic techniques based on linear programs and the like
- change from a goods to a service economy
- alterations in the character of work, whereby the interplay is between persons rather than between producer and physical nature
- a view of humanity not against a backdrop of nature but, rather, within a framework of an environment composed of machines, organizations, information, transportation, and other technologies
- the bounded rationality of human beings challenged by the alleged absolute rationality of the computer
- technological inventions outpacing administrative innovations[61]
- legal decisions shaped by hitherto inadmissible scientific evidence[62]

The ultimate meaning of technology's impact on the culture is, of course, impossible to perceive. A distinguished French commentator, Jacques Ellul, has won many disciples to his thesis that the new technology is brutalizing society in ways more ominous than the first industrial revolution.[63] Reinforcing this theme is Norman Lear, creator of *All in the Family* and other television hits, whose warning to managers might well be engraved on entrances to executive suites:

> The computer is now so pervasive in our society, its language and logic so wrapped up in our daily lives, that it is something of a metaphor for our imagination. In the computer mentality, all data are distilled into binary codes, either one or zero, and then elaborate chains of these binary codes are strung together to assemble entirely new "images" of this world. This tendency to boil the world down into significant numbers and analytical abstractions comes to us, however, at the expense of human values—values which cannot be mechanistically manipulated with numbers or codes. And the wondrous resources of the human mind, which normally include values and priorities and attitudes, are replaced with something I call the *binary imagination*—a two-dimensional understanding of things which distorts and oversimplifies the richness of life and the human condition.[64]

Certain it is, therefore, that managers who make sure that essential human needs are not smothered under the technological blanket will be the survivors. Computers "think" but do not feel; robots work but do not weep. Primacy on humans is one value that must be in place in every organization, and it will not occur if managers continue to mind the store only in terms of the traditional model, namely, finding the most rational and efficient technique to get things done.

Economic Elements

Unlike psychosocial elements, which reveal why Americans behave as they do, or religious elements, which indicate how Americans should behave, or political elements, which tell them how to govern, the economic element moves more silently and, in some respects, more powerfully. Economists who wrangle over many things agree that there are only three bases on which an economy can be organized: (1) tradition, (2) command, and (3) exchange. Tradition influenced ancient Egypt, where children were expected to follow the occupation of the father; in the less industrialized nations today, it still plays a significant role. Tradition explains why members of India's different castes have different occupations or who gets what part of a kill among South African bushmen. In command economies, by contrast, policy goals and modes of meeting those goals are established by a centralized agency. Totalitarian governments follow this form.

The third form is the market system, whose theoretical features were spelled out in 1776 in *The Wealth of Nations* by Adam Smith. Possibly his two most remembered sentences were related to enlightened self-interest: "It is not in the benevolence of the butcher, baker and the brewer that we expect our dinner, but from their regard for their own self-interest. We address ourselves not to their humanity but to their self-love, and never talk to them of our own necessities but of their advantages."[65] Self-interest was to be disciplined by competition and not conflict, a differentiation with important nuances. Whereas competition operates under rules accepted by players who believe that they and others can survive and prosper, conflict views the "other" as an enemy to be destroyed or immobilized. Competition was thus perceived as a moral good in much of the Protestant creed because it built character, helped people adjust to the real world, enhanced self-respect, and resulted in such productivity increases that greater social justice would prevail.

Adam Smith abhorred concentrations of economic power, yet large corporations dominate the landscape; he gave scant attention to non-profits, which are of great importance in a service economy; he did not anticipate the advent of large unions; and he downplayed the role of lawyers, who today hold great power over society. The distance between the theoretical capitalism sketched by Adam Smith and the business system created by corporations can be appreciated in the following contrast.[66]

Market System	Business System
Free competition	Fair competition
Profit maximizing	Profit satisfying
Efficient production	Effective production
Very unstable	Fairly stable
Uncertain	Planned
Consumers' sovereignty	Producers' primacy
Democratic in consumption	Elitist in production
Decentralized markets	Centralized bureaucracies
Individualistic	Corporate
Personal autonomy	Paternalistic direction
Minimal government	Activist government
Free choice	Appropriate choice
Rational for the self	Rational for the organization

REPRISE

Successful managers perform capitalistic, entrepreneurial, and administrative functions: as capitalists they need money for the enterprise; as entrepreneurs they innovate; and as managers they rely on people to get things done. Getting things done requires constant attention to the values people live by, which is their culture. In this respect, managers teach and are taught. Never easy, signal reading is now inordinately difficult because the culture is rent by divisions. Old-line individualism competes with the interdependence factor of industrialized societies; belief in progress confronts fear of change; traditional optimism is muted by undercurrents of pessimism; the stabilizing influence of the church has been challenged by secular humanism and the civil religion; and Madison's confidence that factions would not work effectively against the common good is no longer an article of political faith. Finally, there is the economy itself, no longer a reflection of Adam Smith's capitalism and yet not socialistic in any real sense of that term. Often called a mixed economy, it gives off the same kind of mixed signals that emanate from other parts of the culture. When collisions occur, managers tend to scramble or manipulate—two reactions that will prove less effective in the future. What fundamental values are at stake must be known because, in the long run, the commonwealth prospers only when managers perform efficiently *and* ethically.

3
IDEOLOGIES, IDEOLOGUES, AND ORGANIZATIONS

THE VALUES QUIZ   *(Mark True or False)*

1. _____ Church leaders should not take public stands on political or business issues.
2. _____ There is an instinctive dislike of business among intellectuals.
3. _____ Private property is the best bulwark of political liberty.
4. _____ Corporations should not follow Mobil Oil's lead in talking publicly about major national issues.
5. _____ Corporate PACs are pernicious and should be outlawed by Congress.
6. _____ Not only is there no business ideology but there should not be one.
7. _____ Capitalism rests on the idea of self-interest—an idea that, by its very nature, should worry church leaders who stress sacrifice.
8. _____ With the decline of church influence in modern times, intellectuals must and should assume the role of society's conscience.

Ideologies are answers to questions. They may not be right answers, but they are satisfactory ones to the interrogator. For example, when confronted by a new rule, children frequently ask, How come? The parent is challenged to explain and defend the precept. Parents, in turn, question other things, such as traditional school practices: How come the teaching of Latin in the middle ages was restricted to males? How come in Denmark student councils run the entire operation while in the United States they supervise class proms?

The "how comes" can be applied to Americans in general and to managers in particular. How come they:

- *praise individualism, which Europeans find somewhat repugnant?*
- *prefer market competition over government planning?*
- *restrict congressional power when the equally freedom-loving English operate under an all-powerful Parliament?*
- *exalt self-interest when others, like the Chinese, promote group interests?*
- *emphasize personal liberty when others stress social justice?*
- *resist the welfare state that Scandinavians embrace?*
- *think that big is better when others say that small is beautiful?*
- *prefer capital to be raised through equity financing rather than through bank lending, as practiced by Japan?*

Obviously, the list is illustrative rather than exhaustive. Answers to such basic questions are shaped by common social experiences and expressed in creeds that are frequently grounded in logic, and yet may occasionally be both illogical and ahistorical. In the aggregate, however, the answers flow into a pattern because they "make sense," and making sense to what a particular group believes is the chief function of ideology. Like the word culture, *it is a term that also sparks controversy.[1] Some scholars dismiss ideology as unworthy of serious discussion;[2] the editors of the* Columbia Encyclopedia *and the* Catholic Encyclopedia, *omit the term altogether while those of the* Encyclopaedia Brittanica *gave it short shrift. Since, however, ideological debates divide the country, it is important to clear up terminology if such debates are to be understood and properly assessed. It is a task of some moment to managers who are increasingly concerned because of ideologically based attacks on the legitimacy of their organizations.*

MAKING OF THE MODERN IDEOLOGY

Definition

Values are the criteria upon which important decisions are made; culture is society's constellation of core values; ideology seeks to provide comprehensive and coherent answers to these questions: What are we about? Why are we doing this? How can I explain my life and my society to myself and to others?[3] Managers have a vital interest in knowing how ideologies are formed and interpreted because the very legitimacy of their organizations, as well as the legitimacy of their own roles, depends on belief systems rationalized by ideology. If, for example, Americans fear bigness—which they do—that part of the ideology works to make them skeptical of behemoths like General Motors and General Electric. The ideology explains in part why AT&T was vulnerable to Justice Department attack even though the citizenry had second thoughts about the economic wisdom of the enforced dissolution.

Banners of the ideologues fly from top masts when people identified as important to their causes are nominated for positions of power. Often the Supreme Court is in the eye of ideological storms. In 1916, seven past presidents of the American Bar Association opposed Louis Brandeis's nomination of the Court because he had continued to press the view (first stated in 1905 before the Harvard Ethical Society of Justice) that there was too much emphasis on corporation lawyers and far too little on the people's lawyer.[4] In 1986 congressional investigation into the fitness of Justice Rehnquist for the post of chief justice led to what many called a "rehnquisition." In 1987 Robert Bork's fitness for nomination to the Court led to ideological debates that vulgarized the confirmation process of the Senate. Since the law shapes and is shaped by ideology, it is not surprising to find the legal community involved in discussions with ideological overtones. One example is the bitter debate among Harvard Law School faculty between traditionalists and activists, with the latter insisting that present law is no more than an instrument of social oppression to preserve the powers of the ruling elite. How intense this ideological warfare is waged can be understood in the words of Paul Bator, who, upon quitting the Harvard law faculty after a quarter-century of teaching, spoke bitterly of activist ideologues as "philistines" bent on turning a great law faculty into a group of mediocrities. Ideologies, important to lawyers, are also important to managers who live under laws drafted by lawyers, interpreted by lawyers, and applied by lawyers. Ideologies espoused by professors are also important to managers who hire their graduates. When disputes over policies and people appear, it can be generally assumed that ideology has turned words into weapons.

What, then, is ideology? It consists of propositions that give reasons for people to cling to the values they take for granted in their culture; thus defined, *ideology incorporates a complete system of concepts, images, myths, and representations that, in a given society, supports a specific hierarchy of values and certain patterns of individual and collective behavior.* Modern ideologies have been shaped by the Enlightenment (roughly 1600–1800) and reactions to it during the following centuries. Inspired by Sir Isaac Newton's vision of a universal order of nature, by Descartes's rationalistic skepticism, and by Francis Bacon's empiricism, the champions of the Enlightenment (though differing strongly on specific issues) agreed that society's three major enemies were medieval feudalism, religious dogmatism, and state mercantilism. The new ideology would, as a consequence, replace status by contract, dogma by science, and mercantilism by competition. Merchants, industrialists, and financiers had warmly embraced the Enlightenment because it provided justification for their attacks on such old enemies as priests, kings, and nobles. In this climate, laissez-faire economists from the so-called Manchester School found a congenial home. The happy consequence of all of this was an accelerated rate of economic progress and an expansion of the material base of society justified by an ideology that defended the capitalist system that made both possible.

The intellectuals who forged the Enlightenment, however, lacked both an institutional base and a social role (they were not members of the church or university) in their own culture. This lack was to become very important in understanding what might crudely be called the psychology of the new ideologists. They were aggressive, individualistic, and drawn to voluntary rather than institutional associations; Enlightenment ideas were used to justify assaults on any institution exercising power because power was evil and power holders were dangerous. The seeds of antiestablishmentarianism had been sown. As children of the Enlightenment, contemporary ideologies often contain a series of "antis": anti-state, anti-church, anti-authority, anti-organization, and anti-bigness. Conversely, pro-individual, pro-science, and pro-smallness are its positive elements. To say we are prisoners of an inherited ideology may exaggerate the case; nevertheless, every leader deals with "tilted thinking" because what is sweetly reasonable to him or her may be bitterly irrational to another. One way to understand the modern world view is to contrast the Enlightenment ideology to an earlier one through the use of "captions," a term chosen over "concepts" because it suggests, rather than defines, the dominant social values.[5]

Captions

Classical World View (Greco-Roman and Judeo-Christian)	Modern World View (Enlightenment)
Religious faith	Religious skepticism
God is	God is not—or may be
Future-world orientation	This-world orientation
Ends (teleological)	Means (instrumental)
Mysteries to be accepted	Problems to be solved
Centralized moral authority	Diversified moral authority
Language of metaphor	Technical argot
Intuition	Rationality
Religious obedience	Religious dissent
Blessed are the poor	Blessed are the prosperous
Sense of community	Sense of individualism
Charity	Self-interest
Justice	Liberty
Status	Contract
Routine	Innovation
Individual stability	Individual mobility
Static economy	Growth economy
Just price	Market price
Cooperation	Competition

While ideologies can be put to perverse uses and while they are culture bound and hence parochial, they do serve four useful and sometimes inconsistent functions:

1. They act as an apologetic for dominant institutions, professions, and class structures.
2. They mobilize individual and collective energies for a common goal.

3.   They present a particular world view as universal by eternalizing specific values.
4.   They serve as a vehicle of mystification.

In summary, ideology tells us what to expect from (1) institutions, (2) institutionalized roles, and (3) persons holding significant power in society. Ideology provides justification for action, legitimacy for institutions, and acceptable reconciliations among contradictions. Without it, society lacks a set of "oughts" that tells individuals and organizations what to do as almost knee-jerk reactions. If this seems irrational, it is important to remember that, faced with new problems for which there is no value referent, individuals and entities can become paralyzed or, worse, make decisions on the basis of irrelevant and inapplicable norms. So ideology is invariably marked by tension because it rescues decision makers from paralysis even while it simultaneously contains within itself a virus that can induce paralysis.[6]

If not always admired, ideologies, to repeat, are invariably needed because they give coherence to political, religious, and economic elements that sometimes contradict one another. A classic example is the United States, which has a political system based on democratic criteria borrowed from John Locke and an authoritarian business system resting on the efficiency norm propounded by Max Weber. Leaders of organized groups, public or private, usually follow the ideology of Locke and Weber and see no contradictions in their positions; as a consequence: ideology survives because it makes "sense" out of contradictions, thus legitimizing the way people go about fulfilling essential needs for sustenance and security; it explains how and why people can be bonded together by sufficient mutual loyalties and affections to create a community.[7] Every society needs an ideology, and America is no exception.

The American Ideology

The Political Ideology.   In symbolic ways, early American leaders revealed their Enlightenment traditions by speaking of the "Great Mr. Locke." The Founding Fathers fashioned a form of government designed less to make citizens virtuous—as Aristotle wished it to do— as to make them free, which Locke insisted it must do. Operating on the same premise of freedom, the market system sought to make people richer and thereby fulfill Locke's vision for a country of prosperous owners. Liberty was the cord that bound the ideologies of both systems together, even as each operated within its own sphere. An interesting facet of America's evolution was that its ideology separated society from community; the former stressed fulfillment of role, and the latter fulfillment of self. Building community was left to churches, schools, and families; building society was the burden of a limited republican form of government resting on John Locke's ideas of individualism, property rights, and competition.[8] The Lockean content was grafted upon the work/thrift ethic of John Calvin so harmoniously that ideology and theology thereafter enjoyed a love affair lasting almost to the twentieth century.

More is needed, however, to understand the nation's ideology, and this requires a perspective narrower than—and less dependent on—the European Enlightenment. This parochial view spawned a home-grown ideology that included belief in steady progress, faith in the common man, a sense of special national destiny, and procedural rather than substantive concepts of justice. The result was a commercial republic that tolerated, but never exalted, the high culture of Greco-Roman philosophy and English literature. It was a land of "misters" and "ma'ams," not lords or ladies. It would surpass England in gimmickry, salesmanship, sports, hobbies, fashions, and the like.[9] America was quintessentially bourgeois—prosaic people reading books written in unexceptional prose, promenading not along gracious boulevards but along plain main streets, trusting mail-order catalogues and avoiding fashionable boutiques, interested in town politics and unconcerned with international diplomacy. After the Bible, the popular stories were about rags-to-riches lives, not the heroic exploits of Homer or the spiritual pilgrimages of Dante.

Acultural in the European aristocratic sense, America encouraged culture in another sense. Often noted is the fact that "without hereditary wealth, privilege or rank, Americans found strength within themselves. Their minds were weapons and tools, and individuals with no taste for pure knowledge nevertheless recognized its utility. Americans preferred books easily procured, quickly read, and which required no advanced education to be understood."[10] The dominant ideology was invariably suspicious of liberal arts educators on grounds that they would disturb the ordinary citizen. It was right, moreover, to build technical institutes, agricultural and mining schools (the "aggies"), and professional schools of business because these were in harmony with an ideology that stressed practical results. The consequence was tension between that older part of the ideology influenced by the Enlightenment and the newer part formed to explain and defend the special qualities of American life.

Because it was a society with built-in contradictions, its ideological content would necessarily be eclectic and pragmatic, its intellectual history enlivened by competing interpretations shaped by different ideological preferences. Ideology was used positively to reconcile many Americans into one America; it was used negatively as an instrument for selective indignation. Since each major societal institution developed its own ideology to explain and defend its role and position, it is appropriate to examine the one used by American business.

The Business Ideology.   In its evolution, business ideology passed through successive stages characterized less by change in fundamental content and more by change in focus and emphasis. Nonetheless, two distinct strands are discernible, and these have been called the classical and the managerial ideologies, respectively. The classical strand had direct links to three men: John Calvin (who taught that the road to prosperity was through hard work, thrift, and strict attention to duty), John Locke (who held that private property legitimized public power), and Adam Smith (who made consumers the ultimate sovereigns over the economy). The combination produced an austere creed that emphasized acceptance of personal responsibility and self-reliance for a world wherein no one was owed a living.[11] Horatio Alger was the ideal in fiction and Andrew Carnegie its embodiment in reality.

The twentieth-century advent of large organizations managed by salaried managers meant that some elements of the austere model simply could not survive.[12] Private property alone could not provide legitimacy for corporate power; stress on economic efficiency had to be balanced by social responsibility; stockholder rights had to be weighed against employee and consumer claims. Such new elements as corporate social responsibilities, employee rights, and "satisficiency" rather than maximization were blended into what has been called the managerial creed. Cronyism and nepotism were jettisoned in favor of neutral decisions that rewarded people not by relationships but by performance; price competition was complemented, and sometimes replaced, by product and service competition; the jack-of-all-trades yielded to the specialist; intuitive management fell before scientific management; and corporate giants pushed ahead of small partnerships.

What remained in the ideology was a conviction that business operated according to fundamental laws and that attempts to circumvent them were bound to fail.

THE IDEOLOGUES

That the traditional ideology, both national and sectoral, should be under strain today is to be expected in a country wherein growth is everything—growth in profits and prosperity, people, and territory.[13] When organizational behemoths like U.S. Steel and General Motors came on the scene, people identified themselves more by their affiliation with a business than by anything else, so much so that Americans literally drifted into the late twentieth century with slight awareness that administrative systems had become the dominant force in their lives. Indeed,

> large organizations have influenced us profoundly, but so quietly and so benevolently, that we are scarcely aware they are the major agencies of value change in our country. Therefore, the serious moral issues presented by modern organizations simply are not a matter of interest to most Americans because the changes have not yet caused concern.[14]

Even when the majority is indifferent, there is nonetheless a vocal and articulate minority ready to do battle over both the austere and the managerial creeds.

Intellectuals and Issues

In ideological warfare, intellectuals feel the power of Percy Bysshe Shelley's message that they "are the unacknowledged legislators of the world." While their initial role has been noted, it was only in the nineteenth century that Western history dotted two significant "i's": intellectual and industrialist. As intellectuals became acutely aware of their own importance, they explicitly defined their mission as "the duty to doubt everything that is obvious, to make relative all authority, to ask all those questions that no one else dared to ask."[15] Declining church influence led them to assume that they had an even heavier duty, namely, to serve as the conscience of society. Free from institutional discipline, they could pick and choose their targets and adjust their dogmas as needed. In short, intellectuals-turned-ideologues formed and re-formed mobile strike forces.

This reason makes it important to note their two generally shared qualities: (1) love of humanity transcended affection for individuals and (2) causes were sacred and people bothersome. Examples include Karl Marx, who was cruel to his parents and more interested in writing about capital than in working to acquire it, and Ayn Rand, the redoubtable defender of capitalism who humiliated many who admired her. While the generalization needs qualification, it is nevertheless true that love of ideas, playfulness with words, and self-righteousness characterize the activists. Such attributes make friendly ideologues stalwart allies and unfriendly ones deadly foes when corporations and professions are under seige.

Contemporary ideologues, taking a lesson from the past, marshal their arguments on the basis of a particular slice of the total ideology. Contradictions in the national culture stimulate such selectivity, and not all with negative results. In everyone lurks an ideologue, and the difference between those who are stridently vocal (intellectuals, clerics, and journalists) and those who are largely silent (managers and blue-collar workers) is due to their activities, not their proclivities. Like the ideology itself, the ideologue is useful. Both merit respectful hearing, and both bear careful watching. So far as the economy is concerned, both critics and apologists have concentrated on the three "p's": performance, power, and philosophy. Views of the critics can be captured through the lens of their arguments on each.

The Critics

Performance.   When industrial productivity slackens, criticism naturally intensifies. The Great Depression of the 1930s fanned the fires of hostility, and from Communist fringes came demands for dismantling the market system entirely. While slowdowns in the past decade elicited less strident criticism, a widely shared view was that too much was going into defense and too little into social welfare[16] and that production processes had become too inflexible because of a commitment to high volume and scientific management. America was losing to others the race for superiority in electronics. Statistics were paraded to show how bleak was the picture—a 7 percent unemployment rate, consistent decreases in the rate of productivity since the 1960s, trade imbalances, and slides in the capital investment rate. The country's huge technological edge of the 1950s and 1960s had disappeared.[17] Economist Lester Thurow expressed a popular view when he wrote that "if American industry fails, the managers are ultimately account-able. While we cannot fire all of America's managers any more than we can fire the American labor force, there is clearly something wrong with management."[18] Nobel Laureate Wassily Leontief made the same point when he accused managers of having tunnel vision.[19]

There is evidence to support such pessimism. In 1975 the U.S. national debt stood at $1.7 trillion; in 1988 it was astronomical, and these almost incomprehensible numbers meant that every American had a personal mortgage of $7,000–$10,000 that was growing at a rate of $1,000 per year. The portion of our federal budget allocated to paying the interest on this debt was $155 billion, a sum larger than the entire federal government budget in a year as recent as 1966. The situation became so bleak that the *Wall Street Journal*'s respected editor Robert L. Bartley expressed fear that, given the surge of pro-tectionism in the country, America could relive the ghastly depression of the 1930s.[20]

Numbed by numbers, Americans see the larger picture in smaller snapshots—Lansing, Michigan, home of the Oldsmobile plant and the state university, where Datsuns are used in driver education classes; the Marine Corps, which purchased Japanese pickup trucks;[21] and the underground economy (now estimated to be as high as 10 percent of the GNP), whose denizens pay little or no taxes, heed few government regulations, and create distortions in statistics used to influence public policy, and in farm and real estate tax scams. Especially hard hit are industries in which the United States once had commanding leads— steel, automobiles, textiles, electrical and metal-forming machinery, petrochemicals, and consumer electronics. Many insist that traditional economic theory is unfit to provide responses to new challenges and that insights from "institutional economics" are needed to bring re-newed dynamism to the market through forms of planning not here-tofore tried.

At the same time, government's role became confused and confus-ing. The government broke up AT&T, the most successful and efficient utility in the entire world, while simultaneously permitting Texaco to acquire Getty Oil for $10 billion.[22] To encourage foreigners to buy more of its bonds, the government in 1984 stopped withholding taxes on interest owed to foreigners and issued bearer bonds on which no ownership records are kept; it backed off in its efforts to collect billions of tax dollars not reported on interest and dividends when the banks loudly protested. The system is unhinged. Mixed signals from captains of the mixed economy have convinced critics that even the classical business ideology seeks to make sense of the nonsensical.

Power.   In addition to dismay over performance has been a resurrected fear of corporate power, a fear based partly on historical and partly on contemporary evidence. Adam Smith himself disliked concentrated economic power, and since the American colonists operated small-businesses, they readily embraced Smith's doctrine. The industrial revolution, by ushering in large organizations, shook the old ideology. As America's island communities dissolved, a national network of industrial associations arose to bring the entire nation under its aegis.[23] This process of incorporation provoked debate over not only what America was to mean but also who should have the right to define that meaning. To early critics, the most appropriate symbol of corporate power was the 1892 Chicago World's Fair, possibly the most spectacular cultural event in American history. The fair "settled the question of the true and real meaning of America. It was the victory of elites in business, politics and culture over dissident, but divided, voices of labor, farmers, immigrants, blacks and women."[24] Of these three elites, business held the best cards.

Nearly a century has elapsed since the business "victory" at Chicago was symbolically proclaimed; everything done subsequently, say the critics, has simply ratified the conquest of the giants over the little people. The small corporations of the nineteenth century have become the massive aristocracies of our time.[25] These towering impersonal organizations move vast capital across borders and actually pride themselves on their rootlessness; they are ruled by princes whose decisions lie beyond the reach of the democratic process and are therefore beyond society's control.[26] The corporation that, in the hallowed business ideology, was an organizational servant has now become the absolute despot so that the real struggle is not between rich and poor but between the organized and the unorganized. Critic Michael Harrington made clear his view of corporate power when he said he would prefer to be on the board of General Motors than on the City Council of New York.[27]

Compounding the evil was government's unholy alliance with big business. Because business was the supplier of prosperity, political leaders not only dared not to ignore it but actually catered to it because they believed that industry-engendered economic growth alone would restrain unemployment. The net result was a distorted market and the imposition of a tax on the rest of society.[28] An added irritant was the fact that a few grew fat from profits garnered by shrewd investments and not through salaries earned by productive work. Twentieth-century America, it was said, is reliving Britain's eighteenth-century experiences when a financial revolution, superimposed on the commercial revolution, created a new investor class who lent to the government and then lived comfortably on handsome government repayments. Antagonistic British ideologues then denounced ownership of government investments, not tangible property, as a corrosive evil because capitalism was now built on speculation rather than calculation, on fantasy rather than reality.[29]

To critics, the American story is similar to England's. Business ideology today is used to justify the unjustifiable as it was used in a fractured Whig ideology to defend a system of financial capitalism that was concerned less with productivity or commerce than with relationships between public debtors and private lenders. What followed then has come now—a change in the business ideology to trick the people by using old words to provide new meanings. The final irony is that the very same giant organizations essential to economic growth are now heavily responsible for national impoverishment because they divert more and more resources to maintain a complex and expensive administrative system that provides fewer products and services. In short, the critics conclude that society is so bedeviled by empire building, self-aggrandizement, and dirty tricks that solid values have been displaced by meretricious ones.[30] But even if performance improved, even if business power were curtailed and obligations between business and society sharply defined, a problem would continue because of the deformed philosophy on which capitalism is built.

Philosophy.   Critics of capitalism stress its natural alliance to philosophical liberalism, which allegedly rests on a false and exaggerated form of individualism. This explains why there exists an acquisitive, possibly avaricious society composed of people consumed by a pernicious hedonism. Karl Marx, for example, argued that capitalism meant the accumulation of wealth in fewer and fewer hands, dehumanization of the worker, and creation of a society divided into two classes, the victorious capitalists and the exploited proletariat.[31] Karl

Polanyi said that the philosophic problem was caused not by industrialization but by the claim that people, land, and money were all
subject to the self-regulating market—an inherent absurdity "and the
weirdest of all undertakings by our ancestors."[32] Unlike Marx and
Polanyi, who saw capitalism's demise caused by its inherent defects,
economist Joseph Schumpeter saw capitalism doomed by its success:
it destroyed or impaired intermediate institutions, like churches, universities, and small businesses, that were essential to its survival; it
created economic surpluses that sustained the elites, who then became
the bitter adversaries of business; and it created expectations that only
a government could provide.[33] Finally, there is fear that since the
system is built on the self-interest principle, it ignores or subordinates
the interests of others. Capitalism is, therefore, ethically flawed.[34] The
American dream is America's nightmare.

Progressive emancipation of the individual from the so-called irrational social constraints of the past have actually resulted in less
freedom for corporate serfs who populate factories and lubricate assembly lines with their own sweat. In some ways, G.K. Chesterton
encompassed all the ideological arguments against capitalism when he
wrote that it broke up households, encouraged divorces, and treated
the old domestic virtues with more and more open contempt; it

> has forced a moral feud and a commercial competition between the sexes;
> has destroyed the influence of the parent in favor of the influence of the
> employer; has driven men from homes to look for jobs; has forced them
> to live near their factories or their firms instead of near their families;
> and, above all, has encouraged, for commercial reasons, a parade of pub-
> licity and garish novelty which is in its nature the death of all that was
> called dignity and modesty by our mothers and fathers.[35]

What might be called Chestertonianism has been carried to new
extremes by theologian Rudolf Siebert, who wrote that "no adequate
theodicy can possibly be developed in the context of organized capitalistic society, the ability of which to cause suffering and death—
colonialism, imperialism, two world wars, slums, profitable production of carcinogenic food, economic depressions, fascism, Dachau,
Hiroshima and Vietnam—is so out of proportion to its capacity truly
to help . . ."[36]

So deafening has been the rhetoric that much of it can be dismissed
as polemics without proof; however, when influential economists and
church organizations speak out forcefully, the business community

cannot afford complacency. Robert Heilbroner, whose name conjures up images of the West's great economists as our "worldly philosophers," sees the present system as fulfilling Marx's description of the capitalist production system, M-C-M (from money to commodities and back to money); he strongly suspects that the executives who run the system are ruthless, unloving, uncaring characters whose MBA training disguises their nastier side.[37] Church criticism comes from both Protestant and Catholic ranks.

The World Council of Churches, established in Amsterdam in 1944 and composed of leaders from three hundred churches in a hundred countries, has moved from mild to sharp criticism. The council's basic theme is that since capitalism means expansionism and impersonalism, exploitation and pollution, it is necessarily a destablilizing force in human affairs. At the same time, Catholic church leaders, long hostile to the ideology of laissez-faire capitalism and uncomfortable with many of its unintended consequences, have shown signs of increasing disenchantment. A review of its teachings makes clear the fact that, over the past century, the Catholic church has made an increasing commitment to the poor, coupled with a sense of urgency that social justice will not come about unless religious leaders take a stand. Taking a stand means, of course, a movement from pulpit to politics and raises the question of whether theology and ideology can really be divorced under such circumstances.[38] Consistent with this trend was the action of the American bishops who acknowledged capitalism's superiority in producing wealth but abhorred its unintended by-products: five million Americans living at or below the poverty level, foreign-aid programs based on military support for dubious "friends," and denial of aid to those in dire need.[39] When attacked as ideologists, the bishops responded that capitalism itself is an ideology whereas Christianity is not, that ideologies are partial and Christianity is comprehensive, and that ideologies deal with particular meanings and religion with ultimate meanings.[40] In simple terms, it was a question of capitalist self-seeking or Christian self-denial.[41]

It differs little to business whether the attacks are theological or ideological because the message is the same: capitalism is doomed—by its structural defects, according to Marx; by its barbaric treatment of people, according to Polanyi; by its stultifying self-interest principle, according to Chesterton; by its successes, according to Schumpeter; and by its callousness toward the poor, according to church leaders. Taken together, critics have conjured a Catch-22 scenario so that capitalism, whether spectacularly successful or spectacularly un-successful, cannot and should not survive.[42]

The Apologists

What disturbs supporters of the market system is their fear that both church and lay critics have moved beyond being society's social con-science to become the voice of a left-wing ideology and unwitting supporters of groups committed to increasing their own power over society. Sociologist Peter Berger called the secularist critics the New Class who derived their livelihood from the knowledge industry and their power through manipulation of symbols rather than the making of things.[43] Berger cited the Environmental Protection Agency as the perfect example of how ideologues establish a power beachhead within the federal government while simultanteously garnering profits from policing the atmosphere. Particularly annoying to conservatives is their perception that this new class consists of self-righteous breast-beaters whose rhetoric rivals that of the most bellicose Marxist.

The neoconservatives, according to one of its best known leaders, Irving Kristol, feel that in the symbol-waving, mudslinging world of ideologies, critics have all the advantages because neoconservatives champion what is without doubt the most prosaic of all possible societies, namely, "a bourgeois world of ordinary men and women, a world popular among common people and unpopular among artists, writers and thinkers who take themselves to be Very Important People. Consequently, these VIPs are outraged by a society that merely tol-erates them."[44] When neoconservatives like Peter Berger, Michael Novak, and Irving Kristol and conservatives like Milton Friedman, F.A. von Hayek, and Henry C. Simons of the "Chicago School" of economics address the specific problems of performance, power, or philosophy, their answers tend to run along the following lines.

Performance. Rather than compare capitalism's performance to some utopian scheme, it is, say its defenders, intellectually more honest to contrast it with other ongoing systems. Socialist economies, for ex-ample, are always sellers' markets with scant incentive for product innovation. Fear of failing is nonexistent because the state is unable to discipline inefficient bureaucrats and reward entrepreneurs who create the wealth. Even Japanese-style planning is viewed skeptically by the neoconservatives, who rebuff the common view that Japan's economic miracle is due primarily to a superb industrial policy developed by the Ministry of International Trade and Industry when, in reality, if MITI had had its way, Sony would not have produced a magnetic tape recorder or a transistor radio, and Honda never would have produced a single car, much less the famous Civic. MITI had found Sony's idea of a transistor radio to be preposterous and Honda's motorbikes unworthy of support.[45]

Record, not rhetoric, is the issue, and on this score the American economy wins the race hands down: "Industrial capitalism in the West has produced a better material life for a larger number of people than any system in history. Furthermore, if human betterment is not judged by some utopian ideal but by both higher living standards and greater protection of liberty and human rights, then capitalist arrangements are surely a better risk than any known alternative."[46] Long before the ideological wars, the common man voted for industrial capitalism with his feet, tramping from farms to towns, first in Britain, then throughout Europe, and later in the United States. No queues of immigrants wait to enter the Soviet Union or Bulgaria or Cuba.[47]

Even what America has done between 1974 and 1987 (the "ominous" decade, to critics) is impressive—more jobs created in a record never before achieved in peacetime, as contrasted with the period 1970–84, when Western Europe lost between three and four million jobs. Critics have, say free-market apologists, focused on the trees (Fortune 500's loss of some five to six million jobs) and missed the forest (the 600,000 new businesses started annually in the United States), which, together with small-and medium-sized entities, has made the country the best hope for all workers. If job creation is one index of the overall health of an economy, then say capitalism's supporters, the United States looks very good indeed.

Finally, it is argued that those who concentrate their attack on the multinationals because it is good strategy ignore what global corporations do for the home society and for the world. Domestically, of the four major costs of production (the value of which becomes the final selling price), two account for 93 percent of all costs: wages take 50 percent, and taxes eat up another 43 percent. Of the remaining 7 percent, 4.5 percent goes for after-tax profits and 2.5 percent for depreciation. In the international sphere, American multinationals make four major contributions to world economy:

1. *Product flow*, which means cheaper goods for all customers because of the law of comparative advantage

2. *Finance flow* through investments in the host country
3. *Technology flow* (although inadequate because multinationals want to control it), which helps people in developing nations to understand what innovation can do
4. Managerial flow, which teaches nations how to organize complex operations[48]

Power.   The issue of power is more hotly contested than that of performance record, which can more easily be assessed by facts. Critics, it may be recalled, charge that too much power has slipped toward the corporate side, substantial power to the union side, and little power to the unorganized sectors.[49] Seasoned observer Edwin Epstein of the University of California at Berkeley wrote that the public feared that corporations would "overwhelm other social interests competing in the political process and, thereby, achieve dominance over the formal and informal institutions of American government."[50] The managerial state is perceived as resting on the same overly tight relationships between government and business that existed in eighteenth-century England. Government has primary responsibility for economic stability and business primary responsibility for economic growth;[51] each so needs the other that the legendary "little fellow" is ignored.

Business, however, is not the only wielder of political power. Unions have never been quiet. While efforts to seek protection for the automobile and steel industries have been amply documented, less noted were actions by machinists and the United Auto Workers (who represent more than 100,000 aerospace workers at dozens of companies) to pressure the Pentagon to accept cost escalations occasioned by wage increases.[52] And, of course, there was the historic decision in 1984 by the AFL-CIO Executive Council to move forward its presidential endorsement date in order to provide greater support for Walter Mondale, an obvious reflection of labor's determination to solve major union problems in Washington and not at the bargaining table.[53] That decision triggered other decisions by labor leaders. To appeal to women's organizations, they supported the comparable-worth doctrine; to curry favor from the blacks, they endorsed job quotas; and to win over the powerful National Education Association, they opposed peer review of teachers. If the strategy had worked, it could have meant a major new coalition in American politics.[54] The point is that interest groups other than business are so active in politics that victory ebbs and flows between the pro- and anti-business forces.[55]

Defenders of business argue, therefore, that corporate executives exert no political monopoly because their voice is only one of many crying in the political wildernesses of Washington and state capitals. Futher, business rarely reflects the unanimity of opinion found in other pressure groups. The interests of USX are not those of Alcoa, General Electric does not depend on Exxon, and Apple Computers sues its founder, Steve Jobs; industries compete with other industries and companies compete within industries. Even interlocking directorates do not produce unifying political strategies. There is the further reality that business executives themselves run the spectrum from liberal Democrats to conservative Republicans. Bendix's Michael Blumenthal served as Secretary of the Treasury under Jimmy Carter, and Merrill Lynch's Donald Regan held the same position with Ronald Reagan.

Executives even disagree sharply on who should be the business voice. Don Gevirtz, head of a thriving Los Angeles finance company called Foothill Group, has been associated with the American Business Conference, whose members are from smaller and fast-growing companies. Sponsored by Arthur Levitt, chairman of the American Stock Exchange, conference members are convinced that small businesses have more to offer than the "managerial aristocrats" of the giant corporations. For Gevirtz, the early failures of Chrysler and International Harvester demonstrated that business leadership should not remain with the declining dinosaurs of big business.[56] The inefficient giants should be allowed to fail and public support given to the new entrepreneurial companies that promise future contributions. Standing in sharp contrast to a widely shared Gevirtz view is Irving Shapiro, former Du Pont chairman and member of the Business Roundtable, a select group of two hundred executives from the Fortune 500. In Shapiro's view, needed is a politically balanced approach that (1) preserves the strength of traditional industries crucial to the economy's performance and (2) provides government incentives to big and small firms so long as they continue to innovate.[57] Shapiro made the point that Silicon Valley is not Shangri-la since the five largest categories of workers associated with computers represent little more than 0.5 percent of the total work force. The point here is that different lobbies reflect different ideologies, and such contradictions prove that no monolith stalks the land.

If lobbyists are the "friendly persuaders" in the power game, then political action committees (PACs) hold the friendly purse strings. John White, chairman of the Democratic party during Lyndon Johnson's 1960 vice presidential campaign, told the story of his first meeting with Bobby Baker, a Johnson aide. White reported seeing "a big fat man with a pot belly—until I saw him take off his coat!" Today the bulking money belts are seen less often, but there is more money than ever before. By enacting the Federal Election Campaign Act of 1971, Congress simply abrogated its policy of limiting corporate and union electoral activity and made the PAC mechanism an easy device for large organizations to use in campaign financing.[58] Apologists for the corporate world have their greatest difficulties in trying to show that business PACs are not evidence of business's overwhelming power; indeed, when Congress attempted to control PAC groups, it was the politician, not the executive, who figured out ways to beat the system. "Special purpose" accounts, tax-exempt foundations, creative accounting, and independent spending on behalf of favorite candidates were established or practiced. These special purpose accounts permitted donors to exceed the $5,000 limit on PAC direct contributions through loose interpretation of credit that allowed bankers to lend depositors' money to favorite candidates without requiring collateral.[59]

Not only corporate PACs have aroused fire storms. During the 1982 campaign, for instance, doctors contributed slightly more than $2 million and lawyers gave twice that amount. The president of Common Cause, Fred Wertheimer, said that spending by the professions, and especially by lawyers, holds out no pretense of help to any given constituency; it is straight-access buying and "an extension of the hired-gun principle."[60] So despite the fact that labor had been long involved financially in the electoral process, business and profession-affiliated PACs that came later have become special targets for those who fear that the separation of public and private powers will collapse.[61] But apologists say that overreaction by the media, corporate lobbyists zeal to proclaim victories, and inattention to the public needs for education have been the problem, not corporate power itself.[62]

The business defense of PACs parallels its position on lobbying: so many actors are involved in the drama that no one holds center stage. Influential corporate executives have denounced PACs as strongly as the nonbusiness critics have. The conclusion, say the apologists, is that neither large industries like steel, which competes with other large industries, like plastics, nor even the entire business community, which is fragmented toward its basic ideology, holds dangerous power. Certainly private power is not beyond the control of Congress, the courts, and regulators; not immune to the power of labor unions and pressure groups; and not stalwart before presidential persuasion. On this last point, Congressman Clarence Brown (R-Ohio) told the story of corporate leaders who, vehemently opposed to federal control of gas pricing, vented their views in no uncertain terms to their congresspersons. But Brown added:

That was before the White House invited the chief executive officers of major U.S. corporations to Washington for breakfast with the President and a little straight talk about the realities of doing business in a regulated environment. . . . And they heard some not-so-subtle threats. The steel industry executives were told, according to press reports, that if they didn't back off opposition to the Administration's flawed energy package, the Administration might not set a high priority on the problems of the steel industry when tariff negotiations were next under way with the Japanese. The CEOs of textile companies and others similarly afflicted by foreign imports got the idea about the use of "administrative judgment" in an area vital to their survival.[63]

These "omnipotent" executives heard the message—and buckled under. Brown concluded that business shows not strength but servility, not leadership but followership. Probably the issue that really divides the ideologues is not so much corporate power but corporate philosophy, coupled with the widespread loss of civic conscience.

Philosophy.   It may be recalled that ideologists critical of capitalism denounced it because of its reliance on an exaggerated form of individualism found in the tenets of Adam Smith and John Locke. Yet the pair provide refutations. When Smith talked of self-interest, he did not advocate selfishness; when he espoused the profit motive, he opposed excessive profits and favored high wages. When Locke hailed the merits of private property, he did so in the belief that property rights were "part of the civil rights essential to individual freedom and, in the form of freedom of contract, constituted the governing principle of a free market economy."[64] This Lockean point has always been emphasized by capitalism's supporters, who argue that the market reduces greatly the number of issues decided by politicians and thereby minimizes state involvement in people's lives. Minimum government intervention is good because business can only persuade, whereas government can coerce. This point, so emphasized in the business ideology, was made more than twenty years ago by apologist Ayn Rand in *Capitalism: The Unknown Ideal* and was deemed so important that her view was featured again in the November 19, 1984, issue of *Barron's*: "The moral justification of capitalism does not lie in the altruist claim that it represents the best way to achieve 'the common good.' The moral justification of capitalism lies in the fact that it is the only system consonant with man's rational nature, that it protects man's survival *qua* man, and that its ruling principle is justice."

More remarkable is the fact that, in that twenty-year period between Rand's first pronouncement and its restatement, a new group of intellectuals had emerged to defend capitalism. Historically, the intellectual community had presented a fairly solid front against business, so much so that managers were hard put to find allies among any of the opinion molders. But neoconservatives like Irving Kristol and Norman Podhoretz, *Commentary's* feisty editor, changed the environment.[65] Business was no longer isolated in the ideological fight. Furthermore, a theological defense was introduced by Michael Novak and George Gilder. Novak wrote that the corporation provides "metaphors for grace: creativity, liberty, birth and mortality, social motive, social character, insight, and the rise of liberty and election."[66] Gilder advanced three other propositions: (1) free minds are God's greatest gifts and capitalism provides more liberty to use them than any other economic system, (2) investing should be seen as charity because investors never know whether there will be a return to themselves but do know they will give something to others, and (3) capitalism sees the future as good and is therefore a tangible expression of the theological virtue of hope.[67]

To say that capitalism and its most visible symbol, the corporation, are theologically rooted is to oversimplify their historic origins and purposes. University of Rochester president George Dennis O'Brien (whose wit and wisdom were evident in his book, *God and the New Haven Railway: And Why Neither is Doing Very Well*) decried efforts to depict any political or economic system as sacred: "The liberation theologian's attempt to canonize Marx is as inappropriate as Michael Novak's attempt to canonize Adam Smith."[68] A more modest theological defense of capitalism was offered by Andre Delbecq of the Santa Clara University Business School, who suggested that "building a water reservoir or manufacturing a pump is providing the water when 'I was thirsty' and is therefore a theological imperative."[69]

Fortified by both philosophical and theological arguments, advocates of corporate capitalism have turned their guns on the "hostile elites," including various church groups. Particularly irksome has been the position, already noted, of the World Council of Churches. As the WCC needle punctured corporation more deeply, so did critism of its behavior. The *Wall Street Journal* (August 12, 1983), in reporting the organization's meeting in Vancouver, noted that the members had descended from a mountain with a stone tablet saying that the focus of all evil was the United States: "All of this may come as a surprise . . . but it shouldn't. The Council has long supported many of the same leftist revolutionary causes aided and abetted by the Kremlin and its proxies. The World Council is supported by the mainline Protestant denominations. After its Vancouver revelations . . . its supporters have some explaining to do. A good time to start would be with Sunday's sermons."

The Catholic bishops have not escaped unscathed. In one sense, their critics jumped the gun by denouncing the hierarchy's November 1984 draft even before it had appeared. *Fortune* editors had predicted it would be a paean to planning because the economics of the National Council of Catholic Bishops were "well to the left."[70] A group of Catholic laymen, headed by former Secretary of the Treasury William Simon, reminded the bishops that Catholic social thought rested on three basic principles: (1) the dignity and uniqueness of every single human person, (2) the social nature of human life, and (3) the principle of subsidiarity, which holds that social decisions ought to be taken by the community closest to the concrete realities.[71] The United States was one of the few countries that had turned these principles into realities.

CONCLUSION

Assessments of the positions represented by critics and defenders of the American economic system bring mixed results. Hostile elites, among whom are well-known scholars and church leaders, are accused of going to extremes. Apologists are censured for burying their heads in the sand. Winnowing out the merits of the contrary positions seems an almost insuperable job for managers, whose temptation is then to stay uncritically with friends or stay aloof from the sound and fury of ideological warfare. Yet there is value in these hotly waged debates even when antilogisms lurk in every statement. They draw attention to the basic core of America's culture and to the need for necessary adaptations; they lead to syntheses that may represent a renewal of the best elements in the traditional ideology; and they enrich the old with insights more appropriate to current realities. There are signs of reconciliation. Writers as different in their ideologies as John Scharr, Sheldon Wolin, Daniel Bell, Irving Kristol, and Robert Dahl have agreed that the decline in civic consciousness must be halted. Managers themselves have acknowledged that a new business ideology must be forged. *The admission is one of the most powerful proofs of our hypothesis, namely, that managers must not only know the culture but know how to deal with ideologues of pro- and anti-business persuasions.*

Seeking to stimulate further discussion on a possible synthesis, George Cabot Lodge outlined an ideology that is best appreciated through comparisons.[72]

The Traditional Ideology	*The Contemporary Ideology*
Individualism	Communitarianism
(personal effort and self-interest)	(identity with the whole and common interests)
Equality	Egalitarianism
(fair chance to earn)	(equal share of product)
Competition	Cooperation
Limited state	Activist state
Specialization of labor	Integration of work

Lodge's contrasts challenge managers to reformulate their own ideology by reconciling differing contributions from the ideologues. This reconciling process may, in the end, turn out to be one of the most important challenges to corporate managers, union chieftains and government officials, on the one hand, and to church leaders, academics and journalists, on the other. It is, after all, an attempt to give reasons for what America is and answers to what America should become—the long moral journey that responsible people cannot refuse to take.[73] But the process bears careful watching. If, in the ideological wars, the idea of total victory is anathema, so, too, is the notion of compromise at any price. Reconciliation of contrary views must be based on something more than crowd pleasers. While the American society is one of substantial merit, its culture is a human creation subject to human improvement.

Who, among the scholars, will help managers play their appropriate role in social reconstruction? Not historians alone even though Americans need to know where they have been before they can wisely determine where they are going. As a group, however, historians are extremely cautious in thinking that Clio is a great teacher. Not the economists, even though they are important in helping governments forge instruments for fiscal and monetary policy. But economists restrict themselves largely to analyses of means to meet change, not to social causes of change. Nor are the anthropologists who have, perhaps more than others, enriched our understanding of cultures. Anthropologists most frequently operate on the persuasive premise that what is good for one society is not necessarily good for another. The premise is true—to a point. Missed by anthropologists (as well as others who make moral relativism the sole criterion for judgment), are the implications that flow from each person's need for justice and freedom without which human dignity is meaningless.

At this critical point biologists and moralists have things of importance to say. The former seek to tell us what the human body is. The latter seek to tell us what the human soul needs. The moral manager is concerned with both.

II THE "ETHIC" OF CONCEPTS

4

FROM PERSON TO PRINCIPLE
Scientific and Moral Perspectives

THE VALUES QUIZ   *(Mark True or False)*

1. _____ The more we learn from biology, the surer we are that human values are genetically predetermined.
2. _____ It is all right for employers to use psychologists to program workers so that they behave as their employers want them to behave.
3. _____ There is no moral responsibility without free will.
4. _____ The best guide to ethical behavior is to follow the rule "When in Rome, do as the Romans do."
5. _____ Executives facing a moral dilemma should resolve it on this rule only: if it helps the company and the country, it is morally correct.
6. _____ Ethics and religion are the same thing.
7. _____ Management is a profession, and managers therefore need a code of ethics just as other professionals—lawyers and accountants—have codes of ethics.
8. _____ Doing right and doing good are the same.

Management effectiveness begins with understanding human nature, something John D. Rockfeller sensed when he said, "I will pay more for the ability to deal with people than for any other ability under the sun."[1] Du Pont chairman Irving Shapiro made the same point: "A CEO is first and foremost in the human relations and communication businesses—what else could the job be?—but the point is too important to leave to inference. No other item on the chief executive's duty list has more leverage on the corporation's prospects."[2] Possibly the most relevant comment came from an anonymous source: "Henry Ford knew cars. Alfred Sloan of General Motors knew people. Despite a substantial head start, Ford never caught up to GM." Managing people well, of course, depends on understanding people well, and such understanding encompasses the many qualities possessed by that multisplendored creature called a human being. Every peer and every employee walks, as managers do, to the beat of many drums—

the beat of the mind, which is the cadence of reason;
the rhythm of the soul, which is the cadence of conscience;
the throb of the heart, which is the cadence of emotion;
the pulse of the body, which is the cadence of nature.

Since the organization is influenced by the cadences of its members, those who claim special expertise on the nature of human nature deserve a respectful hearing. Some scientific investigators claim to know how the mind thinks, the conscience works, and the emotions react. If they are right, managers face mind-boggling changes in the work force and the old "trickle down" theory (so evident in the human relations themes of George Homans and Elton Mayo) may become a "deluge."[3] Awareness of what certain scientists claim to know about human nature is of obvious importance.

Moralists also feel they can be helpful. They speculate, for example, on possible differences between doing what is right and doing what is good; whether people should be forced to do the good as diligently as they are forced to do the right; whether rights are innate, conferred, or grabbed; and whether telling the truth is always required. Eventually their speculations lead to formulas that help managers to be what they have always wanted to be: practical in the fullest sense of this abused word. In their practical worlds, moral evaluations are important in such things as performance appraisals, compensation packages, golden parachutes, strikes and boycotts, collective bargaining, investment policies, and affirmative action. Responses are ultimately shaped by the way two questions are answered: (1) What is a human being? (2) What is "being

94

human"? Scientists concentrate primarily on the first and philosophers on the
second. Managers need to do both.

WHEN SCIENCE SPEAKS

The philosophical and ideological content of the Enlightenment, as
previously noted, has conditioned Americans to accord a hallowed
place to scientists. Science is the sacred cow because its product is
seen as sweet milk for present and future generations. People almost
instinctively resonate to the conclusion of the late Carl Madden of the
U.S. Chamber of Commerce that ethics cannot be divorced from
science because "the power of scientific concepts, discoveries and tests
of truth is sufficient to change ethical standards before our very eyes."[4]
Shock waves have indeed engulfed cherished values after major
scientific breakthroughs. The religious view that the earth was the
center of the universe collapsed after Copernicus; belief that God
created humans with no connection to the animal kingdom was modified after Darwin; and emphasis on the primacy of conscious decision-
making weakened after Freud. Of the three, Freud made the most
direct frontal assault on traditional moralities by saying that many
saints were mentally ill, that God was nothing more than the image
of the beloved but feared father of early childhood, and that the idea
of sin was a myth created by religious simpletons.[5]
If Western culture's core values have been influenced by major
scientific themes, so, too, have particular organizational practices been
affected by science's lesser findings. One illustration is the T-group
training programs designed in the 1960s to improve self-awareness;
another is "subliminal advertising," the buzzwords among marketing
specialists in the 1950s;[6] changing employee behavior to increase productivity was promoted after World War II by organizational theorists;[7] and Neuro-Linguistic Programming became popular during the
early 1980s when psychotherapist Richard Bandler and linguist John
Grinder theorized that everyone experienced the world through one
of three primary perceptual systems: visual, auditory, and kinesthetic.[8]
Visual people ask: "Do you *see* what I mean?" "Have you got the
picture?" Auditory types use sentences like these: "Does this name *ring*
a bell?" "You are coming in *loud and clear*." Kinesthetic people inquire:
"Do you *grasp* what I mean?" "Are you *comfortable* with the idea?" "Is
your boss a *pain* in the neck?" More than 60,000 persons (executives

and salespeople, public relations and advertising personnel, lawyers and doctors) have already been exposed to the Bandler-Grinder approach, and the number continues to rise despite criticisms that individuals may be so manipulated that they will lose control over their own behavior. What has started in a science will end in morality.

The foregoing theories, however, have stirred tiny ripples compared with the tidal waves caused by the theories of certain sociobiologists, experimental psychologists, and neurophysiologists. Some challenge such basic tenets of our moral patrimony as liberty and equality; others look skeptically at old ideas about communication and competition; and conventional understandings of the individual as a responsible agent are equally under fire. Since today's scientific esoterica may be tomorrow's conventional wisdom, surveying the landscape is no longer a management luxury but a necessity. Small examples tell a big story.

Biotechnology

In 1953 two English scientists, Crick and Watson, published their findings on DNA in a journal article of only 128 lines. It was a declaration so brief and so historic that its impact will likely exceed that of the Declaration of Independence.[9] The theory holds that any of various nucleic acids are the molecular basis of heredity in many organisms and are constructed of a double helix held together by hydrogen bonds. One practical result of the DNA theory is gene-splicing, which John Naisbitt in his popular book *Megatrends* called

> the most awesome and powerful skill acquired by man since the splitting of the atom. If pursued humanistically, its potential to serve humanity is enormous. We will use it to synthesize expensive natural products—interferon, substances such as insulin, and human endorphins that serve as natural painkillers. We will be able to create a second "green revolution" in agriculture, to produce new high-yield, disease-resistant, self-fertilizing crops. Gene splicing has the potential to synthesize new substances we can substitute for oil, coal, and other raw materials—keys to a self-sustaining society.[10]

Judicial imprimatur was placed on gene-splicing on June 16, 1980, when the Supreme Court handed down a historic 5–4 decision that human-altered life-forms can be patented.[11] The decision's momentous implication is found in the questions it poses: Has the Supreme Court ensured this country's technological future? Has it laid the groundwork for corporations to own the processes of life for centuries to come? The new scientific advance represents a quantum leap over discoveries made during past centuries by plant breeders. Drug companies are already doing cell biology in great vats; tiny corporations are sprouting up at the edges of university towns; and genetic engineering by means of DNA and some RNA technology may produce new microorganisms with the potential for far-reaching economic consequences to major industries—pharmaceutical, agricultural, food processing, chemical, and energy.

That biotechnology is laced with moral booby traps is obvious. If serious damage is caused by biotech products, who is morally responsible—researchers, manufacturers, government? Are patent-granting procedures fair? Can researchers really know the impact of their discoveries on environment? Such questions will occupy the courts and challenge managers well beyond the present century.

Brain Research

That better understanding of the brain has direct relevance to organizations was shown in a mining/manufacturing company in Ogden, Utah. Brain scientists showed management how its shift schedules were so out of sync with the brain's normal "clock" that employees were irritable, easily fatigued, and indifferent to results. When the schedules were rearranged to conform to the brain's own rhythm, productivity shot up fantastically. But the brain has guarded its secrets jealously—secrets that, if deciphered, may reveal more clearly how humans behave and why they behave as they do. Both the "how" and the "why" impinge on value questions, and obviously both are of great interest to managers who need to speculate on scientific questions such as these:

1. Does the mind have two brains? Or does the brain have two minds?
2. Is the brain driven to seek values? If so, where are values located?
3. Are we prone to violence? to hate? to selfishness?
4. Can the nervous system become so "drunk" that individuals are unable to make rational moral decisions?
5. Can we then "detoxify" drunken nervous systems?

6. Is the current morality actually a threat to human survival?
7. Can we alter and improve an individual's values and behavior by engineering the environment?[12]

A more important question touches free will because on it rests the common-law view of personal responsibility, church teachings about sinfulness, capitalism's tenet of consumer sovereignty, and representative government's reliance on citizen choices. Dr. Richard Restak said that this most valued of human possessions may be an illusion: *"Free will may thus be nothing more than a sort of ex post facto delusion."*[13] The conclusion outraged philosophers, who felt that such deductions rest on strained and shaky evidence.[14] But indignation is not refutation.

Sociobiology

The biggest bombshell on traditional values was dropped in 1975 by sociobiologist Edward O. Wilson in his landmark study *Sociobiology: The New Synthesis*.[15] Since its appearance, it has drawn high praise and violent criticism. Why reactions run from positive to negative extremes can be appreciated simply by noting certain, sometimes tenuously substantiated conclusions Wilson has put forth:

1. All forces of good and evil are rooted in the hypothalamic-limbic system of the brain.
2. Since the philosophers' canons of morality, like everyone else's, come from the hypothalamic-limbic system, philosophers have no special competence on value questions.
3. Religions, like other human institutions, evolved in order to enhance the influence of their practitioners.
4. Humans are genetically inclined toward cold-blooded aggression against those who are not part of their kin or social unit. Like lions and chimpanzees, they kill, eat, and conduct themselves in accordance with a set of implicit values shaped by evolution for survival. What sets humans apart is only their ability to talk about it with their fellows.[16]
5. In sexual matters the human male is a tomcat—aggressive, promiscuous, and impulsive.
6. Women lean toward monogamy because domesticity has had a higher survival value for them than other life-styles.

7. Altruism exists among humans because the brain is a value-oriented decision system forged by evolution to ensure survival of the gene pool, not necessarily the individual's survival. Morality, therefore, has no other function except to ensure continuation of the race.

Specification of some of the moral implications for managers that flow from biological determinism include the following:

1. Severe modification of the idea of accountability. Company codes that stress individual responsibility are predicated on wrong beliefs.
2. Leaders are born, not made. Executive development programs are largely a waste of money.
3. Cooperation between management and labor is a chimera since struggle for survival is nature's law.
4. Ethics experts know no more about morality than anyone else. Recommendations of those who urge organizations to establish moral audit teams should be rejected.
5. Ambition for top jobs means a willingness to step on and over other people.

To enumerate possible outcomes of adaptation to a deterministic view of human nature is to alert managers to the high stakes they have in understanding the practical effect of scientific theories. If the determinists are right, then the way children are taught, employees recruited, and management development programs conducted will vastly change. If, on the other hand, the determinists are wrong, managers need to resist training fads that will be advanced by organizational theorists whose ideas are derived from the Wilson brand of sociobiologists.

Experimental Psychology

The person most frequently associated with controversial answers is B.F. Skinner, who said that human behavior can be as much controlled as that of the pigeons on which he experimented.[17] Needed were minimum use of negative reinforcements and maximum use of positive reinforcements, the so-called operant conditioning. It can be taught and it can be learned. Managers have been urged to use Skinner's fundamental concepts because operant conditioning has been empirically validated in laboratory and field settings.[18] The tests, it is said, show how optimal results can be achieved for individuals and organizations.[19] Skinner himself argued for his system in these words:

> Look at the so-called contingencies of reinforcement. All gambling systems pay off on what is called a variable-ratio schedule of reinforcement. That's true of lotteries, roulette, poker, craps, one-armed bandits. They all pay off unpredictably, but in the long run on a certain schedule. Everyone would benefit if work could be organized so that it also pays off on that schedule. People would then work, and they would enjoy the excitement that goes with possessing a lottery ticket that may pay off at the end of the week. Management could solve some of its problems by adding a bit of a lottery to its incentive conditions. Suppose that every time a worker finished a job he got a lottery ticket, and at the end of the week there was a drawing. More jobs would be done, with greater pleasure.[20]

The moral manager confronts a troublesome question: Is it ethical for managers to employ Skinner's techniques in efforts to have employees internalize the organization's values? The answer is yes if (1) the technique itself is ethically neutral, (2) the employee gives informed consent, and (3) the results are also positive for the individual. In Skinner's view, enlightened managers have a responsibility to use employees for benevolent ends. Skinner's operant conditioning is somewhat suspect, however, in that subordinates rarely have opportunities to give informed consent; moreover, the environment is changed by others so that often the quality of work life becomes "something the top tells the middle to do to the bottom in organizations"—elitism without tears.[21] In such circumstances moral alarm bells ring. Furthermore, Skinner is prepared to shatter some precious concepts of a democratic society. For him, behavior is a function of previous experiences and since old experiences are inappropriate for today's problems, it is necessary to curtail individual freedom.[22] Rather than an unaffordable luxury, freedom is excess baggage because it assumes people are rational—a myth, in Skinner's view, verified by no empirical evidence. The startling conclusion seems so morally repugnant that managers are tempted to reject it out of hand.

Nevertheless, Skinner has many positive things to offer. If operant conditioning works to the benefit of both individuals and organizations, all profit; "accentuating the positive" through systematic recognition and reward for desirable behavior is better than the seek-out-

and-destroy policies of some bureaucracies; and finally, operant conditioning is presumed to involve more teaching than manipulation, with greater harmony between individuals and their environment as the result. That it can work has been suggested by the experiences of Emery Air Freight Corporation, at which the password is "positive reinforcement." Hundreds of Emery employees have gotten daily feedback on how their work measured up to company goals and standards, many of which they helped to set. In the first full year after operant conditioning was launched, sales jumped from $62 million to nearly $80 million, a gain of 27.8 percent compared with an 11.3 percent rise the year before.[23] The manager's job is to make certain that operant conditioning is used in morally acceptable ways, defined here as respect for the employee's freedom and adequate disclosure of what is being done. Otherwise, the organization, too, can be victimized by its own success.

ENTER THE PHILOSOPHER

Former British prime minister James Callaghan:

> In my judgment, a leader should have some core philosophy and belief against which he can judge the important issues as they arise. Unless he has that bedrock to fall back on, the unexpected storms that blow up will toss him about like a cork. Without such a foundation, a leader may be able to survive, but he won't be a leader in the sense that I use the term.[24]

Philosophers distinguish themselves from scientists by turning the question of the human being into the question of being human. The turnaround is particularly important to managers who deal with the by-products of the industrial revolution. There was in America a sharp increase in number and power of organizations and the people responsible for managing them.[25] Of all values, bureaucratic rationality (using means economically and efficiently to achieve ends) was most prized. Father of this form of rationality is Germany's Max Weber, whose progeny are the graduates of various schools of management. While Weber's heirs recognize their indebtedness to the intellectual father, they have not appreciated the full implications of his stress on cost-effectiveness.[26]

Weber saw clearly that questions of ends are questions of value. In the intellectual climate of his time, however, values were increasingly viewed as expressions of individual preferences, a view based on a philosophy called moral egoism that, if relentlessly pursued, meant that all beliefs had equal value and "doing one's own thing" made the best sense.[27] If managerial authority lacked objective moral criteria, what better external standard was there than efficiency measured by profitability? Yet Weber's norm has been challenged as the primary one for corporate and professional legitimacy. The reason is simple: preferences that result in action cannot be judged without standards. What does it mean to call an act right or wrong? Does power make right? Or do purpose and content define what is right? The relationship of humans to machines and of individuals to institutions drives managers to ponder philosopher Gilbert Ryle's comment that people are not "machines, not even ghost-ridden machines. They are men—a tautology which is sometimes worth remembering."[28] In that tautology lurk clues to the meaning of personhood—a creature possessed of reason and will, imagination and memory, consciousness and conscience. Well-tempered organizations are judged by the way they increase their output *and* enhance the personhood of their people.

If engineering and economics provide criteria for judging output, ethics provides criteria for measuring the quality of interpersonal relations. Individual choice is key to understanding human behavior, and, as a consequence, philosophers are strongly attracted to probe its meaning: How is choice made? What choices are more important than others? What are the consequences of the choice on the chooser? on others? One philosopher, John Finnis, suggested an experiment wherein people were asked to imagine themselves plugged into an "experience machine" that could afford the individual all the experiences wished for at that moment. There was only one trick: the person must plug in for a lifetime or not at all. What would a person do? Finnis's reply is that people would not plug in, because they know instinctively that growth comes from freely chosen activity over a period of time in a range of basic goods. The inference to be drawn from one philosopher's story is that proper choosing among goals is the cornerstone of ethical reasoning and that a life organized around realizing those goals cannot be simulated. It must be lived. What, therefore, marks a human being is the spontaneity with which he or she moves from experiencing "something" toward efforts to understand that "something." Such spontaneity is neither blind nor aimless but clear and purposeful, revealing the drive within everyone for reasons to explain actions. This instinct to understand operates prior to the formulation of principles;

human judgments move from examination of facts to judgments of values.

The central question of ethics can also be approached negatively: *What robs people of their dignity?* The answer is anything that denies them access to justice and equality, to liberty and truth. Such denials work to depersonalize and dehumanize people—to make them slaves or serfs, strangers or aliens. While heroic souls have preserved their integrity, even when all that is essential to its preservation was removed, the vast majority mature only when treated as free and equal agents entitled to justice and to information that affects their well-being. These are basic rights, not the entitlements of contemporary usage. Individuals who see themselves as holders of rights are properly proud because self-respect is necessary to gain the esteem of others. Conversely, to lose the concept of people as rights-bearers is to admit that individuals are means, not ends—slaves with nothing to protect against their owner.[29] If, on the other hand, rights are rooted in the state or in the corporation, what they create they can destroy. And the stronger of the two—the state—can destroy the weaker of the two, the corporation. Managers have, therefore, a vested interest in what might be called a taxonomy of rights, a sort of crude "moral geometry" that deepens sensitivity to basic values and the priorities they occupy. It has been observed repeatedly that leaders have an especially heavy obligation to become, in a sense, moral geometers. While obviously not incarnations of the philosopher-king ideal of the Greeks, they are archons who direct the destinies of corporate principalities. Managers absorb values, sift values, share values, and, if needed, impose values. Visualizing the package of "goods" they handle is helped by distinguishing between *axioms* (what Jefferson called self-evident truths) and *theorems*, which are derived from them by a process of logic and experience (Table 4-1).

Tying Pieces Together

Since asserting rights does not solve specific problems, it could be inferred that the assertions are meaningless; nevertheless, rejection of the inference comes rather easily by examining certain consequences of nonassertion. Denial of the right to freedom put American blacks in shackles; denial of the right to equality kept American women in shadows; and denial of the right to truth placed workers in jeopardy.

Table 4-1. Axioms and Theorems

Axioms	Theorems
Freedom and Equality	
Every person has a basic right to	Every person has a derivative right to
not be enslaved or dominated;	form private associations;
pursue what brings personal growth;	hold private property;
be protected from war, fear, want, and hunger;	make contracts;
make his or her destiny.	participate in decisions affecting his or her welfare;
	speak and assemble;
	privacy;
	responsible dissent.
Justice and Equality	
Everyone has a claim to what is his or her due.	The right to
	receive income proportional to output;
	resources for basic needs;
	use ability;
	equal opportunity;
	share equitably in society's wealth.
Truth	
Everyone has a claim to know those things which affect his or her welfare.	The right to
	education;
	reliable and effective communications;
	protection against dishonesty and deceit.

Such denials improverished society and organizations. A right is a claim, and implementing the claim changes the face of institutions. As often as not, managers who accept the existence of rights nevertheless face conflicts between two "goods" or between two "bads." Looking to ethicists for clarification is sometimes like looking to Epimenides, who said, "All Cretans are liars' said the Cretan." However, if paradoxes cannot be solved, they can be managed.[30] This managing process takes into account the interplay between cultural, philosophical, and theological values (Table 4-2).

Reviewing the table drives home four important lessons: (1) bedrock ethics are not relative to different times or cultures; (2) specific adaptations and legal interpretations are nonetheless required to make them realizable in different circumstances (water consumption in Alaska is different from water consumption in the Sahara); (3) institutions are needed to give theorems a consistency in practice; and (4) ideologies are propounded to provide legitimacy for the institutions themselves. When basic ethical principles are tied to institutions (secular and religious), the result is a community wherein people, persuaded that societal and personal values are complementary, act voluntarily to preserve it and make it work. In short, moral consensus supports the moral community called the State, the economic community called the Market, the spiritual community called the Church, the intimate community called the Family, the learned community called the University, the working community called the Union, and the service community called the Profession. Interactions flow constantly among them, and the interactions are powered by—back to square one— justice and equality, freedom and truth. Since the principles appear in various guises, it helps the moral manager to know what level (and what kind of ethical analysis) is required.

Levels of Moral Reasoning

Stipulating the levels and then noting the kinds of ethics that appear at the relevent level are a practical response to a practical need.[31] The three levels of ethics are as follows:

1. *Descriptive ethics* seeks answers not to what *ought* to be done but to what *is* being done in ways acceptable to the community. Telling it "like it is" constitutes a descriptive ethic, and anthropologists are good examples of this type of moralist.
2. *Metaethics* (or analytical ethics) deals with age-old puzzles like the meaning of truth or goodness, or the roots of ethical disagreement and ways to resolve them. At this level, sophisticated theories and subtle distinctions abound.
3. *Normative ethics* tells what principles are needed to distinguish right from wrong and how to apply them. This heartland of ethics seeks answers to the is-ought question; while the norms are often

Table 4-2. Cultural, Philosophical, and Theological Values

Types	Primary Values	Validation	Extent	Terms
Cultural	For the state: pluralism For the economy: competition For the self: individualism For society: progress	Common experiences	Particular (the United States)	Mores
Philosophical 1. Moral axioms[a]	Basic right to: Justice and equality Liberty and truth	Reason	Universal[b]	*Basic ethics*
2. Moral theorems	Institutionalized rights: Fair wages (unions) Private property (corporations) Contract (not status) Due process Etc.	Reason and experience	Derivative and particularized	*Applied ethics:* Managerial Professional Legal Medical Accounting Etc.
Theological[c]	God's will, obedience to God, hope and charity	Faith and reason	Universal and particularized	Religious ethics or Biblical ethics

Notes:

[a]Axiomatic rights, being the possession of all humans, are universals.

[b]Universals take precedence over institutionalized derivative rights when conflicts occur.

[c]Religions, by calling people to contemplate the Divinity and to partake of the Divine Plan, have elements that may not be open to nonbelievers and hence can unite or divide a community.

106

incorporated into the legal system, frequently there are misfits between the two, since law may only reflect crudely normative values. Within the normative level are three subsets:

a.   *Managerial ethics* (role ethics) deals with the obligations imposed on individuals by virtue of their position in an organization.

b.   *Business ethics* examines the marketplace (as well as its legal environment) to determine how the organization should behave toward other organizations, customers, and the environment. The self-interest and profit-maximization principles are very relevant to this area of inquiry.

c.   *Professional ethics* consists of the principles derived from special obligations due to clients and enforced through codes of ethics established by peers. Lawyers, for example, are not required to tell the whole truth even though the witnesses they call to the stand are.

THE LOGIC OF MORALS: THREE APPROACHES

How can managers know they are on the right moral track? One response is to ask whether their decisions are responsive to the needs and values of others, but this requires, in turn, decision makers to know what counts as responsiveness.[32] Stipulating the nature of responsiveness has caused lively debate. Egoists say an act is ethical when it responds to the desire of the actor; altruists take the opposite tack, saying an act is ethical when it promotes the good of everyone except the actor. So-called schools of thought help to improve the decision-making process but, like all decision trees, require the exclusionary rule.[33] Exclusions would include (1) a crude Machiavellianism that justifies anything that preserves the leader's power; (2) the "great man" ethic of Nietzsche, which asserts that leaders are not bound by a morality applicable to ordinary people; (3) the belief, derived from Socrates, that knowledge of the moral life is little more than intuitional or speculative; (4) radical existentialists and emotivists who assume that whatever an individual thinks is right, is right; and (5) the Hobbesian ethic (Thomas Hobbes) that all power resides in the monarch. A process of elimination leads to utilitarianism and deontology.

Utilitarianism

Utilitarianism has the most powerful hold on the American conscience: judges have been molded by it; administrators like utilitarianism because it is results oriented; and the economics of American public policy has been relentlessly utilitarian. When asked what utilitarianism has going for it, one philosopher answered: "A lot of things. It seems to harmonize with scientific thought; it stresses this world's needs; it seems to fit the canons of rational validation as these were understood . . . ; it became especially attractive in a secular culture where people could abandon the commands of God, natural rights, and virtue in favor of individual calculations."[34]

Defining utilitarianism with precision, however, is difficult because even its originators never said utilities were set in concrete. Despite ambiguities, all forms of utilitarianism hold individuals responsible for foreseeable effects—with a better-or-worseness of the action for themselves and others. The fathers of utilitarianism are David Hume (1711–76), Jeremy Bentham (1748–1832), and John Stuart Mill (1806–73). While Hume brilliantly defined the role of consequences on ethical reasoning, it was Bentham's definition of utilitarianism as "the greatest happiness of the greatness number" that became historically its simplest and clearest explanation. While this could conceivably be interpreted to mean a majority's right to trample a minority, a more accurate interpretation of Bentham suggests that, since every person counts as one, the more widely that good is distributed, the better it is for everyone. Mill went beyond Bentham to propound the view that ethics is best understood in psychological terms: since people avoid pain and seek pleasure (the psychological base), the resultant duty to promote the greatest happiness of the greatest number becomes the normative foundation.[35] Maximizing social utility (or the social welfare function) is thus the basis criterion of morality and, say utilitarians, the authentic managerial ethic.

Critics, however, argue that utilitarianism is flawed on many counts. Consequences are notoriously difficult to assess, particularly when actions have far-ranging impacts. Apposite is Nicholas Monsarrat's story about a British captain during World War II whose ship was in a position to rescue many survivors from a destroyer sunk by German torpedoes. While willing to take some chances with the lives of his own crew, the captain worried over his own vessel's vulnerability to another German attack. With great reluctance, he finally decided to let the shipwrecked sailors drown—only to learn later that there was no enemy submarine in the vicinity. The further point is made that under utilitarianism, when majority "push" confronts minority "shove," individual rights are jeopardized. In short, the consequential ethic is helpful but flawed.[36]

Deontology

Derived from the Greek *deon*, meaning duty or obligation, deontologists deny that rightness is defined primarily by reference to the results an action is likely to produce. Ethics deals with rights, and it cannot flourish when duties are not acknowledged. If Mill and Bentham are the great teachers for utilitarians, Immanuel Kant is the mentor for deontologists. To him, the essence of morality is strict respect for certain duties and such respect supersedes any other goal. Kant believed that (1) one's duty in a given situation could be deduced from fundamental a priori principles that were open to the careful inquirer and (2) such principles were independent of experience. Reflection provides unwavering certainty that (1) duty is distinct from pleasure, (2) moral virtue is the supreme good, and (3) moral worth is measured neither by the consequences of a person's actions nor by his or her benevolence but, rather, by the person's intention to obey the moral laws. There are, therefore, certain self-evident truths that provide "the categorical imperative" for moral behavior.

One persuasive expositor of Kantianism is Harvard law professor Charles Fried, who observed that

> if deontology, the theory of right and wrong, is solicitous of the individual, it is primarily solicitous of his claim to preserve his moral integrity, to refrain from being the agent of wrong, even if such fastidiousness means forgoing the opportunity to promote great good or to prevent great harm. In this respect the primacy of right and wrong is a doctrine that shows its traditional religious origins in contrast to the secular, melioristic foundations of those theories which hold that it is consequences alone which count.[37]

Deontological norms *direct* the administrator's choices and differ from other value judgments that provide reference points, not directives. Moral *directions* provided by a culture and moral *directives* demanded by duty must be distinguished even when it is known that rights and duties do not occupy the totality of moral space.

When utilitarians and deontologists go at each other with vengeance, doubts arise whether reconciliations are possible. At first blush, the prospect seems bleak. When deontologists insist on inviolable rules, utilitarians counter with violable rules; when deontologists challenge anyone's capacity to anticipate consequences correctly, utilitarians reply that the test is not simply results, but good results.[38] When, however, intellectual controversy rages and no effort is made to provide a satisfactory compromise, one theory may be used as a foil against another, thus permitting the decision maker to employ whichever weapon best suits his or her purposes at the time.[39]

Deonutility as Compromise

Careful review of the conflict reveals a common ground between utilitarian and deontological ethics: it is the shared view that ethical inquiry rests not on ideology but on principles that are objective, important, and unusual. One effort to reach a compromise was undertaken by a British scholar, W.D. Ross, who advanced the view that there are several types of duties that do not derive from Kant's categorical imperative. When, for example, people contract, the parties voluntarily take on special duties; when chemical firms pollute the environment, their actions create a duty to make reparations.[40] Perhaps Ross's compromise can be expanded into what might be called *deonutility*, defined as respect for rights *and* responsibility for consequences. Differences are muted when deontologists and utilitarians agree that (1) decision makers should act on the premise that good principles bring good results, which deontology and rule utilitarianism do, (2) particular cases determine selection of the preferred principles after all relevant ones are considered, and (3) the morally autonomous person sees principles and consequences as inseparable in the pursuit of justice.[41] If these points are accepted, it is possible for deonutility to extract the best elements of the "duty" and the "results" approaches. Implicit in the deonutilitarian approach is the idea that universally recognized duties are a generality in search of specificity.[42]

Perhaps the best example of deonutilitarianism at work is the "just war" theory. From Augustine the saint to Adenauer the statesman, warfare was defended on two deontological principles: (1) leaders had a duty to defend their people from unprovoked attack, and (2) all combatants had a duty not to slaughter the innocent if war came. But having posited these two deontological norms, theorists added two utilitarian principles, stating that leaders (1) must be reasonably sure they can win the war and (2) must decide, by a crude form of cost-benefit analysis, whether gains from victory will outweigh the losses from acquiescence.

Whatever the preferred form of moral reasoning, specific decisions on particular cases clearly involve a certain amount of overlap between deontological and utilitarian reasoning. What managers should avoid is settling into the belief that the mode of moral reasoning is irrelevant to decision making. This belief leads ultimately to loss of consistency in exercising authority because the logic used in one case may be completely contradicted by the reasoning on a similar case. Careful attention to each form of moral reasoning forces managers to consider the duty ethic toward the individual and the consequentialist ethic toward many others.

Consider, for example, the case of a senior manager who is asked to recommend a subordinate for a management development program at a prestigious university. After surveying possible nominees, the manager reduces the list to three. The first is an able 53-year-old who has nearly thirty years of satisfactory work with the company. For this individual it is a now-or-never point. The second candidate is equally able but has five years less of service. What makes this individual's company service distinctive is a documented record of superb integrity and loyalty to the organization. The third possibility is a 37-year-old who is noted for intellectual brilliance and enormous energy.

While it is impossible to predict the final judgment, it is not unfair to suggest that if the decision were governed exclusively by deontological criteria, the first would probably be chosen because three of the criteria for selection—ability, experience, and tenure—are clearly met. To ignore these criteria would be unfair. The utilitarian would counter, however, that the choice violates a more important criterion, namely, the organization's well-being, and so the choice should be the third candidate, who can provide maximum benefit to the enterprise over a longer time frame. Weighing the two lines of argument, the manager could well make a decision that ignores these two equally relevant criteria by adopting a deonutilitarian approach which strikes a balance between a worthy person and a worthwhile organization. Achieving a balanced decision would require attention to other factors, such as the existence of an employment contract as well as its nature, careful assessment of the organization's short-as well as long-term requirements, the condition of the job market, and the effect of the choice on employee morale. Propelled on the one hand by deontological reasoning that tells what must be done for an individual and on the other hand by utilitarian reasoning on what ought to be done for the organization, the decision maker could combine both to make a morally, hence logically, defensible decision by choosing the second candidate. This individual has more ability than the first candidate and higher prospects for valuable service to the organization possessed by the third. In addition, the second candidate possesses the added elements of loyalty and integrity, both of which will command the respect of subordinates. These are the elements that deonutility brings into play. Moral managers test their decisions against all relevant facts and all relevant ethical principles.

The Theory of Agency

It is understandable that managers are inclined to believe that they instinctively know what is the morally right thing to do and that the cause of its not getting done lies elsewhere: with government regulations, union intransigence, consumer fickleness, inadequate resources, poor communication, and the like. From moral perspectives the attractive simplification of reality is a half or three-quarter truth. An added complication is the fact that changing values in the culture have greatly enlarged the manager's fiduciary responsibilities. Unlike lawyers who shrewdly restrict their obligations to clients, managers deal with an expanding number of constituencies—stockholders, consumers, workers, governments, the local community, and the larger society. Determining a manager's moral responsibility is not adequately encapsulated in law. Yet the reality is that managers must obey the law and respond to claimants. Continued pressures lead managers to seek help from corporate counsel and from business economists and to avoid moralists. Lawyers and economists are "realists"; philosophers are mere theorists. Overlooked is an important development in the thinking of economists, as well as other social scientists, called the theory of agency.

The theory of agency regards all social relationships as contracts between principals and agents.[43] While the courts have obviously been concerned with fiduciary relationships, the agency theory emphasizes another factor, namely, that loss of control is inevitable for principals since the agent has goals not always congruent with those of the principal. The loss-of-control factor applies to directors, consultants, regulators, accountants, and, of course, managers. To reduce the costs of control, stockholders rely on government regulations and outside auditors; to reduce administrative costs, managers depend on organizational structure, employee wage incentives, discipline, and the like. For present purposes the key point is that the theory of agency goes beyond what lawyers see as a fiduciary responsibility and what economists have historically seen as simply a cost factor. The implication is that there is an "ethic of economics" and an "economic of ethics." The implication requires elaboration.

Because managers are agents, it is useful to identify two relevant premises of agency theory: (1) every sizable organization is built on long-term contracts between owners (principals) and managers (who are their agents),[44] and (2) moral hazards arise when the principal, unable to monitor the agent, looks only at bottom-line results. As moral questions increase, so do costs; the link, therefore, between ethics and economics becomes so visible that even skeptics are driven to acknowledge the importance of the connection.[45] According to the theory of agency, ethics is good business. There is even room for an ethic of altruism, because altruistically motived managers know that helping an important institution of which they are a part—and from which they draw their livelihood—does, in fact, benefit them.[46] So in affairs of the world, the altruistic instinct really does matter: important institutions are preserved, freedom of choice is maintained, the health of the organization is enhanced, and the wealth of the organization is increased.

Nobel Laureate economist Kenneth Arrow told business that the presence of what, in slightly old-fashioned terminology, is called virtue plays a significant role in the operation of the economic system and the organizations that operate within it. He amplified the point by saying that

> one way of looking at ethics and morality . . . is that these principles are agreements, conscious or, in many cases, unconscious, to supply mutual benefits. Societies in their evolution have developed implicit agreements to certain kinds of regard for others, agreements which are essential to the survival of the society or at least contribute greatly to the efficiency of its working. The fact that we cannot mediate all our responsibilities to others through prices . . . makes it essential in the running of society

that we have what might be called "conscience," a feeling of responsibility for the effects of one's actions on others.[47]

The message is simple: A good conscience marks the good manager. It is a conscience responsive to the morality that governs everyone and to the special accountability that goes with any fiduciary role.

CONCLUSION

Problems do not present themselves to managers with labels of good or evil attached; therefore, to analyze value problems managers realize that, for all their attachment to hard facts, they must often work *from* a hypothesis and not *to* a hypothesis, *from* theory and not *to* theory. The better versed that managers are in the general principles of moral theory, the more probable are the prospects for solid and consistent policies. Because ethical concepts provide reference points and not precise answers, managers strive to (1) understand why certain norms are acceptable and others not, (2) see what relationships exist between moral norms and, when they conflict, know how to prioritize among them, and (3) select and apply the most relevant value criteria to specific cases. Understanding the right concepts helps managers form a right conscience. Defective morals ultimately mean defective managers. Knowing what is their preferred way of moral reasoning (utilitarian, deontological, and the like) prevents erratic decisions that lead to erratic results in and for the organization. Since moral reasoning cannot be divorced from the goals it is intended to promote, it is always necessary for the moral manager to appreciate the subtle nuances that surround them. Equality and justice, for example, flow easily on manager's tongues even as their essences boggle managers' minds.

5
EQUALITY AND JUSTICE

THE VALUES QUIZ   *(Mark True or False)*

1. ____ People who have lived for a long time in their own ethnic neighborhoods have a right to keep out "aliens."
2. ____ Lawyers who adjust fees according to the size of the settlement rather than the number of hours worked are more just than accountants who charge according to the time spent on the job.
3. ____ It is fair to deny the vote to people on welfare because such people are not contributing to society.
4. ____ If a poor man stopped doing business with one individual to deal with another whom he had converted to his religion, it would hardly be called unfair. However, if a rich man acted similarly toward a poor neighbor, that would be unjust.
5. ____ Insurance companies are justified in charging higher auto premiums for young males than for older ones because the accident rate is higher among the former.
6. ____ While you are driving along a turnpike at ten miles above the speed limit, another driver passes you at eighty miles an hour. Arrested for speeding, you protest to the police but the arresting officer is right to answer: "You can't claim injustice."
7. ____ Immigrants are treated as equals when they are required to learn the English language.
8. ____ People too "dumb" to understand and claim their rights have no rights because they do not know what they are missing.

It is of more than passing interest to speculate how people who have made it to the top—and those who think they will—would honestly answer a simple question: Do you think people are equal? Is the question poorly put? Then add: in mind? in strength? A negative response raises the issue of fair treatment for the less gifted, the less strong. Then the issue becomes one of justice. Take the question further: "Do you think people are equal?" is appended a pair of two other words: before God? in rights? Answers then have to reckon with more complex relationships. If the first pairings (which deal with brain and physical power) turn discussions toward the problem of justice, the second turn justice toward the problem of compassion. Some theorists call the "caring" ethic social justice.

Managers of business enterprises are, by and large, spared the task of dealing with social justice. But political authorities, who cannot escape the burden, may answer in ways having enormous impact on corporations. Taxation—levels and kinds—is the most obvious example, but definitions of corporate social responsibilities are also included. If society is to be a humane society, and if corporations are to be humane organizations, then leadership in all sectors is involved.

Awareness of the kinds of inequalities and injustices that must be addressed practically is sharpened by knowledge of the kinds of equalities and justices that are addressed analytically. Neither equality nor justice is singular, and their multiple meanings can generate conflicts among them even before the problem with which they are connected makes itself evident. Examples are many: affirmative action raises the spectre of reverse discrimination; equality in promotion opportunities clashes with seniority provisions under a labor contract; equal needs confront unequal competences. Problems like these will not go away and, therefore, cannot be avoided. When the complexities that lurk behind them are better understood conceptually, wiser policies may be developed.

One final note: Equality and justice, truth and freedom, constitute such a seamless web that there is little possibility of treating them as separate entities. One has spillover effects on the others. Separation is done, therefore, for reasons of convenience and tidiness—and the world of organizations is anything but tidy. The "right to" issue will be handled in pairs: first equality and justice and then truth and freedom.

EQUALITY

Abraham Lincoln: "When the [political party called] the Know-Nothings get in control, [the Constitution] will read: 'all men are created equal except Negroes and foreigners and Catholics.' When it comes to this I should prefer emigrating to some country where they make no pretense for loving liberty—to Russia for instance, where despotism can be taken pure and without the base alloy of hypocrisy."[1]

John Rawls: "Each person possesses an inviolability founded on justice that even the welfare of society as a whole cannot override."[2]

Robert Nozick: "To have justice, you do not necessarily have to have equality."[3]

Rembert Weakland: "We [Catholic bishops] have clearly accepted the fact that inequality is both expected and a blessing."[4]

Wallace Matson: "Justice is not dead. It has been mugged by intellectual hoods."[5]

William Sloan Coffin. "Unless social justice is established in a country, civil liberties, which always concern intellectuals more than does social justice, look like luxuries. The point is that the three ideals of the French Revolution—liberty, equality, fraternity—cannot be separated. We have to deal with equality first."[6]

An "Ominous" Ideal?

Like all ideals, the value of equality "lies not in its crystalline beauty among abstract concepts, not in its wonderful symmetry, not even in its moral power, but in the countless attempts to realize equality in polity, economy and society."[7] In a real sense, equality is as much process as concept, and how the process can work—even insidiously—was traced by Tocqueville in a way that requires some soul-searching:

> The particular and predominating fact peculiar to democratic ages is equality. . . . Nobody is so limited and superficial as not to realize that political liberty can, if carried to excess, endanger the peace, property, and lives of individuals. But only perceptive and clear-sighted men see the dangers with which equality threatens us . . . [whereas] the ills which liberty brings may be immediate; all can see them and all, more or less, feel them. . . . The advantages of equality are felt immediately, and it is daily apparent where they come from. Political liberty occasionally

gives sublime pleasure to a few. Equality daily gives each man a host of small enjoyments. . . . The passion engendered by equality is therefore both strong and general. . . . It is no use telling people that by this blind surrender to an exclusive passion . . . freedom is slipping from their grasp while they look the other way.[8]

Tocqueville's worry over equality's potential threat to justice and liberty had been anticipated by another friend of America, Edmund Burke, who called equality the "monstrous fiction" of a fantasy world when the real one revealed inequalities that rhetoric could never remove.[9] Yet before his own eyes, the United States and France were giving equality a new dimension. Before these two historic revolutions, the equalizing process occurred only when one group fell from power and another scrambled into it. In those centuries equality was conceived in guns and money as much as in virtue: cannons could demolish feudal castles; musket-carrying peasants could destroy sword-wielding knights; and the invention of credit enabled merchants to use economic weapons against princely political powers. After each successful attack came the victor's ultimatum: "Treat us as equals—or else!" Each new class swallowed the class before it and was, therefore, more inclusionary than its predecessor. Equality's expansion meant power's dispersion.

English and American Attitudes

Successful gate-crashing by the bourgeoisie of the aristocracy's private preserves did not come easily. British elites operated on the premise that the upper class should have the upper hand. Cradling their bourgeois myths as much as coveting aristocratic status, the middle classes accepted, as the true story of their progress, the picture of wonderful impoverished old families reluctantly selling their houses and lands to ambitious petty merchants. In reality this process was more exception than rule. The only groups to whom the elite would sell were highly successful lawyers, distinguished officeholders, military men, great London merchants, or retired Indian nabobs. For more than three centuries the new aristocrats were not the manufacturers, industrialists, or entrepreneurs; not one Birmingham businessman was able to acquire property in nearby North Hamptonshire despite the fact that the region was England's center of industrial development.[10] The few who did buy their way intended not to stay. In England, social and political equality was always spelled in lowercase, if it was spelled at all.[11]

In the history of America, unlike that of England, equality has been a persistent theme. A visiting Viennese woman noted with disgust its early manifestation when Boston servant girls refused to kiss her hand: "They act toward their masters as an equal. *An equal!* What kind of country is that anyway? What kind of world will it be?"[12] Answers are found more in history than in speculation. By the beginning of the nineteenth century—and throughout the rest of it— a sense of equality permeated all corners of American life. With no royal families to honor, every white American male assumed that he was every bit as good as the next man. If English social manners were punctilious, Americans were careless—careless in manners and eating habits, in dress and speech, and toward traditions and precedents. They were even careless about their work, exhibiting little of the pride of craftsmanship so visible in Germany and Switzerland. The factory, more than the individual, made American goods the symbol of excellence. When the Japanese built factories every bit as good as the Americans', trouble was inevitable.

The nexus between carelessness and equality, however, may have been accidental rather than causal. The one certainty was equality's fascination for the American mind. Whereas England's lords knew what was due them as aristocrats, Americans knew what was due them as democrats. When they gathered at church socials or camp meetings, they met as equals; their public schools were great levelers; their childhood sports were open to anyone who could play the game respectably. The way American parents viewed their children was another indication of equality's pervasiveness. With certain exceptions in the antebellum South, leading families did not designate one son for the government, another for the military, another for the church, and still another for the law. By and large, young men were treated as equals when it came to career choice. A clue to the American spirit was the 1841 presidential campaign between William Henry Harrison and Martin Van Buren; both were very rich, but when it was learned that Harrison imbibed hard cider from a jug and Van Buren sipped foreign wines from golden goblets, Harrison's triumph was assured.

Even though economic inequalities intensified with the coming of the industrial revolution, there was then—as there is now—little hostility toward people of great wealth so long as they *earned* it; extremes of wealth and poverty existed in a country that, more than any other, enshrined equality on its political and psychological tabernacles.[13] When dissent finally was heard, the two voices most vehement in behalf of economic equality came from New England, and for good reasons: it was there where large wealth first started and was passed to the hands of a few. Emerson and Thoreau, to be true to the American dream, "had" to be dissenters because both desired a society of equals in all things—politics, business, and religion.

Scar Tissues

Equality's beauty was not without blemish. Women were honored but denied the vote; they were allowed to spend money but not to own property; and if a choice had to be made between a bright brother and a brighter sister going to college, the male was chosen. For women, "stay" was the operative word: before marriage, stay pure; in marriage, stay faithful; toward business, stay out. When native Indians could not be absorbed, they were slaughtered. Most illustrative was Lincoln's Emancipation Proclamation, which promised equality to the blacks but was undermined when the Supreme Court, on October 15, 1883, conceived the infamous "separate but equal" doctrine that effectively returned control to local southern communities over the way black-white relationships would be established. The North did not object because its own mores were developing along the same lines that prevailed among Southerners during the antebellum years. So blacks were technically free and practically shackled. Emerson's or Whitman's dream of Americans being different because they were equal continued the illusion. Southern writers (scholars Virginia Phillip and Alexander Bruce as well as novelist Thomas Nelson Page) went unchallenged when they wrote that blacks were intrinsically inferior to whites, a proposition that surfaces even today.

It was at the point of using their "own hands to earn" that blacks ran into insurmountable difficulties. While deep humanitarian and religious feelings supported equality, pragmatic considerations led whites to believe that emancipation could be used to lower labor costs by creating a more disciplined labor force. But the comforting belief collapsed when blacks balked at returning to the plantations on forced labor conditions; the disappointed abolitionists, in one of America's more tragic ironies, then began to backtrack in their support of equality.[14] It took a hundred years and Martin Luther King's death in 1963 to remind the nation that equality was for blacks more dream than reality.

Complicating society's approach to equality is the subjectivity that marks each individual's understanding of the word. Neither majority opinion nor democratic governments completely control the way ordinary people make ordinary decisions on how to treat other people;[15] hope for equality's future therefore depends on moral education that emphasizes the importance of seeing the other person's point of view.[16] Equality's fate in organizations depends ultimately on each person's moral character.[17] Nevertheless, beginnings can be made by managers willing to confront problems that they might prefer to ignore.

Four Faces of Equality

The practical questions about equality lead quite logically to a recognition that speculations about its meaning could help. Sometimes these speculations become mind-bogglers, even when accurate and compelling. A case in point is philosopher Douglas Rae's statement that equality may mean a concern that is

> individual-regarding, bloc-regarding, or segmental; its domain may be straightforward, marginal, or global; the idea of equality may be applied directly (equal results) or may be a version of equal opportunity (which in turn may equate means or prospects); equality may be based on uniform lots or on lots equally accommodating differences; it may be absolute or relative and, if relative, based on any of several distinct notions of relative equality.[18]

The mouth-filler is a mind-filler. Rae is seeking to demonstrate that careless talk leads to careless results and that there are ways of thinking and talking about equality that give enough coherence to the term so that people know what version is being used when inconsistencies and contradictions arise. Two examples give specificity to Rae's point. His opening sentence speaks of equality as possibly meaning "individual-regarding, bloc-regarding, or segmented." Different interpretations of its meaning were evident in 1985 when the Justice Department interpreted affirmative action to be individual-regarding while the courts leaned toward bloc-regarding equality. In the former view, only individuals actually harmed by discrimination should be helped; in the latter interpretation, all members of a certain class should be helped, even when certain members of that class have never suffered from discrimination. By and large, business organizations have opted for the latter interpretation because of practical, not intellectual, reasons: if equality means quotas (even when historically quotas meant inequality), so be it. Managers simply had to know the judge's rule. A second example is the equal results theory, which is a far cry from the equal opportunity theory in hiring and promotion policies. Equality's meaning, therefore, is not singular but plural, and in the plurality are possibilities of contradiction. There are, in fact, at least three equalities: equality of opportunity, equality in results, and equality of protection.

Equality of Opportunity.   One conception of equality on which virtual unanimity exists is equality of opportunity. Repeated survey results have demonstrated support for this version (Table 5-1).

While commitment to equality of opportunity is pronounced, qualifications appear when race is concerned and considerable modifications when homosexuality is involved. These modifications raise two important questions: (1) Does the fair share principle among equally worthy claimants produce good decisions for organizations *and* for individuals? (2) Should powerful or talented individuals help the less powerful or less talented? Those who see the first as the more relevant are often labeled conservatives because they think that equality means a society of "misters"—not a society of lords or dukes or sirs—who struggle endlessly to get ahead but with no guarantee of ever achieving it. Talent and luck are keys to success. Those who concentrate on the second question, on the other hand, are the liberals, who see the issue as one of social justice because the strong should help the weak. [19]

Since equality of opportunity commands almost universal assent, it is important to identify its three hidden elements that affect other forms of equality. The three are (1) the agent or class for whom opportunities exist, (2) the goals toward which opportunities are directed, and (3) the relationship connecting the agents of an opportunity to the goal of an opportunity. Addressing each in order can clarify meanings. The first element deals with the way in which opportunity for a particular person or class differs from one to another. Illustrations include laws that provide opportunities for blacks *alone*, for women *alone*, for major and independent oil producers and refiners *alone*, and for housing opportunities for low-income persons *alone*. Some states provide equal opportunities only for people within the state.

The second element is the goal toward which the opportunities are directed. Access to jobs, education, medical care, housing, and pro-

Table 5-1. Equality of Opportunity

	General Public (percent)

1. Everyone in America should have equal opportunities to get ahead.

Agree -	98
Disagree -	2

2. Children should have equal education opportunities.

Agree -	98
Disagree -	1
Uncertain -	1

3. Do you think that Negroes in this town should have the same chance as white people to get a good education?

Yes -	89
No -	6
Qualified Answers -	3
Don't know -	2

4. Do you think Negroes should be given just as good a chance as white men to get ahead in the armed forces?

Yes -	72
No -	22
Don't know -	6

5. Do you think a Negro doing the same work as a white man should get the same pay?

Yes -	87
No -	10
Don't know -	3

6. As you know, there has been considerable discussion in the news lately regarding the rights of homosexual men and women. In general, do you think homosexuals should or should not have equal rights in terms of job opportunities?

Should -	56
Should not -	33
No opinion -	11

Source: Herbert McCloskey and John Zaller, *The American Ethos: Public Attitudes Toward Capitalism and Democracy* (Cambridge, Mass.: Harvard University Press, 1984), 83. Reprinted with permission.

motions are good examples. Yet getting one may occasionally reduce chances for acquiring another.

The third element is the relationship connecting the agents of an opportunity to the goal of an opportunity. An opportunity is never a guarantee, and yet it is something more than a simple possibility. Normally, job opportunities are simple possibilities; however, if the law explicitly states that the opportunity must be there, it creates a presumption that the opportunity will be protected in ways not extended to other opportunities.[20] A good example of a "protected" opportunity is the 1979 Illinois Human Rights Act, which prohibits labor organizations from discriminating against people on the basis of race, color, religion, sex, national origin, ancestry, age, marital status, or physical or mental handicap. The agents are specified on the basis of groups previously discriminated against, and the goal is their employment. To speak, therefore, of equality of opportunity without making explicit what kind of opportunity is involved and how that opportunity enhances prospects of achievement is to confuse the issue.

To summarize: to ascribe equality to people is not to ascribe identical characteristics. Two persons can have an equal opportunity to achieve a certain objective even though each faces a different obstacle (ill health, poor education), provided that both are free from the same specified obstacles. Equal opportunity means that certain specified obstacles may be removed. Ambiguities about equality of opportunity have led many to conclude that all talk about it is hypocrisy run rampant. Nevertheless, to speak of equal opportunities by prescribing unequal opportunity may not involve a contradiction; it may be the only sensible method to get out of messes that history, race, sex, or physical handicaps have brought into the marketplace. Imposing unequal opportunity on some may be the only practical way to achieve equal opportunity for others.[21] Furthermore, hope for achievement inherent in the goal of equality of opportunity may provide dynamism to the society. It is important to remember, however, that such dynamism brings collisions of ambitions and energies, wherein some win and some lose.[22]

Equality in Results.   When the very few have very much (the top 1 percent of American families hold almost a third of all the wealth, and the bottom half hold only 5 percent of that total), justice seems to totter, even though equality of opportunity exists. The result of wealth inequalities flows partly from inequality of talent and partly from forms of social organization that not only assign roles and select the role-player but also attach a monetary value to the role.[23] Angered by what seems to be blatant inequality, extreme socialists support distribution of wealth on a share-and-share-alike basis; less extreme versions of socialism support a welfare state wherein everyone is guaranteed all basic necessities. No individual jumps ahead of another if one is harmed—and the consideration applies even if the contribution to the organization's prosperity is negligible. Extreme socialism is a utopia; moderate socialism is a reality, notably in the Scandinavian countries. The socialist perception is that market economies are intrinsically unjust and that government control over production and distribution is essential if the grand ideal of equality is to be fulfilled.[24]

Corporate executives often reject out of hand any form of socialism. It is a bad word embraced by dangerous people. Yet one parallel to moderate socialism is the profit-sharing enterprise. Its advocates admit that employees make varying contributions to the organization's success; nevertheless, all are equally involved, and equal involvement means more equal sharing in the company's prosperity. Not only are all individuals rewarded financially, but they are enriched psychologically because they perceive their personal involvement in the organization's goals. Its goals become their goals; its image of itself becomes their image of themselves. The presence of profit-sharing enterprises, encouraged by some and tolerated by others, reveals nonetheless a rather widespread conviction in the business community that the principle of equality is related to rationality: *to treat people unequally on the basis of arbitrary standards is to behave unreasonably*. Equality holds forth the promise that all individuals are capable of sorting out their own higher interests and that such interests should be under that person's control on a basis equal to the control exercised by others. In this sense equality means (1) respect for others to seek fulfillment of their higher interests unfettered by artificial restraints and (2) a certain commonality in those higher interests, such as dignity, autonomy, and self-respect.

Equality of Protection.   Critical to success in all efforts to transform the idea of equality into practice is recognition that all must be equally protected. If white police officers stand idly by when a bully beats an innocent black bystander, equality of protection vanishes; if fire fighters refuse to respond to alarms from certain neighborhoods, equality of protection is nonexistent. People must be protected in certain fundamental respects. If equal protection under the law is essential for individuals, it is also important for organizations. How difficult it is to understand its practical impact was illustrated by the *Metropolitan Life Insurance Company* v. *Wood* case. The case arose when Alabama levied a tax on gross life insurance premiums so that out-of-state companies paid three to four times as much as their domestic competitors. Alabama defended its discriminatory tax on the grounds that it was needed to encourage the formation of domestic insurance companies within the state (equality of opportunity). In a 5-to-4 vote, the Supreme Court declared that promoting domestic industry by imposing tax disadvantages on foreign competitors was the kind of parochial discrimination that the equal-protection clause was intended to prevent. But a strong minority obviously felt that equal protection for outsiders meant unequal protection for natives. The case illustrates one of the many problems inherent in making the idea of equality of protection work—and because it often does not work, suspicions again arise that the rhetoric is hypocritical. In all cases it is clear that the manager's preferred definition of equality influences the way justice is fulfilled within the organization.

JUSTICE

Scales of justice were used symbolically in ancient Egypt to indicate that the sun-god Ra would weigh conflicts evenhandedly. That it was not perfect scaling is suggested by Job's injunction in the Old Testament: "Prosecute the rich, not merely the penniless; the strong-armed as well as the powerless." Like equality, justice has gone through such various stages of evolution that it seems necessary for each generation to reinterpret it. Easy to accept was the Golden Rule definition of justice—but not to be ignored was George Bernard Shaw's qualifier: "Do *not* do unto others as you would that they should do unto you. Their taste may not be the same."[25] Yet there is, as Chester Barnard asserted, "no escape from the judicial process in the exercise of executive functions."[26] Justice must be managed, and the art of administration is to apply pain when needed, as painlessly as possible. The best way to avoid unpleasantness is to promote justice. But what is it? Consider just two scenarios:

Scenario One

Bill Schulz, deputy director of industrial safety in a large manufacturing company, had begun work with his present employer immediately after receiving a doctorate in industrial engineering. Now, with twenty-five years of experience, he had to admit that a recent heart attack had slowed him down perceptibly. With four children in private colleges and with an ailing wife, Schulz had few options when he was told that prospects for future advancement were slim because he had "slowed up." Pondering the predicament, Schulz debated whether he should (1) offer to work an extra hour or two to compensate for his slower pace, (2) take what was in effect a long-term salary cut, or (3) appeal to his boss's sense of fair play by describing his family situation and the consequent need for more income. Although not putting his thoughts into crisp questions, Schulz was raising age-old issues about a just wage:

- Is it what we can get?
- Is it what we will take?
- Is it what we need to live on?
- Is it what we put into the work?

Which of the above answers is the most logical?

Scenario Two

Five professors were appointed by the university president to allocate scarce parking spaces to the faculty. When one proposed that locations nearest to buildings be charged higher fees than those at distant locations, certain committee members objected on the grounds that the arrangement was unfair to other junior and less well-paid colleagues. When the advocate of the differential fee system rose to defend the proposal, she used this example: Suppose a teacher decides to pay the higher amount of money for the nearby space and foregoes attending two or three ballets, while a colleague attends the ballets and, as a consequence, has insufficient funds for the more expensive parking ticket. Is it fair to deny the thrift-oriented professor the better space,

especially when the committee has already agreed that (1) the handicapped would have first choice and (2) higher fees would subsidize
more remote low-cost parking areas? Her critics called the analogy
irrelevant and argued that lottery is the best road to justice when the
resource is scarce and necessary.

Do you support the differential fee argument?

Definitions

Correct answers depend on raising the right questions. But right
questions depend on accurate understanding of what the relevant terms
mean. Unfortunately, the term *justice* is almost as complicated as
equality. Most involved in defining justice are lawyers and philosophers, and their efforts are like "shovelling smoke," Judge Learned
Hand's famous description.[27] Given their pragmatic bent, Americans
have preferred to define justice in terms of a fundamental constitutional
principle they call due process: no one can be deprived of life, liberty,
or property without correct legal procedures. Having heard the words
so often, Americans think that when lawyers speak of due process the
definitional problem has been solved; managers, too, find it easier to
establish procedures like the open door and in-house arbitration panels
than to wrestle with content.

Yet if due process is the answer, why have courts stretched its
meaning like taffy?[28] One constitutional lawyer noted that, taken
seriously, the assumption that due process is a rational process makes
of courts "lunacy commissions sitting in judgment upon the mental
capacity of legislators and, occasionally, of judges"; what is good sense
to the layperson is often rejected by judges. Even the Supreme Court
tends to believe that what it says three times about due process must
be true, and so "we are left with a term that, denoting neither an
historic fact, a psychiatric insight, nor a moral concept is nevertheless
one of the key words in the vocabulary of justice."[29] The words are
often so mysterious that Americans cannot comfortably live with them;
they are so magical that Americans cannot live without them. Since
due process deals more with technique than with substance, it is
necessary to seek philosophers' help—even when one of them, as noted,
accused his colleagues of being the intellectual hoods who mugged it.
If lawyers have trouble with the procedural aspects of justice, philos-

ophers battle over its substance: what one asserts, another denies. Yet justice always commands respect because it represents a great ideal—not because there is consensus on its meaning.

Because justice looks outward to others' rights, it is first necessary to know who those "others" are, since the recipients themselves affect the process.[30] In socializing domains represented by family, home, school, and neighborhood, for example, reciprocity, not exchange, is the preferred route to justice. In addition, different needs require different responses. The sickly infant gets more of the mother's attention than the sturdy adolescent; the poor neighbor deserves more financial help than the wealthy one. While all are viewed equally, unequal treatment is necessary to fulfill justice.[31] On the other hand, reciprocity is much less acceptable in relationships among people who have no ties of blood, kinship, or friendship. In market relationships the view is that people should receive in proportion to what they give or what the market says they are worth. Recent polls suggest, however, that public opinion is shifting somewhat away from complete reliance on such norms. Sensitive to the importance of pulse-taking, managers weigh the implications of findings that show:

- Rich and poor strongly endorse guaranteed jobs.
- Rich and poor support equality so long as it is couched in terms of need, investment, results—anything except being couched in terms of equality itself.
- Rich and poor—but poor particularly—see poverty more as a result of bad luck or imperfections in the system than as an indication of their sloth or sinfulness.
- People vacillate in their preference between the norm of need and the norm of results when concrete problems require solutions.[32]

Current "Debates"

Whether growing public interest in the meaning of justice has affected the scholarly community is hard to say. There is no doubt, however, that interest is high, as the following two "debates" show.

Rawls versus Nozick.   Among the most distinguished contemporary theoreticians is John Rawls, whose *Theory of Justice* has already been acclaimed as a classic. His opening statement, quoted at the beginning of this chapter, bears repeating: "Justice is the first virtue of social institutions as truth is the first virtue of systems of thought."[33] Rawls has become symbol for a more activist government role, and, because his ideas are put to uses he might often disclaim, it is well to review what he really thinks. With considerable ingenuity he linked equality and justice by assuming that all rational people equally want certain things such as liberty, opportunity, income, and self-respect. These are *primary values*, which should therefore be distributed equally (unless a nonequal distribution of any or all is to everyone's advantage). Upon this "thin" theory of the good (the result of eliminating consideration of other good), Rawls advanced two hypotheses:

1. The *equal rights principle*, which asserts that each person has an equal right to the most extensive liberties compatible with a similar system of liberty for all
2. The *difference principle*, which holds that social and economic inequalities are to be (a) arranged so that they work to the greatest benefit of the least advantaged consistent with society's duties toward future generations and (b) attached to offices and positions open to all persons under conditions of equality of opportunity

If conflicts ever develop between the two principles, the first always takes precedence. Since society cannot survive unless constructed on universally applicable principles accepted by rational people, a question arises: How can we determine what is rational? Rawls's answer was to place people under a hypothetical "veil of ignorance," where they know neither their own nor others' strengths and weaknesses. Free from prejudice and tunnel vision, uninhibited by status or wealth, people would then accept the logic of four maxims related to need, exchange, contribution, and saving, respectively:

1. *Need*. Each person should be guaranteed those primary social goods necessary to satisfy basic needs in the society in which he or she lives, assuming that sufficient resources are available to maintain the guaranteed minimum.
2. *Exchange*. Additional primary social goods should be distributed on the basis of private effort and voluntary agreements and exchanges.
3. *Minimal contribution*. When resources are insufficient to provide the guaranteed minimum to everyone, a minimal contribution to society is required of all those capable of making one.

4. *Saving*. The rate of saving for each generation should represent its fair contribution toward a future society whose members can roughly enjoy the same benefits as the present generation.

Critical to Rawlsian concepts is the fact that the idea of a right comes before the idea of the good, a philosophic expression of individualism because it speaks first to things that separate one individual from others before asking what connects one to others. In the original position represented by the veil-of-ignorance hypothesis, individuals do not reflect on the meaning of justice; it is, on the other hand, determined by unanimity. But unanimity presumes the good is already defined and needs only to be found. Despite this objection, Rawls does force managers to consider what kind of an organization is most likely to promote justice. In the United States the secular scripture holds that justice is best achieved through a market system based largely upon quid pro quo relationships and an organizational structure based on wage packages for nonmanagement employees. Competition among equals disciplines the recreant corporation; fear of firing disciplines the careless worker.

Managers have been joined by several philosophers in their qualified acceptance of Rawls, who has received the treatment authors of significant treatises invariably receive—fulsome praise and sharp criticism. He has been praised for stating clearly that inequalities are presumptively immoral and that, when they exist, they must be logically defensible; he has been lauded for making clear the fact that justice is something more than quid pro quo; and he has appealed to some manager because he holds that people seek to make the most use of their talents. Knowing something will be taken from them to help others induces them to work hard to maintain a living level they deem adequate.[34] The worry of conservatives is that Rawls spent too much energy on what others have called the primacy of welfare rights.[35]

Among the critics is Robert Nozick, who feared that "Rawlsianism" would be used by liberals to support the activist state. Liberals, by his definition, encourage A and B to join forces in determining what C should give to D.[36] Nozick argued that justice is best served when persons, without harming others, acquire things through the expenditure of their own labor, effort, and ingenuity. When the process of acquisition is fair, justice is served—no matter how unequal is the final distribution of goods and services. Any thought of governments determining how to redistribute a person's honestly earned (or inherited) wealth to others is arbitrary because it violates the freedoms of those who have worked hard to achieve their gains. Nozick made the further point that redistributive schemes usually result in income being taken from the productive rich to help the unproductive poor, whereas his "entitlement principle" (what one honestly earns, one legitimately keeps) takes into account the past, present, and future. Government redistribution of wealth is the prattle of socialists whom one wit slyly defined.

> What is a socialist?
> One who has yearnings
> For equal division of unequal earnings;
> Idler or bungler, or both, he is willing
> To fork out his penny, and pocket your shilling.[37]

There are other criticisms of Rawls. It has been argued that justice is not the primary virtue for individuals or for societies. Benevolence is more important because it fills the gaps that even the most just societies cannot fill. This is true because individuals owe others more than justice requires or even permits, not by reason of the social contract but because the way wealth is shared and enjoyed helps define the character of the individual.[38] Rawls has also been criticized for serious omissions and possible contradictions in his list of primary goods. When he talked about the importance of enriching relationships with others, he neglected meaningful work in his catalogue, yet among the primary goods should be an assurance that "every citizen has access to decent work, an income sufficient to sustain self-respect and an equal right in economic decision-making."[40]

Walzer versus Dworkin.   While Rawls and Nozick initially occupied center stage, others moved in to enlarge the discussion. Two prominent additions have been Michael Walzer and Ronald Dworkin. In the former's view, justice cannot be defined absolutely because the worth of things is determined by society and not by a single person. Things take on value because they come into people's heads before they come into people's hands. Justice is a social version of the market system because certain goods are so dominant that they determine the value of related goods. Behind Walzer's theory is a view of equality that says a person's success in one sphere must not spill over to allow that person to dominate in another sphere. For example, wealth should not bring the political power that often occurs in market societies; in technological societies, scientists and engineers should not determine public policy on such things as nuclear power or national defense; and in the medieval world, clergy had power but came to grief when the popes demanded, and got, sovereign political rights.

Distribution of power and wealth is what social conflict is all about; therefore, the perception of a single dominant good (power, money, titles) is created by competing bands of "magicians" whose own social position is maintained when others accept their sorcery. Further, wrote Walzer, even if one envisioned a completely equal society (all supplies are equal, all demands are met, and each person has an equal amount of money), this great "regime of simplicity" would disintegrate quickly under democracy and capitalism. Under democracy, people vie for power to ensure priority for their interest; under capitalism, self-seeking individuals establish meritocracies that eliminate egalitarianism. Only an absolute monarch could maintain a regime of simple equality, yet such a regime would be morally unacceptable because omnipotent government is "the most dangerous instrument in human history."[40] In short, Walzer thinks that justice is best promoted when power among basic institutions (business and government, church and university) is separated and when people do not define justice but describe it through observations of what people most prize.

Walzer's views have not impressed Ronald Dworkin, who maintains that the very existence of cultural and psychological differences means that disagreements over justice can be resolved only when people move outside their own traditions and appeal to general principles. Some inclusive formula is needed to measure justice in all societies; relativistic accounts are essentially doomed because, in contemporary societies, the number of shared understandings is diminishing rather than increasing. Any theory, therefore, that ties justice to prevailing perceptions or conventions is ultimately unacceptable. Philosophers make no contribution to understanding how governments or organizations should conduct themselves—or be erected—unless they pit principle against impulse, concept against culture, generalization against particularity. Dworkin indicts Walzer for relying too much on the status quo, thereby denying possibilities for reopening challenges to the conventional wisdom. Justice is too important to be left to convention and anecdote.[41] It comes only when rights are taken seriously.[42]

Newcomers. Just when it appears that the choice is between a relative and a more fixed view of justice, along comes Yale law professor

Bruce Ackerman with a new twist on the meaning of the right to justice and equality. To Ackerman, rights exist only when a person can participate in dialogues on the nature of justice and can logically defend the statement "I am as good as you are." Because young children can make no such defense, they are not considered citizens; similarly, the mentally retarded are not allowed to vote or sit on juries. To Ackerman the rights of the "talking" ape are more secure than those of a human "vegetable."[43]

Similar reasoning has been applied to the abortion debate by Michael Tooley, who argued that a right to anything, like equality and justice, cannot be assessed by fetuses or infants because they cannot reason on their right even to life itself; because reasons for this most fundamental of rights elude them, they are outside the human community. Then comes a blockbuster: infanticide is as morally reasonable as abortion and, by extension, illiterate workers and the mentally handicapped are properly excluded from a right to be treated equally and justly.[44] If Tooley is right, then when infants cry all night, parents should call out Herod's soldiers. Revulsion at such consequences does not make philosophers irrelevant; rather, it tells why, almost in a perverse way, philosophers are so needed. Their constant reinterpretations of equality and justice have bearing on the shape of debate on affirmative action policies; their interpretations of justice bear thoughtful consideration when compensation programs are being devised; their explorations of why income disparities can be defended only under certain rules of logic affect tax programs; and their efforts, finally, move managers to go beyond due process symbolized by open-door policies to those ultimate meanings of justice that due process is presumed to serve. More important to them than theories of justice are those few practical precepts that help to guide decision making. This preference involves understanding a set of basic principles.

BASIC PRINCIPLES

To review the various theories about justice is to find philosophical support for ideological positions on the welfare state and market capitalism, on inalienable rights and conferred rights, on animal rights and infant rights. Of the foregoing, it was Jefferson's philosophy of "inalienable rights" that most appealed to Americans' instincts, if not to their minds. This instinct would support the following maxims:

1. To each according to his or her contribution to the stock of goods and services
2. To each in ways wherein nonessentials, defined here as "luxuries," are allocated on a free-market principle
3. To the present generation in ways that respect the needs of their descendants
4. To each on the basis of universal principle and not exclusively on the basis of existing circumstances
5. To each an opportunity to share in the community's increased wealth
6. To each so that past wrongs are not perpetuated but redressed[45]

Major Kinds of Justice

Students and practitioners of management eventually must sort out which of the foregoing are most useful to decision making. The sorting-out process is made more manageable when three fundamental relationships are handled in proper order: (1) relations of individuals to other individuals, (2) relations of individuals to the community, groups, and organizations, and (3) relations of the community, group, or organization to those who constitute it. Such basic relationships lead to three kinds of justice: exchange, contributive, and distributive.[46]

Exchange Justice.   Exchange (or commutative) justice approximates a quid pro quo model by asserting that people deserve to receive in direct ratio to what they contribute. The old maxim regarding "a fair day's wage for a fair day's work" captures the spirit of exchange justice. Because exchange justice prevails more fully when markets are genuinely competitive and entry relatively easy, Adam Smith used this definition in his apologia for market capitalism: a competitive market was the best mechanism humans could contrive to meet the twin imperatives of justice and equality.[47]

Contributive Justice.   Contributive (or legal) justice spells out what authorities think is the individual's indebtedness to the community. It addresses questions like these: Who should be drafted? How shall people be taxed? What criteria should one meet to vote? Hold public office? In these instances, the community, as the bearer of rights, asserts claims against persons. Because it is community based, the general welfare holds the preeminent position and citizens or workers may find their individual "freedoms" curtailed in the interest of a larger good.

Distributive Justice.   Distributive (or social) justice, the most controversial aspect of the three, acknowledges that the community has duties toward its members and must therefore aim to promote the good of each individual within that community. It presupposes that markets rarely work in purely symmetrical terms and that some people are enriched while others are handicapped. A relevant example, the first authentic "soap opera," involved two neighboring cities in the English Midlands—poor, dirty Manchester and rich, clean Harrogate. The cost of air pollution fell more heavily on the poorer Mancunians; needing more cleaning materials, their purchases of soap absorbed a larger proportional share of the family budget. In this case an indifferent British government tolerated a festering injustice. In the United States the Harrogates are the Scarsdales, Bel Airs, and Grosse Points; the Manchesters are the Appalachias, McKeesports, and Harlems. Today "Mancunians" in America are making greater claims on the rest of society—part of that "third revolution" which Irving Shapiro talked about and in which he insisted business leaders must play a key part.

Others suffer grievously because of discrimination based on race or sex, physical or psychological qualities, class relationships or social structures. Such persons have a special claim on the community even though they are unable (or are denied a chance) to render a fair return for goods apportioned to them.[48] Distributive justice, therefore, flows from the belief that humans are capable of being known by other humans, of being perfected from within but needing help from without. Primary responsibility falls not on the claimant but on those of power or wealth who are obligated to make equity come alive for all.[49] The obligation is quite different from that in the lender-debtor relationship, wherein the creditor has a right to receive repayment. With distributive justice, nothing belongs exclusively to any one person; all that belongs is a *share* in something common to everyone. In this case, the individual is not a separate party to a contract with claims equal to those of others in the contract but is a partner with a higher ranked partner called society.[50]

So far as distributive justice is concerned, the following should be emphasized: (1) whereas in exchange justice what is due can be calculated (by the party entitled to it, by the party obligated to pay it, or even by an impartial third party), in distributive justice such calculations are not possible; (2) in distributive justice, responsibility for determining what is due an individual falls on one in authority; and (3) whereas in exchange justice the obligation is paid, in distributive justice it is allotted—the difference between them being in arithmetic and geometric calculations, respectively. Reference to obligations under justice is more audacious than reference to rights because, by stressing obligation, people must seek convincing proof for the grounds upon which their obligations rest.

A Special Note on Social Justice

Before closing, it is well to note what contemporaries mean when they speak of social justice. From Adam Smith in the eighteenth century to W.S. Jevons in the nineteenth, economists were very discreet in discussing income distribution—even though Adam Smith said that hurting one citizen to promote the interest of another was contrary to justice,[51] John Stuart Mill, a great proponent of equality, nevertheless refused to support a progressive income tax; and Francis Edgeworth insisted that while the state should tax the rich before the poor, people below a certain intellectual level should not be allowed to have children.[52] Each struggled to express a precise form of justice, and each sensed inadequacies in his definition.

Supplementing these half-definitions was "social justice," a phrase that appeared first in 1795 with William Godwin's *Enquiry Concerning Political Justice* and later in 1840 with Massimo Taparelli, an Italian political revolutionary who then conveniently neglected to give it precision. Nevertheless, it was an effort to get beyond the idea of comparative justice and to the idea of noncomparative justice, that is, what a person is entitled to by virtue of his or her humanity.[53] In an attempt to fill the void, economist Josef Solterer wrote that social justice is a process of institutional restructuring, analogous to the way individual restructure their moral values as they mature: "Social justice is closer to love than the older justice of exchange. Love is the power to increase the dimensions of the universe indefinitely, a possibility because it itself is ultimately structureless. . . . Knowledge of social justice is then another, but not final, piece of knowledge in the transformation of the person and the world."[54] Managers pondering

Solterer's message recognize the relevance of his concentration on human potential and growth as prerequisite to organizational potential and growth. Compassion does not replace justice; it complements it.[55] Employees are seen as valued participants of the corporate community, not as disenfranchised and easily replaced cogs in the organizational machine.

CONCLUSION

Claims to economic rights today are the sequel to those claims for political rights which took firm shape in the Western world after 1865. If political rights were expected to destroy the kingdom of "sinister interests" in the state—as J.S. Mill put it—economic rights are seen today as weapons against the "sinister interest" of individuals and groups having extensive control over capital.[56] In a fundamental sense, the form of justice that best promotes equality is social justice because it is responsive to everyone's potential for greater growth and greater maturity. Because social justice deals ultimately with the transformation of individuals and their organizations, fears persist among administrators that it is simply another shibboleth masquerading as theory. Yet this concern for drawing out the potential in every person and in all organizations is being recognized as the best definition of a leader:

> And leadership means vision, cheerleading, enthusiasm, love, trust, verve, passion, obsession, consistency, the use of symbols, paying attention as illustrated by the content of one's calendar, out-and-out drama (and the management thereof), creating heroes at all levels, coaching effectively, wandering around, and numerous other things. Leadership must be present at *all* levels of the organization. It depends on a million little things done with obsession, consistency and care, but all of those million little things add up to nothing if the trust, vision and basic belief are not there.[57]

So described, leadership is the necessary instrument for justice in all organizations. Managers are marvelously situated to take the lead.

6
TRUTH AND FREEDOM

THE VALUES QUIZ   *(Mark True or False)*

1. _____ Moral freedom means the right to say whatever we want.
2. _____ In the organizational world, managers are ethically bound to tell the truth, the whole truth, and nothing but the truth.
3. _____ While it is ethical for diplomats to lie when the vital interests of the country are at stake, it is not ethical for managers to lie when the vital interests of their organizations are at stake.
4. _____ Although not condoning perjury, lawyers should allow clients to perjure themselves if perjury means victory.
5. _____ To act paternalistically is part of the manager's job.
6. _____ Primary responsibility for helping employees to mature morally falls on employees themselves and not on management.
7. _____ So long as a person does no harm to another, that person should be able to do what he or she wishes to do.
8. _____ Because they are better educated, elites are more tolerant than the masses.

On portals leading to university campuses and on the friezes of city libraries are often found these words: "Know the truth and the truth shall make you free." No one challenges the aphorism. Many have debated its meaning. What is truth? And what is freedom? Criminals hearing the judge's sentence of life imprisonment know a truth as they forever lose their freedom. Patients told by the attending physician of an incurable cancer know a truth that may cause added emotional pain. These surely are not the kinds of truths or freedoms that the aphorism is intended to convey.

To penetrate their meanings is to work at different analytical levels. Oliver Wendell Holmes had this in mind when he wrote:

There are one-story intellects, two-story intellects, and three-story intellects with skylights. All fact collectors, who have no aim beyond their facts, are one-story men. Two-story men compare, reason, generalize, using the labors of fact collectors as well as their own. Three-story men idealize, imagine, predict; their best illumination comes from above, through the skylight.[1]

Truth and freedom need skylights. The two, larger than life, are life. They define man's nature even as they exhaust his energies; they are beacons on a hill shrouded in mist; they have moved people to die so that others might possess them. Strange words. Beautiful words. Yet they relate to what Russian novelists and political theorists of the nineteenth century called the "cursed questions: cursed in the two-fold sense of being misunderstood and of being abused."[2] Intrigued by them as much as by his country's history, Stephen Vincent Benét was moved to write:

There are certain words,
Our own and others', we're used to—words we've used,
Heard, had to recite, forgotten, . . .
Liberty, equality, justice.
To none will we sell, refuse or deny, right or justice.
We hold these truths to be self-evident.

Benét's emphasis on words that are "our own and others' " conveys the critical message: These words are not the flowering of a particular language or the possession of a single people. They are so prized a part of a common patrimony that when war and savagery engulf the world, everyone knows they have been lost or grievously threatened. They are, in short, words and more than mere words. They are definitions of the self and of the society. When they are perverted, their replacements gnaw at the community's flesh. When they are denied, society's corpse is cold. Have the meanings of these words stayed with us? Or are we not moving toward the eighteenth-century world that Alphonse de Lamartine described as

140

times of chaos; opinions are a scramble; parties are a jumble; the language of new
ideas has not been created; nothing is more difficult than to give a good definition
of oneself in religion, in philosophy, in politics. One feels, one knows, one lives,
and at need, one dies for one's cause, but one cannot name it. It is the problem
of this time to classify things and men. . . . The world has jumbled its catalogue.[3]

Catalogues are jumbled when they include words like creative accounting,
nonrevelatory disclosures, cooking the books, hype, leaks, planted
rumors, and disinformation, *each of which contributes to a loss of confidence*
in leadership. Leaders suffer and followers share the pain. Yet Americans'
commitment to truth and freedom gives them a resiliency to bounce back.
President Nixon gave the lie and Judge Sirica found the truth; Ivan Boesky
lived with his deception and the Securities and Exchange Commission discovered
the reality; Admiral Poindexter hid the facts and a congressional committee
discovered them.

But these Nixon-Boesky-Poindexter deceptions were events; they do not define
truth's substances. A forgotten seventeenth-century divine named William Wol-
laston (1659–1724) said that every immoral act is an offense against truth
because immorality consists in going against human nature.[4] *Similarly, every*
denial of freedom goes against human nature. Recalling this old English
clergyman is useful insofar as it suggests how different moralists have ap-
proached the problems of truth and freedom.

TRUTH AS CONCEPT

David Rockefeller, board chairman of Chase Manhattan: "There is absolutely no justification for lying in business, in academics, on ré-
sumés, or anywhere else. Honesty in business is nonnegotiable. In
banking, our business is founded on faith, trust, and public confidence.
Banking is above all a business based on mutual trust, and we demand
absolute honesty in all our affairs, both internally and externally."[5]

Donald M. Kendall, CEO of Pepsico: "I cannot imagine a situation
in business when it would be legally or morally justified to lie . . ."[6]

John Dewey of Columbia University: "Society not only continues to
exist . . . *by* communication, but it may be fairly said to exist *in* . . .
communication. There is more than a verbal tie between the words
common, community, and communication. Men live in a community
by virtue of the things which they have in common; and communication is the way in which they come to possess things in common."[7]

Albert Dondeyne, a European philosopher: "Every time freedom has been separated from truth . . . it has been voided of its very meaning, its internal substance, and has degenerated into anarchy and disorder."[8]

Gerhard O. Forde, a Lutheran minister: "The modern world, since at least the time of the Enlightenment, has been hooked on freedom."[9]

What Is Truth?

A common definition is that truth is a concordance between what is said and what is fact.[10] In dealing with truth, it is as important to know the facts as it is to convey the facts. And in a complex organization, knowledge of facts does not come easily. Managers are "protected" from unpleasant realities by overzealous subordinates; departmental reports have such serious omissions that the half-truth can become the Big Lie; and memories play odd tricks on people. In communicating with others, the necessary elements are (1) possessing facts, (2) stating facts, (3) identifying those who are entitled to the facts, and (4) using language that the hearer understands. Neither can long be absent if the organization is to prosper. However, two critical questions remain: What kinds of truth provide what kinds of certitude? Who has a right to what people know?

Kinds of Truth

Like every other major concept, truth has been dissected repeatedly. Self-evident truths, scientific truths, moral truths, and natural truths are commonly used to distinguish among the word's various manifestations. Yet three classifications used by philosophers over the centuries maintain a sturdy relevance: metaphysical, physical, and moral.

1. *Metaphysical* truths are those which flow from the principle of contradiction used by logicians: something cannot be and not be at the same time; parallel lines in a plane surface cannot meet; sunlight is not darkness. In metaphysical truths, there is no conceivable way of reconciling one proposition to its contradiction without doing violence to one of them.
2. *Physical* truths pertain mainly to the verified findings of science

and are usually called laws. The law of gravity is an obvious example, and anyone who defies it without the help of counter-gravitational forces does so at peril. But when scientific laws fail to work in certain cases, investigators are led to develop new laws, such as Einstein's principle of relativity—or admit that an exception to the law has actually occurred. People then speak of miracles.

3. *Moral* truths, based on probability theory, are the types that managers deal with. No automobile traffic could flow safely in large cities without substantial assurance that most people will obey stop-and-go signals; no factory could meet production quotas without reasonable confidence that a steady percentage of workers will come to work on time; and no school could continue if faculty attendance was grossly inconsistent. Moral truths give a distinctive type of certitude to the expectation that behavior by participants in the enterprise is predictable. Obviously, the margin of error is higher in this than in the other two realms of truth Drivers do ignore signals; employees do not come to work; and teachers call in "ill." But moral truth, and the certainty it allows, enables organizations to so operate that planning can be done with confidence and implementation achieved on schedule.

Truth and Decision Making

Because the margin of error is always present with moral truths, distinctions between judicial/historical decision-making and administrative decision-making are drawn. In judicial decision-making, efforts are made to ascertain what has happened; it is, in a sense, "past tense" decision making. Because the deed is cemented in time, people are under no urgent pressure: trials drag on, hung juries are replaced with new ones, one set of evidence is repeatedly tested against another set. Historians, auditors, journalists, the IRS, and jurors are engaged in judicial decision-making. Managers, on the other hand, are more like football coaches in that they review the past to determine the percentages but then take, usually under time constraints, a decision that thrusts the team and the organization into the future. In short, managers make decisions on the basis of both past performances (where the margin of error can be factored in) and future possibilities (where the margin of error cannot be so readily calculated). For such leaders, the decision process is like riding a bicycle while trying to make it. Uncertainties over consumer receptivity to new products, counter-strategies by competitors, reinterpretations by judges of old precedents, and uneven enforcement of laws by regulators are among the variables that plague the administrative decision-making process. Yet managers are able to estimate the future on the basis of the moral certitudes arising from an understanding of how humans act under given circumstances and a reasonable confidence that such knowledge can be extrapolated to coming conditions. What is unfair is to apply the "Monday-morning quarterback" rule too broadly. Judicial decision-making and administrative decision-making, not being identical, are not to be assessed by the same criteria; nevertheless, the latter is not immune to moral judgment.

Some managers reach the top on the basis of what has essentially been a good "counseling" role for a superior. Once in the hot seat, they may freeze when tough calls have to be made. No one has been able to calculate the cost of work-hours lost through repeated and prolonged committee meetings, the use of consultants to do what management itself is paid to do, and the too-little, too-late syndrome when a decision has finally been reached. Inordinate delays in reaching decisions become not only an economic but a moral problem. The sad fact is that in board-management relations explanations for delays, when they are asked for (which is rarely), are too often given by the same people who created the problem in the first place.

DILEMMAS IN TRUTH TELLING

Given these limitations, it is next necessary to inquire how moral truth should be handled. Having the truth is sometimes easier than telling the truth. The tiny tongue is a mighty instrument for the mind. It can clarify and confuse, confirm and contradict, castigate and console. Sometimes the tongue leaps beyond control of its owner. One manager put it this way: "Sometimes my tongue goes several minutes before I decide what I want to say." And what a person wants to say is conditioned by multiple factors. Memory is one. John Dean (a White House staff member in President Nixon's administration) was acclaimed by Watergate investigators in 1973 for his precise reporting of facts, yet comparisons of oral testimony with written transcripts showed that in some of his reports hardly a word was true.[11]

More difficult to handle is what a Washington bureaucrat asked of a CIA analyst when figures were being doctored on the Vietcong's troop levels: "Sam, have we gone beyond the bounds of reasonable dishonesty?" Is there such a thing as "reasonable dishonesty?" How responses to the question have been made provides the most interesting checkpoints for humankind's journey toward truth.

Taking the question seriously does not mean accepting its validity unreservedly. Concession to exception is not the logician's way to define terms. The fact of the matter is, however, that concessions have been made repeatedly, and usually on the basis of the right-to-know principle. To illustrate: Is it unethical for a government to deceive the enemy? its own people? Must a person tell a burglar where the family jewels are hidden? Should doctors tell the unvarnished truth to a patient who has a year to live? May defense lawyers withhold critical truths from their adversaries? from the jury? Answers have stirred bitter debate. Was Saint Augustine harsh or was he wise when he wrote:

> Little by little and bit by bit this evil (beginning with a lie that seems beneficial) will grow and by gradual accessions will slowly increase until it becomes such a mass of wicked lies that it will be utterly impossible to find any means of resisting such a plague grown to huge proportions through small additions.

The issue, therefore, is whether these "small additions" can be contained in ways that prevent the dam of trust from bursting. Clues to permissible constraints, as well as signals for impermissible ones, have been given by Sissela Bok, who analyzed lying in order to clarify the rules for truth telling.[12] According to Bok, a lie is (1) any intentional deception that is stated which (2) places the burden of proof on the liar and which (3) demands that the burden be capable of public statement and public defense. Remedies against lies are found less in exhortation and more in rewards for (1) whistle-blowing and reporting unpleasant facts of importance to superiors, (2) collective bargaining on an open rather than a hidden basis, (3) truth in advertising, and (4) objectivity in annual corporation reports. Exceptions to the truth-telling requirement are influenced by multiple factors: role, situation, timing, and consequences.

Such rare exceptions must be tested by more than Bok's criteria; indeed, the distinction between lies as a stated proposition and deception as an unstated one, while theoretically defensible, does not represent a real difference. If communication had no other purpose than the exchange of information, the inquiry could stop with one proposition: Truth telling is so important in and of itself that any departure therefrom is unacceptable. If, on the other hand, communication has other purposes in the human community, then a broader—and more ambiguous—arena is opened. Individuals are enjoined to love, protect, and sacrifice for others, and these imperatives cannot be summarily dismissed. Four situations—kindness, role, confidentiality, and the "save from jeopardy" factor—create the hardest dilemmas. After a description of each comes a question that plagues the communicator.

The Kindness Factor

In one of those delightful novels that literary critics ignore, Katherine Cookson told the tale of a little farm girl named Mary Ann who loved her father with a fierce tenderness. Trust between them was perfect because each could rely on the other's word. One day, through her neglect, the father lost his hand in an accident, and the child blamed herself through the long days of her father's hospitalization; indeed, so devastated was she that the mother worried about her daughter's own survival. Returning home, the man greeted his grieving child, but she would have no part of his feigning that all would be well in the harsh world of farm life, where the crippled had no part. It was only when the man fabricated an impressive story of his own sloppy work habits as the cause of the misfortune that she began, very slowly, to listen—still wanting to believe but still skeptical. Aware of her uncertainty, the father, wrote Cookson, put on his most convincing air, "knowing that what was demanded now was that he lie with sincerity and redeem something of himself in absolving the child from all blame."[13]

Was the father ethical?

One story concerns a railroad switchman and his yardmaster. Friends from childhood years, theirs was a relationship built on absolute trust. At work one dark and rainy night the switchman, in a moment of carelessness, pulled a wrong lever, causing three loaded boxcars to crash into a small yard engine. The locomotive's engineer and fireman were killed, and a flagman was seriously injured. After the dead and injured were moved, the erring switchman broke down and wept bitterly. Like a monk chanting a litany, he cried out in a singsong voice: "I killed them. I killed them. I killed them."

Fearing that his friend would collapse totally, the yardmaster put his arm around the distraught worker and repeated softly: "No one could see the switch in that rain. No one!" After a time, the grieving man raised his head imploringly and asked the yardmaster, "Are you telling the truth?" The yardmaster said that he was indeed telling the truth. The response so reassured the switchman that he was able to return to work.

Was the yardmaster unethical?

The Role Factor

Because roles differ significantly, five examples are offered to illustrate the impact of role on the obligation to tell the truth:

1. *Doctor.* By definition, physicians are dedicated to health-restoring efforts. At one time a doctor prescribed a nonaddictive painkiller called pentazocine for a patient suffering from a chronic intestinal problem. Over a two-year period, the patient faithfully followed the doctor's orders by injecting himself six times daily with the drug. His skin and muscle tissue, however, became so scarred that he had difficulty locating places on his body to make the injections. After he complained to the doctor about the problem, another specialist was summoned. Further examinations convinced the consulting physician that the drug was no longer needed. Told of this, the patient raised an outcry, saying that the pain would be unbearable. Confronted by an obdurate patient, the doctors said they would, reluctantly, continue the drug. What they did not reveal was that the drug would be progressively reduced through a saline solution. Only when the dosage contained no pentazocine and the patient reported no pain was he told.[14]

    Did the doctors lie? Were they ethical?

2. *Executive.* An executive knows that he will recommend to the board a two-for-one stock split at its next meeting. Rumors begin to circulate on Wall Street, and a reporter catches the CEO at a

public meeting. When asked if the rumors are true, the executive answers, "Absolutely not." Pressed to respond to questions about whether his company will consider a stock split at a later time, the executive answers: "Not at all likely. We like what we've got. And we've got what we want."

Is the executive ethical?

3.   *Athlete.* Mike Schmidt, brilliant third baseman of the Philadelphia Phillies, was thrice voted the coveted most valuable player (MVP) award. One year Schmidt was paid $5,000 for wearing shoes made by Nike Incorporated of Beaverton, Oregon, and given the use of a $100,000 Rolls-Royce for a year. Finding the Nike shoes uncomfortable on astroturf, Schmidt used shoes made by the Brooks Company and painted the Nike symbol on them.[15] Suppose that a Nike company official had learned of the player's shoe replacement, was asked by a sports writer whether it was true, and answered: "We paid a small endorsement fee to Schmidt and, so far as we're concerned, he is wearing shoes showing the great Nike symbol."

Did the company officer lie? Was he ethical?
Did Schmidt lie? Was he ethical?

4.   *Lawyer.* During the 1980s, Hofstra University law professor Monroe Freedman carried on a battle with then Circuit Court Judge Warren Burger over the proper rules to govern court behavior by criminal defense lawyers whose clients wanted to perjure themselves. The professor argued that if efforts to persuade the client not to lie failed, the lawyer should put the client on the stand and let the prosecution find the facts. This was, after all, a small price to pay for a prized adversarial system of justice. Burger, on the other hand, argued that a lawyer was also "an officer of the court" who was obligated to pursue justice. It was in this atmosphere that a 1981 case, *Nix* v. *Whiteside*, arose. Whiteside was convicted of second-degree murder because his lawyer, Gary Robinson, refused to let him take the stand and lie to save himself; the lawyer threatened to tell the trial judge. On appeal, a judge from the Eighth Circuit Court ruled that, by warning Whiteside against testifying as he wanted and by threatening to inform the trial judge and even testify against him if the warnings were not heeded, Robinson had set his interests against the client's and

denied Whiteside the right to effective assistance of counsel guaranteed by the Sixth Amendment.

Did the court behave ethically?[16]

5. *Diplomat.* A month before President Carter's planned raid on Iran to rescue American hostages in Teheran, Secretary of State Cyrus Vance knew of it. To him was given the task of convincing America's allies that if they did not apply economic pressures on Iran, the United States would carry out a military strike. The purpose was not to trick the allies but to lull the Iranian kidnappers into a sense of false security that would enhance the rescue mission's chance of success. The allies bought Vance's deceit. After the unsuccessful strike, Vance resigned. Journalist William Safire discussed Vance's departure with Dr. Arthur Burns, former chairman of the Federal Reserve Board and

> a man with more rock-like integrity than anyone I know. If he was heading a central bank with a much needed devaluation in prospect, if needs of the impending devaluation would severely damage the national interest, and if he were put on the spot—would he lie?
>
> "I never had to face that," said the former Federal Reserve chairman, "but I was prepared to face it. If the moment came when I saw an overwhelming need to lie in the nation's interest, I would lie."
>
> He sucked on his pipe for a moment and added, "Of course, I would resign immediately afterward."[17]

Had Vance (and potentially Burns) acted ethically?
If so, does resignation provide a sufficient excuse for the lie?

The Confidentiality Factor

For managers, one area of concern is the trade secret. Patents, trademarks, and copyrights are the open ways to protect property, but many new developments do not fall into the protected areas. In 1980 an employee of the Celanese Corporation went to prison for four years for transferring the company's trade secrets to Mitsubishi.[18] The employee did not lie; he did deceive his employer. More relevant is the California Supreme Court's decision against a psychiatrist who allowed a "public peril" to occur by protecting the secrets of a patient who threatened to kill (and did kill) his former girlfriend. Probably the hardest decisions are those created among friends who share information about their private lives. Usually such information has little significance to society or to the organization, but when it does, should the presumption be in favor of the one likely to be harmed? or to the one who shared the secret? A small example illustrates the dilemma.

A personnel manager's best friend was Hubert Cord. The two men had gone to school together, served in the armed forces together, and joined the company together. Cord called his friend by the initials PM. Within the past six months, PM had noted a reticence on the part of Cord to talk very openly about matters—as had been their custom. When PM confronted Cord, he learned that Cord was planning to leave the company for a competitor. But PM was pledged to secrecy until Cord himself announced the resignation. During the interim, the CEO called PM to his office, where he revealed plans to make Cord president of a wholly owned subsidiary. The decision would mean Cord's jumping ahead of two able managers who were senior to Cord. And the move would probably cause an early departure by the pair, each of whom had come to believe that one of them would surely get the post. PM urged his CEO to discuss the matter immediately with Cord, and this was done. However, it became apparent to PM that Cord had not leveled with the CEO. Distraught, PM begged Cord "to come clean," but Cord refused, saying he had promised his new boss to reveal nothing until "certain problems" had been handled.

PM then tried a new tactic: to persuade Cord to tell the CEO that several months were needed for him to consider the offer, during which time neither man would say anything publicly. Cord complied. But the CEO rejected Cord's idea, saying that "this kind of information always gets out." PM was later called by the CEO, who expressed bewilderment that Cord would want to postpone news that was certainly good for him. PM said nothing.

Did PM act ethically?

The Jeopardy Factor

One of the hardest problems in truth telling arises when someone is in a position to save another from danger but the other person has no trust in the speaker's word. Saint Augustine raised the problem this way:

[Imagine] a man who, knowing that a certain road is besieged by bandits and fearing that an unfriendly neighbor for whose safety he is concerned will take that road, tells him that there are no bandits there. He makes this assertion realizing that his neighbor does not trust him and, because of the statement to the contrary by the person in whom he has no faith, will therefore believe that the bandits are there and will not go by that road.[19]

It seems obvious that the man wants his neighbor to know the truth and, consequently, one critical element in lying—namely, intention to deceive—is lacking. Interestingly enough, having given the example, the old saint does not give the answer and we are left in the dark as to how this great theologian would answer his own scenario: Was it a lie? Did the teller act ethically? By inference, it could be suggested that Augustine would reluctantly answer both questions affirmatively—all of which leaves the ethical question of "circumstantial" lying in shadow.

It seems appropriate to conclude with five generalizations:

1. Truth telling is essential to an organization's survival because, without it, trust vanishes and management's word is suspect.
2. Deliberate wordless deception is technically not a lie but is equally unethical.
3. When defenses for lying under certain grave conditions are advanced, the liar should be not praised but excused. To praise is to condone, and that itself is questionable ethics.
4. When a deceptive public or corporate agent is exculpated, that person should make some public act or gesture (resignation, subsequent full disclosure) that tells the public that lying is not a respected form of behavior. To do less is to destroy the trust on which democratic governments and market economies rest.
5. If lying or deception looms in difficult cases, follow a simple maxim: When in doubt, don't.

FREEDOM AS CONCEPT

Freedom is too big an idea for too short a biography. Yet even an incomplete vignette can advance understanding of something that is as treasured as it is misunderstood. To many, Yale economist Henry Wallich was right in saying that money is "crystalized freedom." So defined (and Wallich himself introduced qualifications), freedom means the right to make money. What hold the freedom-money nexus has on Americans was suggested by the experiences of presidential candidate George McGovern in 1972. Speaking to workers in a rubber factory near Akron, he made a promise that he thought would endear him to blue-collar workers: he would increase inheritance taxes so that the rich could leave very little to their families after death. To McGovern's surprise, he was loudly booed. The workers disliked the idea because they themselves wanted the freedom to leave as much money as possible to their heirs. Part of the American dream was to make the next generation better off, and without this possibility, freedom was more a nightmare than a dream.

To its critics this version of freedom has the seeds of its own destruction because it makes easy the step from freedom, defined as the right to get what individuals want, to the idea that all wants are legitimate, especially if the wanters are informed, consenting adults. On this score the well-known federal judge Richard Posner has argued that personal freedom exercised in ways that cause no harm to outsiders—even though causing harm to the freely participating adults—should guide the law.[20] While an attractive proposition, this interpretation of freedom could lead to what one critic has called a fatally flawed kind of freedom: "Good and evil, right and wrong, lose all meaning when all that matters is whether . . . people get exactly what they think they want."[21] The criticism indicates that freedom is bounded and that, in some cases, freedom is bondage—a curious and intriguing thought.

Freedom's Bondage

To be free is to be jailed, and the prison guard is called responsibility. Freedom to own means an owner "possessed"; freedom to contract leashes the signatories; freedom of assembly carries responsibility for orderliness; freedom to vote requires information if it is not to be a throwaway ballot; freedom to marry ends "playing the field"; and freedom to run an organization is constrained by boards and stockholders, regulators and workers, and customers and social activists. Recognition of freedom's bondage has led many to surrender it. In politics the legendary "man on the white horse" has been hailed as a secular savior even though the price of salvation is loss of liberty. In organizations, buck-passing is often a finely honed art and delegating authority, while easy to extol, is difficult to do because both mean a diminution of flexibility. From Max Weber to Henry Taylor, management theorists traditionally operated on the premise that employees had to be told what to do because it is the workers' nature to shirk responsibility, even when accepting it enlarges the personal domain of freedom.

Perhaps the most baffling quality of freedom does not end with the burden of responsibility but begins there. Asked is this question: What does responsibility bring? If the answer is that it brings self-fulfillment through self-determination (through use of reason and passion, body and soul, experiences and fantasy), then a person, in a sense, recreates the self by each new decision. But affirmation is done without self-deceptions. There are no illusions that life does not bring injustices and absurdities, misfortunes and drawbacks. These are the dark sides of life, and freedom requires the ability to admit that life is no bowl of cherries. It is, say some philosophers, freedom's need for "tragic insight" that is its highest expression: Abraham did not complain or evade, Christ freely received the cross, Luther accepted excommunication, and Martin Luther King risked assassination. The tragic insight leads to the full acceptance of the "coexistence of human freedom and human finititude."[22]

This dour view is unpalatable to Americans who see freedom's wealth and resent its tax. However perceived, freedom's riches lighten the person's chains. To be human is to be free. To enslave is to debase. The long struggles to escape Europe's oppressiveness, to win the vote, to form corporations, and to organize unions were ways to enlarge freedom's meaning.[23] Because the efforts have been so relatively recent and so spectacularly successful, it is easy to forget the story.

Freedom as a Western "Discovery"

Sometime between the fifteenth and seventeenth centuries there appeared, for the first time, an idea of individualism unknown to peoples of medieval and ancient times. Rather suddenly, the individual—whose fulfillment had primarily been seen in the past as being a good citizen in a good state or a good artisan in a good guild—was separated from the group. This rupture, unusual and unique, led not to man as a lord or serf, as a member of a town or guild, but to man as a loner, a masterless man. This was the kind of equality and freedom that, as noted, Tocqueville feared, Edmund Burke despised, and most Europeans misunderstood. Nowhere is the contrast between Continental and American beliefs about freedom better illustrated than in the story of England and her colonies. Liberty in England was nothing more than the right to have what was due under the law: "The Magna Carta did not provide for any generic liberty; it only set forth . . . the right to enjoy what the law gives"; and the lawgivers, of course, were once the king and are now the Parliament.[24]

In the United States, on the other hand, the extreme individualism led to a different interpretation. Instead of being given freedom, Americans had it, and instead of a trickle-down theory of political power, citizen consent meant a pumping up. From its conception the nation viewed freedom in a new light. Cecelia Kenyon of Smith College put it well when she wrote:

> The first sentence of the second paragraph of the Declaration is one of the most remarkable in the entire corpus of political philosophy. It consists of only 111 words. In that short space, Thomas Jefferson abstracted from the political tradition of the West two golden threads, one ancient, venerable, reaching all the way back to the Iliad and the Bible; the other evolving out of the older thread but less than two centuries old in 1776 and, leading forth in a new direction, together with the old, created a new fabric of which only fleeting glimpses had been perceived in its past.[25]

Because the fabric was new and the political garment unfinished, it was not surprising that Americans should, at times, be inconsistent in the way they clothed freedom. In the Declaration of Independence were found denunciations of George III's evils but no word about his support of slavery, and for a very good reason: Americans had slaves and were determined to keep them. A helpful Supreme Court later defined blacks as commodities and corporations as persons, workers as quasi serfs and employers as quasi kings. Such ambivalences produced two constitutions—the formal written one that expounded the ideal and the informal unwritten one that accepted realities. Reconciling the two was always difficult.[26]

Those who find the reconciliation unsatisfactory compare Americans' exercise of freedom to Narcissus' spending life staring at his reflection in the water until he eventually fell in and drowned.[27] The emphases on self-assertion, self-discovery, and self-identity are examples, it is said, of narcissism at work—individualism gone amok. "Born free" is to be born wild. David Riesman observed that when people are told all others are out for themselves, they begin to believe it and to behave similarly. One small example is the way people drive in "cities like Boston where, expecting aggression from the other driver, civility actually becomes hazardous."[28] To some people, freedom, American style, is idiocy.[29]

Freedom and Toleration

The problems of freedom arise at that intersection where competing freedoms and needs collide. The organization needs reliable workers, some of whom "need" drugs. Is freedom to privacy denied by mandating drug testing? The public wants freedom to ride trains, but railroad engineers exercise their freedom to strike. Whose freedom comes first? Often laws lag behind the times. In 1979, for instance, the Labor Department, backed by unions, charged a Vermont skiwear maker whose female employees knitted in their homes with violating minimum wage provisions. The women, however, preferred working at home, where they could be with children and did not have to travel to the factory over icy roads in winter. Their demand was for freedom, and the demand led the Labor Department to retreat. In the realm of public speech and assembly the matter of tolerance is even more complicated by two questions: (1) What impels some people to protect the freedom of others even when those freedoms are used for purposes they think are despicable?[30] (2) What leads others to assail the freedoms of others when their own cherished beliefs are under attack?[31]

One answer has been given to the effect that access (to higher education, political office, city amenities like theaters and museums) produces an elite tolerant of diversity and difference. Lawyers and judges, professors and journalists constitute this class, and it is they who are the true guardians of liberty. In this version the young are also liberty-lovers while the masses (unskilled workers, small-town folk, and, of course, the elderly) are not. But the masses have been more respectful of free speech than intellectuals like Herbert Marcuse, who said that while freedom is great, "certain things cannot be said, certain ideas cannot be expressed, certain policies cannot be proposed, certain behavior cannot be permitted without making tolerance an instrument for the continuation of servitude."[32] Under this banner, ultraliberal students at Berkeley, Toronto, Columbia, Yale, and other prestigious universities locked arms to lock out people whose views they found distasteful. In the students' view their act was a necessary "repressive freedom." However distasteful, their behavior raised anew some fundamental questions: What is freedom? If abused, what, if any, corrective measures may be taken? How should personal freedom and organizational freedom be managed?

If freedom means an opportunity for self-determination leading to self-fulfillment, two conditions must exist to explain the limits of toleration: (1) people should act reasonably and (2) when they act irrationally, they should be restrained. Self-fulfillment is not self-degradation. How the restraints are applied (and when they are not applied) depends on specific situations. In making decisions related to these complex issues, managers do not dive into the philosopher's think tank; nevertheless, moralists have thought longest and hardest about liberty's meaning and have had influence on judges and legislators, teachers and artists, and corporate executives and journalists. So it is useful to see how some philosophers think about the concept, even as they voice their own frustrations.

The Three Freedoms

The first notable thing about a philosophical view of freedom is that it is a *process*, first from self-determination to self-development and then from self development to self-fulfillment. Each step involves a different kind of liberty, and managers deal primarily with the last. Charles Van Doren, upon completion of his comprehensive review of the literature on liberty, reported his "melancholy conclusion that, if the idea of rational debate is appropriate to the philosophical enterprise . . . it would be hard to gainsay the fact that what has been accomplished in twenty-five centuries of Western thought about freedom is a very poor performance, indeed."[33] People have been confused about freedom because so many definitions have been thrown at them. The confusion is unfortunate because there are really only three essential kinds of liberty: *natural, acquired*, and *circumstantial*.

The first, an indispensable part of human nature, refers to the individual's capacity to determine what he or she wishes to do and to become. The second, acquired freedom, appears when natural freedom is used to develop minds and skills, characters and personalities. Since its goal is improvement, this stage represents a perfecting process within a moral universe where everyone has a stake in what this perfecting process means.[34] John Dewey put it this way: "We are free not because of what we statistically are, but insofar as we are becoming different from what we have been."[35] One point is extremely relevant: acquired freedoms are the prime responsibility of the individual, not the organization. Education, character development, skill acquisition, and career planning fall first on the person. While organizations can and should help, that assistance follows after, not before, the person's own efforts. Too much organizational involvement with self-development invites paternalism. Too little means insensitive bureacracies.

Circumstantial freedom represents the process of self-realization and is the culmination of freedom's other two aspects.[36] Self-realization can be frustrated by the individual's own physical or psychological handicaps;[37] it can also be frustrated—and this is the important point for managers—by organizational structures in which no single person exercises obvious coercion but in which options are nonetheless restricted or denied. Circumstantial freedom exists, therefore, only when conditions are favorable to individuals who wish to seek a certain goal and follow a certain course. This notion of freedom most involves managers because self-realization occurs within those social, political, and economic contexts that they establish; in this sense, it is the critical freedom—the "space" people create (or destroy) for others. For example: those who see socialism and communism as systems inimical to man come to this view precisely because such societies destroy or severely limit options; those who support capitalism do so because they believe that it provides the most hospitable circumstances for individual fulfillment. This explains why economists like Milton Friedman or F.A. Hayek always link the market economy to a free political system. To them, one without the other is unthinkable.[38]

Because managers are agents of an enterprise, and because the enterprise is part of a social contract, there are constraints on what managers can do for employees who, for one reason or other, have not developed the necessary discipline to make their own self-fulfillment likely. To foster self-realization for employees who have not cultivated self-discipline is risky business. The caveat requires a more detailed analysis.

FREEDOM IN ORGANIZATIONS: PROBLEM AREAS

Because a business corporation is first and foremost an economic entity—and only secondly a quasi-political one—the wholesale transfer of techniques needed to foster political freedom is inappropriate, despite the clamor of some for such transfers. IBM's open-door policy is only crudely related to judicial due process; participatory management is not representative democracy; and employee rights are not a constitutional bill of rights. Freedom of speech, for example, is a precious civil right, but it may be curtailed within the corporation by executives, in unions by presidents, in churches by bishops, and in professions by review boards. Full and fragmented free-speech rights can and do coexist in the United States.[39]

Since, however, freedom and America are indissolubly linked, freedom's expansions in the political environment have impact on the business environment. The expansions raise such problems that Robert Yarnall, Jr., chairman of Yarway, a Pennsylvania corporation, asked, "Can managers handle freedom?"[40] Recalling the closing days of the nineteenth century, when Henry Towne was president of the American Society of Mechanical Engineers, Yarnall noted that for Towne and his colleagues, freedom embraced only two strands: (1) political freedoms of speech, assembly, religion, press, and suffrage and (2) economic freedoms to buy and sell, hire and fire, and save and invest. While these were the "name of the game" in former times, both the name and the game have changed dramatically. Now people expect employment that is "fulfilling," jobs that are secure, wages that are bargained, privacy that is respected, and so on. As a result, managers face new definitions of freedom. These challenges, in turn, raise the question of managerial discretion.

Managerial Discretion

In the present climate, where more and more freedoms are claimed and where "rights are trumps," managers think twice before "granting" new rights.[41] Discretion seems to be the better part of valor. Discretion is prudence—used not simply to maintain power but to soften the rigor of freedom too broadly interpreted. If discretionary authority is indispensable, its use has to be justified and monitored.

Since managers may misread data, use good information in wrong ways, or act at the wrong times, the burden of proof for exercising managerial discretion is on their shoulders.[42] It is, therefore, not implausible to suggest that they examine ways in which others, having discretionary authority, have used it. A first step in that direction might profitably involve a review of those federal regulatory agencies with which their companies have been involved. The survey would yield three items of importance to large organizations:

1. When a policy statement is contemplated, administrative agencies give public notice of the time and place the meeting will occur, the legal authority under which the rule is proposed, and the substance of the new rule. Corporations need not go to the same lengths, but when major employer-related policies not covered by the labor contract are under consideration, mechanisms for worker input are appropriate.
2. The government's policy statement indicates the boundaries within which action will be taken and the reasons for such actions. Organizational drug-testing policies are issues that might profit from this procedure.
3. Affected parties are given opportunities to respond, and the record of these responses is made public.[43]

Driven by so many forces, managers are understandably reluctant to introduce government practices. Nevertheless, if the trend continues toward greater protection of expanded freedoms, prudence suggests that examples set by other organizations be understood; on the basis of such understanding, working papers could be prepared for methodical and careful deliberation. Obviously, present procedures for rule making in the public sector offer no panaceas for corporations—but neither are they irrelevant.

Paternalism

Implied in the foregoing discussion is acceptance of interventions that affect individual freedom under certain circumstances. The implication raises the spectre of paternalism, sensitivity to which has been assiduously cultivated in the United States by those who think that John Stuart Mill was right in holding that the "only freedom which deserves the name is that of pursuing our own good in our way, so long as we do not attempt to deprive others of theirs, or impede their efforts to obtain it."[44] The sweep of Mill's comment raises problems for managers because, in individual-organization relations, the line between doing what is right and doing what is good is hard to draw. To illustrate: Have managers a responsibility to alcoholic employees to warn and to counsel? What should they do for employees whose drug abuse threatens them even more than the enterprise? Have they special duties toward people who eagerly seek work in dangerous industries because high pay goes with high risk? Some say that the answer to each question is no because interference harms a person's freedom;[45] "intrusions" are thus seen as expressions of paternalism. Nevertheless, paternalism may be necessary for the organization's—and even the individual's—good. Caveats are in order. The Kantian no-harm-to-others ethic is, in principle, easy to defend. Harm-to-the-self is less clear as a policy guide. People do learn from mistakes.[46] On the other hand, intervention is not an intrinsic evil, but when it is undertaken, the interventionist should know which liberty-limiting principle is being used to justify the action. The following seven "principles" have been advanced as possible justifications for paternalism:

1. To prevent injury to others (the private-harm principle)
2. To prevent impairment of institutional practices that are in the public interest, such as taxes and custom duties (the public-harm principle)
3. To prevent offense to others (the offense principle)
4. To benefit others (the welfare principle)
5. To prevent or punish evil (the legal moralism principle)
6. To prevent harm to the person him or herself (the lawful paternalism principle)
7. To benefit the person (the brother's keeper principle)[47]

It is possible to justify paternalism by the first five principles, but the last two create problems. Yet to ignore them creates the risk of reducing morality to law—a minimalist ethic whereby moral judgments are made only on public acts. Clearly public law and organizational mores should be minimal in relation to private acts, but this does not mean that the moral realm thereby shrinks. Any society or

organization that calmly views vice as beyond censure is not the health-
iest society or organization. At this juncture, intervention is not the
answer; public opinion is.[48] Influencing public opinion on moral issues,
however, is itself interventionist. Those entrusted with responsibility
may wonder whether there is any way out of the moral swamp. The
best answer takes into account the nature of ambiguity in moral issues.
Life is not a problem to be solved but a paradox to be lived. Despite
the many limitations that characterize paternalism, managers can take
eight actions:

1. Acknowledge publicly that a manager's job is inescapably interventionist and has a paternalistic dimension.
2. Make clear by example and exhortation the organization's basic
   values.
3. Stipulate when infringement of the organization's values will not
   be tolerated.
4. Let employees know what behavior is expected of them on the
   job and in public places.
5. Provide counseling and health services to employees on a voluntary
   and confidential basis.
6. Pledge to take no punitive action against those who avail themselves of such services.
7. Pledge—and take—disciplinary action against those who do not
   avail themselves of support systems when such abstention results
   in inefficient job performance.
8. Publicize within the organization that sanctions have been applied, without identifying the individual.

Critical to success is the employees' understanding of the values the
organization stands for. Employees uncomfortable with those values
should have opportunities to challenge them and to ask clarification
of their meanings; they should also be given opportunities for re-
couping losses (the reconciliation principle). Having taken all these
steps, managers know that neither they nor their employees constitute
a communion of saints. But if the goal sounds too utopian, even with
adjusted expectations, the alternative—an organization of wrongdoers
—is worse. While detailed analysis of every type of freedom is beyond
the purview of this discussion, one small example illustrates the problems related to freedom in the organization.

A Scenario

Jim Speaks, vice president of Scrape-Off, a manufacturing company with a publicly announced affirmative action policy, had traveled to Alabama at his own expense to participate in Martin Luther King's freedom march. This experience resulted in his being featured in local newspapers, which, in turn, led to invitations to address various groups in various cities. Eloquent and impassioned, Speaks began to draw ever larger audiences and gain greater media coverage. His valedictory was invariably the same. In slow cadence he would cry out: "Count the number of blacks who hold senior positions in the banking industry. Count the number of blacks who hold senior positions in the steel industry. Count the number of blacks who hold senior positions in the health care industry. Count the number of blacks who hold senior positions in the insurance industry." After each statement, Speaks would dramatically wave one hand and a few fingers.

A church invitation to lecture took Speaks to a city plagued by racial tensions. It also happened to be a city where the mayor was negotiating a multimillion-dollar contract with Scrape-Off. In the audience that night were some black militants who, stirred by the oratory, organized stronger protest movements designed to snarl traffic during morning and evening rush hours. When interviewed, leaders of the protest quoted Speaks as the inspiration for their action. Their comments also began to appear in newspapers and on daily news broadcasts, and Speaks was often mentioned as their intellectual father.

Angered by the repeated disruptions, the troubled mayor called upon Scrape-Off's CEO to protest: "You either quiet that rabble-rouser or we go somewhere else with our business." When the mayor departed, the CEO called Speaks to discuss the issue. Given the company's dilemma, Speaks expressed sorrow but said that he was as committed to racial justice as anyone and that the Civil Rights Act expressed his philosophy. When asked to go slow until at least the contract was signed, Speaks exploded: "I am no raving zealot. I do not ask to be introduced as a Scrape-Off vice president. I ask reporters not to make my business affiliation known, but they do. What else can I do?"

The CEO answered: "Speaks, old boy, you can shut your mouth in public for a few months."

"No way," retorted Speaks. "As a matter of fact, I have a second invitation from people in that troubled community, and I intend to accept it. I am a free man in a free country. I advocate what is in our company code—fairness. But I do not parade under the company's banner."

The CEO looked long and thoughtfully at Speaks before responding. Then, in measured tones, he said: "The company has a lot at stake here in profits. That town has a lot at stake here in racial peace. The mayor needs a diminution of tension, not an escalation. If you accept the second invitation, look for a new job."

Did the CEO violate Speaks's freedom?
Was the CEO ethical?

CONCLUSION

Dilemmas confront executives who deal with a society that prizes individual freedom more than organizational freedom. Yarnall's question (can managers handle freedom?) will not go away. Identifying and promoting those conditions which enable employees to fulfill themselves while contributing to fulfillment of the organization's goals require future-oriented decision-making that should be assessed morally through a logic somewhat different from that used to appraise past-oriented decision-making.

It is, therefore, always appropriate to reemphasize the practical connections between truth and freedom. If Hitler's mad regime taught any lesson it was that the Big Lie is an instrument to enslave. Less dramatic—but by no means trivial—are two stories about truth and freedom that relate to the investor and workers, respectively. The first occurred under the madcap management of Gordon McCormick at Equity Funding, the Los Angeles corporation that deceived Wall Street, a Big Eight accounting firm, the Securities and Exchange Commission, and state insurance authorities in Illinois and California for nearly a decade. Only in 1973, when the firing of a low-level manager led to disclosure, did McCormick's policy of lies become known. Untruth's victim was investors' freedom to control their own wealth. Freedom to own property was, in this instance, a shibboleth. Freedom to know was equally relevant in the 1984 story of the Film Recovery Systems Corporation. In this instance it was the workers' right to truth and their freedom to take action in their own behalf that were involved.

Three of the firm's senior managers were each sentenced to twenty-five years in prison because they failed to tell all employees that the plant was using cyanamide in one of its manufacturing processes. [49]

The lesson is simple. The lie enslaves. So the old maxim reappears: the truth can make you free.

III THE "ETHIC" OF CHARACTER

7
THE PERSONAL DIMENSION

THE VALUES QUIZ   *(Mark True or False)*

1. _____ The first things a CEO should demand from potential successors are technical competence and total loyalty.
2. _____ Donald Siebert, formerly CEO of J.C. Penney, was right in saying that "the cornerstone of human ethics, which is what business ethics are, is the set of laws in the Ten Commandments."
3. _____ Relatively few people reach that stage of moral development at which they are willing to challenge either authority or consensus belief systems.
4. _____ Freud was right in saying that a woman's sense of justice is more subjective, hence less reliable, than a man's sense of justice.
5. _____ Males, more than females, will "dump" friends when opportunities for career advancement come.
6. _____ Women are more likely than men to give their loyalties to a particular person as opposed to the organization itself.
7. _____ Those at a high level of moral growth are more likely to support liberal causes (antinukes, proabortion, no-fault divorce, and the like) than those at a lower level of moral growth are.
8. _____ In screening job applicants, employers have a right to examine such personal matters of the candidate as records on repayment of debts; reasons for previous dismissals from other companies; drug and alcohol use; and conditions of health.

In recent times there has been much talk about "characters" and little about character, much about rights and little about duties, much about health and less about honor, much about vigor and little about virtue. Words dropped from ordinary conversation signal changes in values. Only when such changes result in serious moral lapses do people take notice. A drug culture is a sick culture. An underground economy is an undermined society. A government marked by quasi-official "leaks" or "disinformation" is a political community of distrust.

Signs of disarray have led thoughtful people to ask, What has gone wrong? One answer is that the attention formerly given to character development has dropped rather dramatically. Whether the most salutary remedy is greater emphasis by teachers on value instruction is hotly debated. Whether virtue can be taught is an old question, but it is again being seriously discussed. A 1985 report from the prestigious Committee for Economic Development stressed the indispensability of that "invisible curriculum" which deals with "such traits as honesty, reliability, self-discipline, cooperativeness, competitiveness, and perseverance. . . . Schools have a responsibility and an opportunity to help instill these habits."[1] The importance of character was made clear two centuries ago when Edmund Burke told a friend never to separate a legislative proposal from its sponsor: "You will be told that if a measure is good, what have you to do with the character of those who bring it forward?" (However) "designing men never separate their plans from their interests and the power of bad men is no indifferent thing."[2]

Burke's view is of particular interest to Americans, who generally believe that personal and private lives should be separated: the errant spouse can be a good president, the tyrannical parent a sensitive supervisor, or the country-club gossip a competent corporate secretary. The wall-of-separation view has not been empirically proved or disproved, and, in the absence of hard data, it is more comfortable to believe with the English that home is the castle and personal privacy the coin of liberty. But this leads to the curious conclusion that private virtue is unimportant to one's public performance.

Managers of high character regularly exhibit such consistency of behavior that subordinates trust them. On occasion individuals of dubious qualities rise to high positions. It is then that expediency becomes the ethic. The resulting confusions seed corporate consternation. Apposite is the story of onetime British Prime Minister A.J. Balfour, who, critics said, could never make up his mind: despite reproach and malediction, he firmly adhered to "unsettled convictions."

168

Settled convictions animate a settled character, the major components of which have been described in classics of Western civilization. But the convictions are meaningless unless applied to life's problems. It is the steady application of these principles that reveals a manager's character. Insights into what constitute appropriate convictions and appropriate applications can be learned. If they can be learned they can be taught —at least in rough-hewn ways— by exposition, by exhortation, and, above all, by example. All are essential to character development.

THE SEARCH FOR CHARACTER

Pulitzer prize winner *Barbara Tuchman*: "Perhaps what is needed more than anything else in government (and management generally) is the well-ordered soul."[3]

San Jose Mercury News (January 23, 1985): "The new generation's ambition is somewhat different than the old. Opinion researchers have found today's strivers are less loyal to their companies, and more willing to step over the bodies of friends on their way to the top."

Robert K. Fullinwider of the University of Maryland: "We need to teach the virtues, which we can divide into four groups: (1) the moral virtues—honesty, truthfulness, decency, courage, justice; (2) the intellectual virtues—thoughtfulness, strength of mind, curiosity; (3) the communal virtues—neighborliness, charity, self-support, helpfulness, cooperativeness, respect for others; (4) the political virtues—commitment to the common good, respect for law, responsible participation."[4]

Charles W. Power of Yale and *David Vogel* of the University of California at Berkeley: "We doubt that personal integrity can be 'taught' in any simple sense; we similarly doubt that managerial integrity can be simply 'taught.' But we do believe that there are teachable tools, skills, and capabilities that will help in the development of managers who understand what an ethical decision requires in the light of personal commitments, the organizational ethos and purpose, and the societal context in which the organization lives and plays its role."[5]

Stanford professor *Harold Leavitt*: "Vision, values, and determination add soul to the organization. Without them, organizations react but do not create; they forecast but do not imagine; they analyze but do not question; they act but do not strive. While pathfinding vision, values, and determination are not enough, we can't go very far without them."[6]

*   *   *

On November 10, 1987, the *Wall Street Journal* reported the results of a survey of more than two hundred company codes of conduct. The most ignored item was personal character—it seemed not to matter.[7] Character, on the other hand, was never a matter of indifference to the classical philosophers. While Plato and Aristotle speculated about principles, they never stopped there but went on to ask how one could incorporate sound principles to become the kind of person from whom correct conduct emanated, almost automatically, because of a "fixed disposition" toward virtue.[8] In today's world, virtue, like virginity, is an old-fashioned and somewhat prissy word. If there is indeed a slackening interest among ordinary folk in being virtuous—a proposition that could be debated endlessly and inconclusively—there is no diminution of interest in the virtue of leaders, even though the cult of personality leads some to think otherwise. Among ordinary people is the sense that when societies or organizations start to fall apart, it is because character has fallen apart. Character development depends mainly on one-on-one relationships: parents for the infant, teachers for the young, masters for the apprentice, and mentors for the neophyte in organizations.

Twenty years ago, when there was much talk about management as a profession, Richard Scacchetti of the Life Insurance Association of America wrote that managers must first be persons of "good moral character."[9] Warren Bennis said much the same thing when he declared that managers must demonstrate authenticity in all their relationships.[10] Preferring to expound principles, philosophers today tend to neglect the job of helping people develop strong moral characters because the assignment appears to involve indoctrination, not education. For this reason disappointment in philosophers was expressed by Mark Lilla, an editor for the *Public Interest*. To him, moral theorizing, while educational, was definitely not moral education:

at high levels of abstraction, ethicists no longer teach people to be moral and may even have made them less so. Disengaged from moral education, philosophers are intellectual housekeepers, clearing up models here and there and checking the foundations occasionally; [but] morality is something we live and . . . a way of life is a complicated thing. It is not merely a set of propositions to be applied with legal precision to certain cases which arise in life; it is an attitude or outlook, a set of virtues and habits which we learn, sometimes rationally but usually not, from our families, churches, peers, and even our schools.[11]

The teaching record of these four instruments is quite uneven.

Some educationists who theorize about moral training at the elementary and secondary levels are often suspect. Philosopher Christina Hoff Sommers of Clark University leveled a hard-hitting critique at a former dean of the Harvard School of Education, Theodore Sizer, and his faculty colleague, Lawrence Kohlberg, whom she accused of working systematically to scrap the old morality.[12] The Harvard pair had enjoined teachers not to discuss the "old bag" of virtues in which are deposited such things as wisdom, courage, compassion, and proper behavior, because any attempt to instill them in students is indoctrination. The result for Sommers is a system of moral education that is silent about virtue. College fare is not much better. Students are told that selfishness is "natural," that all values are relative, and that tolerance of all forms of moral behavior, however idiosyncratic, is necessary. In short, anything goes. To demonstrate the point, Sommers recounted the story of Harvard professor Richard M. Hunt, who gave a course on the Holocaust to more than a hundred Harvard undergraduates. He found that a majority of them viewed the rise of Hitler as inevitable and that, therefore, no one was really responsible for what happened. Hunt's teaching assistant remarked: "You know, I think if some of our students were sitting as judges at the Nuremberg trials, they would probably acquit—or at least pardon—most of the Nazi defendants." Professor Hunt dubbed his students' forgiving attitude "no-fault history."[13] No-fault management is no-win management.

Lifting moral responsibility from individuals requires placing it on something else, and that something is the institution; the transfer partially explains the popularity of the "blame it on the system" mentality. To censure governments, corporations, courts, unions, or professions is the vogue, and often the criticisms appear through a thin garment stitched in conspiracy-theory cloth. The consequence is that persons so indoctrinated think of ethics as learning how to be for or against institutional policies. Whereas Aristotle, Aquinas, Mill, and Kant told people how to behave, the contemporary university moralist is concerned with what we are to advocate, vote for, protest against, and endorse. This is not to demean the importance of vigilance when large organizations move to deny rights. It is to note, rather, the shift from emphasis on personal to institutional responsibility and to invite attention to the consequences of the transfer.

With the family in jeopardy as a teaching agent, with schools divided over their obligation to inculcate moral values, and with the power of the church eclipsed by the state, successful moral training of the young looks unpromising. Yet neglect of character formation is dangerous because it hastens the obsolescence of the concept of honor. Honor implies that personal identity is importantly linked to institutional roles, whereas today's preferred words, integrity and self-respect, imply that a person's character is essentially independent of such roles. The strong and unpalatable implication is that preservation of dignity is best assured in a Thoreau-like solitude: to accept an institutional role is to become morally suspect. Confused by the ignored, and consequently blurred, meaning of honor, organizational leaders have simply dropped honor from their vocabulary, yet people who reject important social roles effectively turn from themselves and thereby limit personal fulfillment.

The Hovering Shadows

Standing alone, concepts are bloodless, lifeless, motionless—shadowlands of the ideal awaiting the light of fulfillment. They do not explain prudence, instill courage, or inspire loyalty—qualities having a debatable correlation to book learning and a clear relevance to managerial performance. Such relevance becomes even more obvious when managers move their roles from purely transactional to transformational ones. Transactional leaders work out trade-offs from the perspective of present desires, present needs, and present commitments; in the transformational role, the leader engages others in multiple ways to raise the organization's levels of efficiency and ethics. If certain corporate executives (like Du Pont's Irving Shapiro or Service Master's Ken Wessner) are correct in holding that managers must take a more active stance in influencing the politics and values of American society, it follows that their transformational role will become more and more important. It also follows that they must have their own values in place before seeking to transform the values of others. Transformations require subtlety and sensitivity. Sensitivity, one of the two requirements for effective change, varies so greatly that some people respond to others only when blatant signs of suffering are evident; others see in almost every utterance or gesture a moral problem. In most cases, however, emotional reaction precedes cognitive operation: managers feel before they think.

How insensitivity collides with morality was revealed in two experiments. The first was conducted by professors John Darley and C. Daniel Batson of the Princeton Theological Seminary. After receiving biblical texts to record on a disc, students were given directions to a recording studio that required them to pass a writhing, gasping student-actor lying in a doorway. The only significant differentiating factor in determining whether a student stopped to aid was the amount of time he thought he had: those who were told that they were late for the recording session stopped much less often than those who were told that they had sufficient time. It made no statistical difference that half of the seminarians had been asked to record the parable of the Good Samaritan. Tyrannized by time, managers can inadvertently overlook the anguish of others—the colleague with a drinking problem, the harassed salesperson struggling to reach impossible quotas, the worker with an ailing spouse.

The lessons are clear: comprehending moral values does not ensure acting on them. Mastery over meanings endows managers with no mastery over themselves; at worst, the conceptual dexterity induces false moral superiorty while, at best, it provides danger signals that may nonetheless be ignored when self-interest is jeopardized. Because sooner rather than later managers must act, they are drawn to what is often called quandary ethics, or problem solving.[14] How to cope with leaders of wildcat strikes, with whistle-blowers who steal confidential company documents for evidence, with lawyers whose legal advice is shot through with ethically unacceptable premises—all are examples of quandaries that demand understanding, and something more: action. And actions reveal character.

Managers, however, are not always engulfed by quandaries. People working in quite ordinary settings under quite ordinary routines can generate value differences; even long-established routines may paper over festering injustices or protect decision-making processes that effectively remove accountability from individuals. The expected pearls from experts who study and write of such things as responsibility and rights, dignity and honor often turn out to be what Lord Hailsham of England called pebbles.[15] Pebbles may have been good for Demothenes' tongue. They are dead weights on a manager's mind.

The gate before which philosophers stop is the one somebody must open if individuals who lead, influence, and shape big organizations are to be assisted. Because institutions operate with charters, bylaws, organizational charts, codes, and sundry other written documents, they exist as ghostly products of ghostwriters, but there is need to create bodies for the hovering shadows. That "body," quite simply, is character—character of individuals and character of institutions. How it counts in leadership positions becomes a burning issue when crisis strikes. For example, speaking of her old nemesis, Richard Nixon, the acidulous Mary McGrory observed how the former president once showed to an audience of "dazzled editors the intelligence for the job he was forced out of. It was only character that was found wanting."[16] Yet one writer with decidedly leftist instincts showed how the former president walked from a humiliating defeat in a 1962 California election to the White House in 1968, and from a "coconspirator" in 1974 to an elder statesman in 1984. "Going through fire," observed Nixon himself, "makes soft iron into steel." That he has climbed from the deep pit of public hatred to a higher perch of public respect is probably due as much to Nixon's courage as to anything else.[17] Courage, however, does not exhaust the list. Subordinates want their managers to be thoughtful and helpful, while managers look to workers for loyalty and cooperation. Both sides want people of integrity and honor.[18] Management is, therefore, a particularized form of statecraft, and the craft is not well served by the crafty.[19]

So far as character training is concerned, contemporaries are, in a sense, reliving the debate between Socrates and Aristotle. When the former contended that knowing what's right would produce right-acting individuals, Aristotle countered that right knowledge does not necessarily lead to right action because passions, circumstances, foibles, and cowardice make that transfer anything but sure. The old master insisted that "it is hard, if not impossible, to remove by argument, the traits that have long since been incorporated in the character. . . . Passion seems to yield not to argument but to force. But somehow character . . . must be there already . . ."[20]

"*The character must be there already*." Six words of one short sentence drive moral inquiry from concept to character. Character leads a person to do well because that individual is well; it is an amalgam of virtues. But the virtues that make a reliable character are differently ranked in different cultures and in different times. For ancient Greeks, the exemplar of greatest character was the warrior; for the Japanese, it was the hero ready to die for the cause;[21] for the English novelist Anthony Trollope, it was the gentleman; for Thomas Aquinas, the saint; and for Ben Franklin, the honest entrepreneur.[22] Barbara Tuchman, when asked what was needed to cure leaders from the folly of "wooden-headedness," answered:

> Experts first prescribe education. The Chinese tried it when preparing the Mandarins for administration, the Ottoman Turks educated the Janissaries and, in modern times, Prussia required civil service applicants to study politics, philosophy and the social sciences. Failure marked every case because training for government did not touch character. . . . Perhaps more than anything else in government, what is needed is the well-ordered soul. The final problem is to ensure a system in which the well-ordered soul will rise to the top.[23]

Good character defines the well-ordered soul as well as the well-ordered organization. Ben Franklin, the idol of pragmatic administrators, exemplified Tuchman's points when he wrote of having "a tolerable character to begin the world with; I valued it properly and determined to preserve it. . . . I grew convinced that truth, sincerity, and integrity in dealings between man and man were of the utmost importance to the felicity of life; and I formed written resolutions which still remain in my journal book to practice them ever while I lived."[24] Happily, the infant American colony had a system that allowed Franklin to rise to the top. Organizations need the same system for their own Franklins to rise. If the needs are to be met, three questions must be addressed: (1) What is character? (2) How is it acquired? (3) What power does it exert over others?

The Meaning of Character

Character is more than what simply happens to people. It is what they do to themselves. To speak of a person's character is not to discount the significance of fate or luck or genes. It is known, for example, that height is directly related to salaries, promotions, political approval, and the like. Using a sample of 5,085 men who had passed an Air Force cadet qualifying exam, one study showed that after twenty-five years, shorter soldiers were earning $2,500 less per year than the six-footers; in another study, 72 percent of 140 job recruiters said they preferred taller over shorter applicants. Of all American presidents, only Madison and Harrison were shorter than the average American male living at the time of their election.[25]

While physical handicaps, economic deprivation, and natural disasters can hinder an individual's progress toward Tuchman's well-ordered soul, they do not destroy it. Of all living creatures, only humans have the power to shape their own character, to choose between honorable and dishonorable behavior, to tell the truth or deceive, to exploit or respect others, to work hard or slack off. Each decision so shapes the person that subsequent behavior is more predictable. Predictability is important to every human relationship (marriage, work, associations, leadership) because it flows into the decisions and choices individuals must make. Persons act only in the world they see, and seeing is partially determined by the kind of beings they have become.[26]

Character development can, of course, go in wrong ways. In 1827 Thomas De Quincey wrote satirically that "if once a man indulges himself in murder, very soon he comes to think little of robbing; and from robbing he comes next to drinking and Sabbath-breaking; and from that to incivility and procrastination. Once upon this downward path, you never know where you are to stop. Many a man dated his ruin from some murder or other that perhaps he thought little of at the time."[27] The reverse is, of course, true: the purse snatcher becomes the bank robber, the schoolyard bully the gangland thug, the "snotty" child the insensitive boss.[28] Since all leaders face temptations to get power at some cost and to hold it at all costs, Will Durant's shrewd characterization of them deserves to be remembered:

> He is domineering and likes to feel that men are bricks to his trowel, to build with them what he likes; and that they find a secret zest in being led by him. . . . His activity makes him healthy, and leaves him no time for thought or gloom. He enjoys life, bad as it is, and does not ponder much on the future or the past. He is skeptical of utopias, and had as leave that all radicals should be shot at sunrise. He abhors ideologists—people who make speeches or write articles, and settle international affairs from their garret eminence.
>
> Nevertheless, in some of his avatars he is a man of ideas: not a poet, nor a painter, nor a theoretical philosopher, nor a scientist who buries himself in test tubes or ancient tomes; but an inventor, an architect capable of original designs, an engineer brave enough to span great rivers with poems of woven steel, a sculptor commanding marble into life, a scientist willing to face all the world in defense of his new truth. Nevertheless he has a hundred lives of action for one life of thought.[29]

Applied narrowly, Durant's profile defines the leader as the almost thoughtless agent who leaps from unexamined premises to inconsistent practices. Applied liberally, the manager's "hundred lives of action" depend on how that "one life of thought" is directed. Character, therefore, is more complex than a character trait. When directed toward developing a constellation of qualities like sensitivity, loyalty, courage, fairness, honesty, and openness, the manager reveals a particular and visible moral identity. Direction, determination, movement—all reflect the operation of a developed character guided by a developed conscience. Conscience can remain undeveloped; it can be lost; it can be recaptured and, once regained, become a cause of jubilation.[30] What we do morally is determined not solely by rules or responses to one particular situation but by what we have become through our past history: "Experiences like facing death and falling in love are very important for what we are and do; yet they are often ignored in the analysis of moral experience simply because they are not in propositional form. It is our character that gives orientation and direction to life."[31] Emphasis on character shifts attention from the act performed to the performer of the act, from emphasis on thinking to emphasis on being, from the single act to the series of acts. Character becomes the conduit through which an individual's past and present flow and the future is designed; while shaped by conviction about what is right and wrong, significant and insignificant, tolerable and intolerable, the connection must explode in deeds.

Acquiring Moral Character

Raised earlier—and left unanswered—is one of the oldest questions, perhaps *the* oldest, in moral philosophy: Can virtue be taught? Those who say yes feel that the only way to become virtuous is to learn what virtue is; others insist that good habits come from being with good people. The medieval Jewish theologian Maimonides wrote that "a man needs to associate with the just and the wise continually in order to learn from their actions, and to keep away from the wicked who walk in darkness, so that he avoids learning from their actions."[32] So the question is not whether virtue can be taught but how it may be taught. Example, not exhortation, and practice, not principle, take priority: carpenters become carpenters by building houses; pianists become pianists by playing the piano; managers become leaders by leading. The same is true of character: people become virtuous by practicing virtue and by living with moral mentors. If, for any reason, an organization becomes sidetracked, only managers of sound character can restore a sense of direction. Disciplined organizations reflect disciplined leaders whose honed abilities lead them to behave consistently, almost instinctively, in moral ways.

CHARACTER IN THE CLASSICAL TRADITION

Contemporaries often differ on the essential components of a good character, as did the Greeks. The Athenians were united, however, in believing that the good person was the good citizen and the good citizen was one who accepted responsibility for actions, spoke the truth, and acted courageously. Things dear to nineteenth-century Americans—like thrift, hard work, conscientiousness, and commitment—did not appear in the Greek catalogue. There is, nonetheless, a rather startling similarity between old and new thinkers in their insistence that good character depends on possession of four qualities: prudence, fairness, courage, and temperance. Because contemporary interpretations of each differ from traditional ones, it is well to specify the meanings.

Prudence

To many careerists today, prudence suggests self-preservation, small-mindedness, and even cowardice; however, older generations saw prudence as a sort of "ways and means committee" of the mind that related appropriate resources to legitimate ends. Prudence involves two capacities: (1) the ability to make correct assessments of opportunities and (2) the capacity to evaluate accurately likely consequences. Prudent managers do not accept legal systems or absolutes mandated by others as sufficient guidebooks for conduct but seek instead to discover their reasonableness. Because it does not rely on scientific rules, prudence possesses a certain tentativeness. Its bottom line is possession of an uncommon amount of common sense that keeps managers from going too far too fast and seeking too little too late. If one word captures the meaning of prudence, it is foresight—that unusual capacity to understand and act in accordance with reality. Foresight requires managers to be open to advice, willing to have their initial judgments challenged, and ready to take appropriately appraised risk.

In this sense, prudence is "the mold and mother of all the other cardinal virtues."[33]

Fairness

If prudence helps a manager to determine what and when things should be done, fairness says how they ought to be done. Fair managers do the "right thing" almost instinctively because they accept obligations toward others and because those "others" are not simply commodities or replaceable parts, but persons. It is the reverse of "me-tooism," the counter to egoism, the disciplinarianism of self-interest. In one sense, fairness is an antidote to the sociobiological ethics with its stress on aggression and clan interests; fairness also mitigates the "tribal" ethic used to justify acts done for the organization at the expense of others. A tribal ethic operated among the robber barons in the United States who exploited the weak because traditional intermediary institutions (churches and guilds) were ineffective. Tribalism always means a "marginal ethic" that, following its own Gresham's law, drives high values downward.[34] Fair-minded managers resist a Gresham-like morality. They recoil at cheap shots directed against any racial, ethnic, sexual, or religious group; they go beyond narrow and legally defined contractual responsibilities to accept some responsibilities for indirect claimants. James Madison saw the tribal ethic in the special interest mentality that placed group good ahead of the common good. What Madison saw, Madison feared. Self-respect is, therefore, intimately bound to respect for others.

Courage

The Polish writer Artur Miedzyrzecki once observed that people may never realize what evil passes outside their own windows and that when they do, it is too late to do anything: "Heroism is first and foremost the courage to see in time"—and to act on time.[35] When Stanley Teele was dean of the Harvard Business School, he was once asked what distinctive lessons he hoped his faculty would impart to students. His almost laconic reply was "courage." Pressed to defend an answer that seemed to denigrate the intellectual role of the professoriate in favor of something that smacked of indoctrination, the dean admitted that while university faculties, of course, want students to think critically, they must also recognize that managers need courage to act when risks are high—and courage to try again when decisions turn out to be wrong.[36]

The two singular attributes of courage are (1) the ability to face danger and (2) the capacity to sustain actions. Whereas the confrontational side of courage is often put to sudden and brief tests, the endurance component requires long, plodding, and determined effort. Paradoxically, perseverance is the obverse side of the courage coin that works often to challenge reason, a point made by Harold Leavitt, who wrote: "Reason and resolve often take opposite sides in our own heads; reason estimates the odds and behaves accordingly. Resolve either ignores bad odds or thrives on long shots. Determined people try to make it happen because they believe in it, not because the odds are on their side."[37]

Temperance

It has been the word's fate to have been both undervalued and overvalued. Its undervalued meaning is found in its equation with "moderation in drinking" or "restraint in sex." Medieval casuists, for example, gave much attention to unchaste thoughts, lustful desires, insinuating words, suggestive books, and the like; nevertheless, the greatest mind of the period, Thomas Aquinas, gave relatively little attention to sex matters in his acclaimed *Summa Theologica*. Aquinas realized that temperance meant something more than controlled indulgence of alcohol or sex; it was essential to intellectual fulfillment, a point not lost on Adam Smith when he wrote of qualities needed by actors in the market economy. The temperate executive is preferred over the intemperate one, and for one very good reason: overindulgence is bad ethics and bad business. Its manifestations are the spendthrift, the freeloader, and the hedonist. Its opposites are the thrift ethic, the work ethic, and the long-term ethic. For managers, temperance means careful budgeting of all resources—financial, physical, and human—in order to make the organization continually viable in serving human needs.[38] It means living a life of apparent contradiction in its admonition that it takes courage to be cautious in the face of unanalyzed opportunities, to be restrained when no others can impose restraint, and to behave with reserve when followers call for daring.

The four cardinal virtues are not anchors but hinges: certain acts are let in or closed out. Robert E. Wood of Sears had character because he knew, almost instinctively, when to open or shut the door on certain organizational practices. IBM's Thomas Watson, Jr., David Packard of Hewlett-Packard, John Bogle of Vanguard, and Charles Zimmerman of Connecticut Mutual are exemplars of men of character in the world of business. Possibly an unbecoming humility prevents business from establishing its own hall of fame. A similar reluctance characterizes business school faculties who shy away from biographical case studies that illustrate in actual practice leaders who left something grander than even extraordinary growth and financial success for their organizations.

CHARACTER IN THE RELIGIOUS TRADITION

It is important to begin with a restatement: religion and ethics are not identical.[39] The religious individual is not necessarily endowed with special insights, special virtues, or special organizational skills. Why, then, go beyond the cardinal virtues to discuss the theological ones? One answer is that, by stressing obedience or sacrifice, religion fulfills the utility function noted by Mill, who said it was necessary for social cohesion. In a more profound sense, however, religion gives to individuals a feeling for the transcendent, a spiritual identity, and a different way of viewing other human beings.[40] While Judaism and Christianity hold that the basic moral law is knowable to both believers and nonbelievers, they nevertheless insist that the prophecies and teachings of the holy ones are necessary enrichments of human understanding.[41] The rabbis of old spoke of "the Seven Laws of the Sons of Noah" that condemned commercial trickery, false weights, state favoritism, and failure to support those in dire circumstances.[42] Maimonides applied such biblical insights to the world of business when he wrote that "the business conduct of the disciples of wise men is truthful and faithful. His 'no' is no and his 'yes' yes. . . . He obligates himself in matters of buying and selling in circumstances where the Torah does not obligate him, so that he stands by his word and does not change it."[43]

Christians continued the Jewish emphasis on a God concerned always with justice for the poor and the lonely, tolerant of human evils, forgiving to the penitent, and demanding high moral quality in all corners of social life. When Augustine and Ambrose spoke to the early Christian communities, their emphasis on "social morality" reflected rabbinical thought and anticipated Maimonides; when the American Catholic bishops presented their 1984 draft statement on the American economy, their judgments were made from the biblical perspectives of creation, covenant, and community.[44] Religion, therefore, summons men to supplement the classical virtues with the theological virtues of faith, hope, and charity.

Practical Implications

When all is said and done, what special use has religion for managers? When mystics suggest that spiritual experiences can be so powerful that they change a life forever, psychologists answer that peak experiences are not necessarily religious;[45] when it is implied that spiritual people lead more enriched lives, others counter that the behavior patterns of the religiously committed are really no different from those of the nonreligious; and when a catalogue of saints is compiled, "sinning saints" appear with disturbing regularity.

There are nonetheless some differences. Religiously motivated people use a distinctive form of reasoning in the way they view human actions, the procedures by which they judge them, the rules of preference by which the actions are ordered, and the values that determine and guide detailed decision-making. One such way has been succinctly expressed in the *Book of Discipline* of the United Methodist Church, which holds that actions shall be governed and judged by scripture, tradition, reason, and experience—the so-called quadrilateral. Not all churches emphasize the same criteria. Catholics have relied primarily on tradition, revelation, and reason; Protestants have looked to Scripture and experience; and fundamentalists often call on Scripture alone. The quadrilateral holds that *all* are needed, a view endorsed by Joseph Cardinal Ratzinger of the Roman Curia, who said that, taken in isolation, each source leaves some questions unanswered but in combination they become the path to moral behavior.

As churches emphasize certain parts of the quadrilateral, so, too, do individuals. Religious norms are therefore like the streets we travel in our cars and seldom think of leaving, "the single road we share with others. But our itineraries differ. Other people live, work, shop and play in different parts of the town, hence they take different routes, even to identical destinations."[46] So it is for religious precepts that reveal a gestalt, an overall configuration, more than a spiritual essence. What is made explicit is belief in God and a conviction that this faith not only supports a meaningful moral community but supports individuals during periods of suffering and doubt.[47]

Ultimately the issue comes down to two questions: How do we face reality? Is God meaningful to it?[48] From religion come the following responses:

1. Unlike human law, which is primarily interested in a person's deeds, Divine law is also interested in a person's motives—not simply what gets done but what is willed.[49]

2. God's laws are not negotiable. They exist, and people accept them or else pay a price.

3. Taking seriously the presence of evil in the world, religious individuals see all utopias (the fictional one of Thomas More or the real one of Robert Owen) as foundations too fragile on which to build healthy institutions.

4. The religious person accepts many tools in the learning process. British economist E.F. Schumacher caught this perspective when he wrote: "The answer to the question 'what are man's instruments by which he knows the world outside him' is . . . quite inescapably this: everything he has got—his living body, his mind, his self-aware Spirit. . . . Restriction in the use of instruments to cognition has the inevitable effect of narrowing and impoverishing reality."[50]

5. Without the graces God alone bestows, people live one-eyed lives, relying "largely on the eye of the mind to form images of reality. But today, more and more are opening the other eye, the eye of the heart, looking for realities to which the mind's eye is blind. Either eye alone is not enough. We need 'whole-sight,' a vision of the world in which mind and heart unite as two eyes make one in sight."[51]

6. Religious individuals, taking human limitations as a given, frequently invoke the metaphor of contraction and enlargement: shrinking of the moral self by evil acts and enlargement through gratitude, repentance, and renewal.[52]

7. Looking over the vast array of moral problems, the religiously committed person concludes that certain real-world cases involving "tragic choices" are best handled by recourse to the teachings of Moses and Abraham, the examples of Christ and his saints, Scripture, traditions, and church teachings. Intellectual pride is perceived as a most dangerous vice.

8. Because God made humans to the image and likeness of the Divine, persons must be treated as ends and not as means.

9. The bottom-line ethic of business (money talks) is counterbalanced by an upper line of religion that "faith talks"—and faith touches the individual's deepest corridors of communication, namely, love, justice, compassion, and community.[53]

10. Related to respect for others is a sense of gratitude for life, a view not easy to sustain when lives are taken brutally and suffering affects millions.[54]

11. In a civilization plagued by pessimism is the religious reality of hope, the Parousia (God will come again—to Jews for the first time, and to Christians for the second).

12. The religiously committed feel that prophets and saints, not rulers or philosophers, provide exemplars for building a truly humane society; it is holy people like Albert Schweitzer and Mother Teresa who bring light to dark corners.

13. Everyone is called to a vocation, not simply a career. Behavior is to be "professional" in the root sense of the word, namely, living in terms of decisive values and humane purposes that must be professed.

14. For managers, one very important lesson is in the imagery of the "good shepherd" who cares for the flock—the stewardship theme expressed by many business leaders.[55]

15. In a religiously formed character is a powerful sense of repentance and humility. Repentance is not self-recrimination but a returning to the purposes of personal and common life consonant with God's will. Repentance, in turn, fosters humility, which is "a readiness to revise one's purposes, to acknowledge one's mistakes, to redress the harmful consequences of one's past actions. It takes the form of willingness to question one's own judgments, to listen to others whose wisdom and insight might help us."[56]

16. Religiously committed people perceive social life as a covenant, not a contract. Max Stackhouse spoke to this perspective when he wrote that

in contractualism it is presumed that there are no objective moral guidelines for human mutuality and we humans must, by unfettered mutual consent, construct our own agreements on whatever terms seem advantageous to the parties involved. . . . Covenant, on the other hand, recognizes the necessity for different levels of accountability in social organizations, but it sees leadership as necessarily accountable to another.[57]

17. The covenantal ethic differs from the contractual ethic in its insistence that obligations arising from relationships among employees, owners, suppliers, competitors, and governments must be responsive and reciprocal and not simply quid pro quo. Whether managers use covenant or contract to describe their obligations provides clues to whether they are primarily concerned with stockholders or stakeholders. Whereas the primacy of stockholders flows from a contractual ethic, the primacy of stakeholders flows from a covenantal ethic; people once considered "outsiders" (employees, suppliers, society) have a real stake in the organization because of the covenant.[58]

18. Responsiveness and reciprocity demand sacrifice, and both influence the way people reason; logic alone makes obvious the fact that no one can fully repay debts owed to parents, colleagues, teachers, employers, and society and that obligations exist, therefore, that no law can enforce. Sacrifice is one way to make restitution or compensation to those for whom complete justice can never be returned.

19. Related to sacrifice is loyalty. Philosopher Josiah Royce said that all the recognized virtues can be defined in terms of loyalty that, when rightly interpreted, becomes the person's whole duty: "You can truthfully center your entire moral world about a rational conception of loyalty. Justice, charity, industry, wisdom, spirituality are all definable in terms of enlightened loyalty."[59]

In sum, religious moral reasoning differs from nonreligious moral reasoning in its emphasis on *process over logic*. Logic relates to the criteria of right and wrong within a given universe of discourse, whereas process means the multiple ways (imagination, intuition, faith) in which a person determines whether a rule, action, program, or institution conforms to those standards.[60] By joining philosophic and theological analysis, better answers may be given to what historian Ralph Henry Gabriel said were always life's two most important questions: "'The first is: what is the relationship of the individual to the society of which he is a part? The second is: what is the relationship of the individual to the mysterious and largely unknown cosmos in which he finds himself? These two questions cannot be disassociated."[61] It is argued that religion provides such a nexus.

Religion and the Managers

Is religion "piety in the sky"? Or does it offer skyhooks?[62] It is evident that loyalty, sacrifice, and covenant are particularly important to a society whose legal system is adversarial and whose economic system is competitive. But rare indeed is the leader who does not call for sacrifice and loyalty. Kennedy's inaugural speech ("ask not what your country can do for you; ask what you can do for your country") was only an added commentary to the religiously tinctured vocabulary of many American presidents. Iacocca's challenge to Chrysler employees and Roderick's plea to steelworkers to sacrifice for a common organizational goal are examples of similar messages. Not one of these men would attribute his exhortations to a religious source. But others have. Robert E. Wood of Sears once told the Rotary Club of Chicago in 1951 that the organizational world would become a truly human world only if individuals held to their "belief in God, had sincerity in their beliefs and practiced the ethics of their religion in their daily lives and in their associations with their fellow man."[63] Several years later, James Worthy, a Sears vice president at the time, wrote that when people's obligations to God are obscured, "concern for a fellow man comes to be seen as a matter of social convenience rather than a consequence of brotherhood under the fathership of God."[64]

Since Wood's time, an impressive array of comments by business executives could be assembled to demonstrate the generalization that religion is important to CEOs—like former J.C. Penney's Donald Siebert,[65] Lincoln Electric's James Ellington,[66] Thomas Murphy of General Motors, and J. Irwin Miller of Cummins Engine. Miller's observation reflects the common theme. Acknowledging that religion can be put to pernicious uses even by well-intentioned leaders, Miller nevertheless felt that

> religious values [temper] an organization's single-minded pursuit of its own good and the single-minded pursuit of self-interest. Religious values lead people to rebel at the enforced unemployment of millions, challenge

a culture which denies responsibility to the persons doing the work, and reach out to make meaningful the Proverb's plea: 'Let not loyalty and faithfulness forsake you'.[67]

That the statement reflects conviction, not fluff, is shown by the fact that Miller's company promulgated a credo called Cummins Practice that reflects broad ethical and religious precepts. From Abraham and Moses to Christ and his disciples, people have shaped their lives and careers on a religious basis.

MORAL GROWTH PATTERNS

In recent times, clinical psychologists, more than moralists, have stepped forth to provide answers about how character is formed and how moral growth is achieved. They assume that people's values are revealed by their stands on social issues, by their ideologies, and by the way they allocate praise or blame.[68] While psychologists have long been interested in the process of moral growth, the big names from the immediate past are the American George Mead and the Swiss Jean Piaget.[69] Of late, Lawrence Kohlberg tends to dominate the field. Although Kohlberg, as has been noted, is not interested in inculcating traditional values, his theories are interesting.[70]

Kohlberg's Three Levels

According to Kohlberg, individuals progress through three levels— preconventional, conventional, and postconventional—each of which has two stages. In the first stage of the preconventional level, people are (or behave like) children who follow an obedience/punishment orientation; at the second stage of this first level, individuals define right action as that which brings satisfaction to themselves and oc- casionally to others. The third stage marks the beginning of the second, or conventional, level and defines good behavior as that which helps others and is approved by others. The fourth stage, where, according to the theory, most of us arrive and stay, is marked more by a law- and-order orientation: right behavior is doing one's duty. At the postconventional level, the two respective stages take dramatic upward turns. At the fifth stage, right action consists in recognizing the rights of others according to standards that have been critically examined and agreed upon by the entire society. At the final stage, right action is defined by a conscience that has sought out certain ethical principles having logical comprehensiveness, universality, and consistency and by living according to that conscience.

The attitude of individuals at each stage in each level differs. At the preconventional level, the person often feels like an outsider who, at great disadvantage, must contend with authority figures (parents, uncles, aunts, bosses). At the conventional level, individuals move more from a selfish or egoistic view to recognize the value of the group and the attendant values of group practices and group roles; at this level, individuals develop loyalty to the organization and recognize that the maintenance and support of that organization or the existing order is critical. Loyalty and self-sacrifice are seen as important in determining whether an action is good or bad; motivations count, and to mean well is to do well. When good motives, however, produce bad results, the individual is shaken and begins to probe for better justifications for conduct; this leads to the law-and-order orientation of the fourth stage, where rules are accepted as essential to personal safety, security, and prosperity.

Only at the postconventional level are found individuals who really have thought through their problems in terms of moral principles. At both the fifth and sixth stages, individuals go through "principled reasoning," whereby right action is defined in terms of individual rights and standards have been critically examined and agreed upon by the thoughtful elements of society. Rational acceptance is the key. The highest level of moral reasoning is the sixth stage because only here do individuals affirm the right of everyone to his or her dignity. It is really a one-for-all and all-for-one morality, manifested by people prepared to challenge the dominant value structure if it denies justice to certain persons or groups.[71] Persons at the sixth stage are now fully autonomous moral agents who know who they are, what they believe, and why they believe it and who act in accord with those beliefs. Autonomy differs from heteronomy, which implies credibility, gullibility, complacency, submissiveness, interdependence, and servility.

Having postulated the levels of moral growth, Kohlberg went on to make or imply these additional points:

1. Moral development is invariant, so that an individual must progress through the stages in sequence.

2. Once a way of moral judgment has become established (which defines the level of reasoning), that method will not deteriorate because levels are not reversible.
3. If people cannot fall from a higher to a lower level, neither can they jump from the first level to the third.
4. Careful observation allows supervisors to identify the level that has been reached by their subordinates.
5. Individuals at one stage cannot comprehend moral reasoning at a stage more than one beyond their own.
6. In stage development, individuals are cognitively attracted to reasoning at one level above their own.
7. Movement through the stages is affected when a person's cognitive outlook is inadequate to cope with a given moral dilemma.
8. While culture is important, the development of modes of moral reasoning is the same everywhere.
9. As persons advance into higher levels of moral development, they tend to prefer liberal over conservative positions.
10. The vast majority of people never reach the third level and are, therefore, not fully autonomous moral agents. (See Figure 7-1.)

Kohlberg is not without critics. He has been charged with neglecting the impact of envy, low self-esteem, insecurity, and the like on a person's cognitive development;[72] his sampling at the so-called advanced level of moral growth has been deemed inadequate;[73] he is wrong in implying that individuals at a high level are more politically liberal than persons on lower rungs;[74] his scorn for traditional religious values divorces his approach from time-tested wisdoms; he has concentrated on how people think and neglected what people do; and the autonomy he cites as the highest expression of moral maturity could actually mean individuals who are laws unto themselves.[75] In the end, Kohlberg's model is too cerebral because it rests only on cognition, too narrow because its sampling base is restrictive, and too limited because it forecloses possibilities for self-fulfillment that transcend the bounds of civil society.[76] To buttress their position, critics have pointed to the experimental Chester School in Cambridge founded by Kohlberg in 1974 which was in shambles when he terminated it—faculty sharply divided, sex and theft rampant, and Kohlberg fighting bitterly with the teachers.[77]

If, on the other hand, Kohlberg turns out to be right—or even half right—managers will want to know the practical implications of

Figure 7-1.   Kohlberg's Three Levels

LEVEL	STAGE	SELF-PERCEPTION
Preconventional	1. Obey or pay 2. Self (and sometimes others') satisfaction	Outside the group
Conventional	3. Win others' approval by helping them 4. Law-and-order mentality: doing one's duty	Inside the group
Postconventional	5. Respect individual rights and abide by critically examined values 6. Act in accord with logically developed and universally accepted principles	Above the group

his theory. For example, how should managers handle personnel if Kohlberg is correct that the vast majority never go beyond the second level in moral development? Is participative management a theory whose time will never come? Or will the hunger for approval and the orientation to duty make participative management necessary? Can testing reveal an employee's moral level? Should executive development programs be reexamined to see if they can help individuals advance more rapidly from lower to higher moral levels? Some organizations, like Allied, Champion, and General Electric, to cite only a representative sampling, have already addressed these questions, and more are evaluating them.[78]

The Gender Gap

Perhaps the sharpest challenge to Kohlberg has come from women investigators who say his findings reveal a sex bias because he, like most researchers, has worked overwhelmingly with male subjects. The stage was set before Kohlberg by Simone de Beauvoir, who painted the relationship of women to men on a wide historical canvas and concluded that women were never allowed to define themselves but were defined by men. If change is to come, two things are needed: (1) an admission by males of their lack of understanding of the way women approach moral problems and (2) a redefinition of the meaning of moral maturity. Misunderstanding could be corrected if men would revisit old questions and reassess old answers such as these:

- Was Freud (whose influence has been profound) right in saying that women (1) are swayed more by emotion than by reason in their moral judgment and (2) possess a less developed sense of justice than men?[79]
- Do women hold back on career commitments? Years ago Charles Kettering of General Motors said that he wanted no one who "has a job working for me. I want the job to get him in its clutches when he goes to bed at night and, in the morning, I want that same job to be sitting on the foot of his bed telling him it is time to get up and go to work. And when a job gets a fellow that way, he is sure to amount to something."[80] One notes the male emphasis on other males.
- If indeed women do hold back, are they revealing cowardice or are they saying that something is rotten in the organizational Denmarks when success is defined exclusively as having better results than anyone else?[81] To women this kind of success is distress.
- Are women less suited than men for the competitive worlds of business and politics?[82]

Carol Gilligan has become well-known for her challenge to these male assumptions and their implications for different definitions of moral maturity by men and women.[83] Kohlberg defines moral maturity in the way males presumably define it: individuals who honor contracts, play according to the rules, and are governed by a high sense of abstract justice. Gilligan argues, on the other hand, that male researchers have neglected the importance that attachment and separation play in the cycle of human life. For men there is a willingness to separate from family, from friends, and from the hometown if separation is necessary for achievement in the work force. To fail at work is to fail the self. Male friendships, therefore, are as rare as golf-club buddies are numerous.

Women, by contrast, go through a different type of moral develLopment, resulting in behavioral patterns that reflect a caring and compassionate ethic. There is always a relationship deemed so important that the woman is ready to sacrifice herself to maintain that relationship. Loving others is like loving yourself.

How, then, does the crisis necessary for moral development occur for men and women, respectively? For the former, it happens when, having achieved certain successes in business or profession, the male somewhat belatedly acknowledges that intimacy with other human beings is important. And at this point, intimacy is the transforming experience for men. A woman, on the other hand, reaches her crisis when confronted by conflicting demands between caring for others and caring for herself. If the woman lapses into a continuation of the caring ethic at the expense of herself, she risks living the life of a hypocrite who privately laments the lost opportunities. It is only when a firm decision is made to accept responsibility to oneself *and* to others that moral development occurs.

Implications

These different perspectives are reflected in two different moral positions: the ethic of rights and the ethic of care. The morality of rights, predicated on equality, focuses on the concept of justice, whereas the ethic of care concentrates on responsibility. It relies not on a contractual but an equity notion of justice, wherein no one is ever to be hurt needlessly and everyone is to be helped. Therefore, although men and women start from different moral perspectives, each reaches adulthood only as there is a greater convergence in judgment on the importance of both justice and care.

Positing these two different modes of moral thinking enables managers to understand more completely the meaning of fiduciary responsibility. These qualities fall largely within the orbit of "religious" virtues—the "outer banks" infrequently visited by hardheaded pragmatists. If Gilligan and her associates are right, the implications for the organizational world are very substantial. For one thing, women may move to a McGregor Theory Y form of leadership more naturally than men. Carol Coston (who has served on the boards of Common Cause, the National Center for Urban Ethnic Affairs, and other catalytic groups) wrote that "feminist leadership is more . . . small scale, *empowering of* rather than *towering over*. . . . A feminist style encourages a variety of leaders to emerge."[84] It is likely that when a new management style becomes dominant it will be called Theory A or B or C, not Theory F (feminine), because the male tradition is not yet prepared for so revolutionary an admission. And this reluctance may be due in no small part to the male conviction that "feminine" management style suggests weakness, sentimentality, and romanticism. Yet *caring for* is not *caving in*.

Applying the "caring" concept to organizations may not be so illogical as once supposed. When Richard Ruch, business dean of Rider College, and Ronald Goodman surveyed workers at General Motors, they concluded that the "image at the top" had a more profound impact on employees than any other single factor in the work setting. And the best image was the caring leader:

> For most American managers, the use of the word "love" in connection with the workplace seems inappropriate. "Love" invariably brings to mind notions of romantic attachment or perhaps some unbusinesslike religious teachings. These associations are so deeply ingrained into the consciousness and culture of traditional American management that it is extremely difficult for many persons to see beyond them. The thought of "loving relationships" makes most managers nervous and mildly embarrassed. But the love to which we refer is neither romantic nor particularly religious. It is simply a form of relating to others effectively and in a genuinely caring manner.[85]

It is clear that a sense of justice *and* a sense of caring are both needed if individuals are to become what Bowen McCoy, managing director of Morgan Stanley and Company, called the authentic administrator—one deeply concerned about the organization's performance and viability, about eliminating waste, about serving clients and customers, and about meeting competition. The authentic manager is comfortable in "dealing, arguing, pushing the limits, making trade-offs, firing employees and living with ambiguity and paradox" —and yet always aware of the importance of the caring ethic to ultimate effectiveness.[86] The authentic manager has "character" in this dual sense of justice and compassion. From the duality comes a developed conscience prepared, when necessary, to challenge defects in either the ethic of culture or the ethic of concepts.[87] Character's companion—indeed, its twin—is conscience, the ability to discriminate right from wrong, to prioritize values, to blame or approve an act, to rejoice over good acts and repent over evil ones. To repeat for the sake of emphasis, good conscience animates good character so powerfully that it becomes the moral manager's special quality.[88]

While decisions affect—and are affected by—a person's moral stage, they do not necessarily result in moral advances. Some people, sadly, have moral characters that have not moved beyond a preconventional level. Not all who enter the adult world are moral adults. But describing the elements that good character represents and tracing the path of growth toward a developed character prepare managers to see what are desirable traits and optimum growth patterns for themselves. Whether it prepares them to see themselves and others in a clear light is another question. As a Harvard MBA graduate lamented: "I learned to read everything—except people . . ."

But is not reading people the key to an organization's ultimate success?

CONCLUSION

Character and charisma are not one. Yet managers who add competence to character are likely to be charismatic. Like the proverbial city on the hill surrounded by small villages, moral managers surround themselves with good people. This is not to suggest that goodness' payoff is greatness. Rogues have risen, and will continue to rise, to the top. They may stay there by virtue of the nonvirtue inherent in their rascality. There is, however, the comforting thought that in that illusive "long run," the best organizations are built by the best and the brightest of managers.

8
THE ORGANIZATIONAL DIMENSION

THE VALUES QUIZ   *(Mark True or False)*

1. _____ Every CEO should make sure that the organization's credo conforms to the culture of the people with whom the firm does business.
2. _____ Managers should place the well-being of their employees ahead of efficiency or productivity.
3. _____ The best reason for building ethical organizations is that it pays off: good ethics means good profits.
4. _____ The maxim "When in Rome, do as the Romans do" is the best ethic for a worldwide organization.
5. _____ Large organizations tend to be more ethical than small ones.
6. _____ Bureaucracy generally enables people to dodge responsibility.
7. _____ Organizational "openness" is as likely to encourage unethical behavior as organizational secrecy is.
8. _____ Since an enterprise cannot begin to operate until it has money, those who provide the money (the stockholders) should come first in the corporation's philosophy.

Organizations have been with us since Adam and Eve—and with mixed results. Even during that Edengate period when the first family was organized, things were not totally satisfactory. The wife blamed a slimy serpent for breaching the house rules; the husband passed the buck when challenged by the Lord; both behaved so badly they were exiled; one son murdered another son; and their progeny have built civilizations and destroyed them. From Genesis to contemporary times, the story of organizations has been one of rocky starts and resounding successes.

That everyone has interest in the character of an organization is reflected in the way people ask questions. Potential employees inquire whether the company is a good place to work; customers ask whether it is worth patronizing; suppliers wonder whether it is worth doing business with; and security analysts probe into management's competence and uprightness. If something untoward happens, observers quickly smell a story. More enduring and more intriguing for organizational theorists, as well as for managers themselves, is the question of the degree to which leaders can put the stamp of their own character on their organization's character. Is IBM's number-one ranking on Fortune's chart of highly regarded companies related to the moral values of the Watson family? Did Sears, Roebuck outperform Montgomery Ward because Robert E. Wood, as has been noted, had a more humanistic value system than Montgomery Ward's Sewell Avery? Has Toyota lurched ahead of American automakers in the small-car field because its leader, Taiichi Ohno, follows a corporate philosophy that holds that Toyota's foremost aim is to make not better cars but better people? The unstated assumption, of course, is that better workers will indeed make better cars.[1]

A related question deals with how value systems are conveyed to employees. Is good example enough? Or must the value system be made explicit by codes of conduct? Hard-nosed executives differ sharply in their answers. Should the ultimate responsibility for ethical behavior in business fall on such government agencies as the Securities and Exchange Commission, the Federal Trade Commission, the antitrust division of the Justice Department, and the IRS? Or does it fall—squarely and completely—on the shoulders of corporate managers themselves?

Throughout any discussion of an organization's character is woven a tantalizing issue that, at the moment, holds great fascination for philosophers and little for practitioners—namely, the notion of an organization having a "conscience," and hence bearing not only a social but a moral responsibility *as well. Despite the lack of interest in the theory, however, the issue raises critical practical questions: What precisely defines the range of an organization's obligations? Is a firm's ethos different from its conscience? Who is primarily at fault when things go wrong—the entity or the individual?*[2] *Are morale and morality transferable terms? It is quite possible that inability to resolve such questions explains why managers and scholars have moved away from the 1950 concept of corporate social* responsibility *to the 1980 idea of corporate social* responsiveness.[3] *Responsibility is essentially a moral question, whereas responsiveness is a practical one. The difference suggests that more is at stake than purely speculative interest in how the definition of an organization is finally made.*

AN ORGANIZATION'S CHARACTER

Quantum leaps were made in organization building during the nineteenth century when railroad managers had to coordinate vast networks to serve passenger and freight needs; these managers, driven by both technology and societal expectations to become pioneers, found that their efforts required the development of some form of organizational philosophy.[4] Some credit the Pennsylvania Railroad with being the trailblazer because, after the Civil War, its managers clearly defined relationships between departments, spelled out lines of communication, and established reporting chains. The "Pennsy" created a central office group consisting of department heads who worked with the president in coordinating plans and activities for all departments.

Critical to the success of this once great railroad was management; critical to Ford's and Apple Computer's successes were their entrepreneurial founders. The difference raises an interesting question about the relative importance of the manager and the entrepreneur to organizational success. While debate has occurred over the topic, it seems that a safe generalization is this: As long as the original entrepreneur was in effective control, the enterprise prospered; when it became too large, the entrepreneur proved inadequate for the job. Something new was required. Recognition came gradually that management itself was being institutionalized as a function related to, but distinct from, entrepreneurship; not only must markets be captured and held but worker loyalty and societal trust had to be captured and held as well.

Public Concerns

Despite uneven performances and ingrained public fear of organizational giants, larger and larger organizations have multiplied to meet the changing needs of changing people. The nineteenth- and twentieth-century organizational revolutions differed from the commercial revolution in that, during the latter, business people showed remarkable entrepreneurial daring but little skill at creating true organizations. One good example is the Mines Royal and the Mineral and Battery Works, respectively (both established in 1768 under most favorable circumstances), whose leaders never developed good organizational techniques. The joint stock company was condemned for preferring monopoly over efficiency. But, as noted, large organizations were always suspect by Americans, who instinctively feared size because it represented a concentration of power. This fear was intensified during the early part of the twentieth century when Adolf Berle and Gardiner Means spoke of the managerial revolution and propounded the thesis that large corporations "belonged" more to managers than to their stockholders, a view not likely to warm the hearts of investors. As a consequence, there lurks in the background of every discussion about big business the suspicion that managers take care of themselves first—the "catering to amenity" potential—and then of others only on the basis of their respective capacities to cause trouble or embarrassment.[5]

Skeptics wonder aloud whether high moral character is vanishing. Consultant Robert Allen reported that of fifteen hundred respondents in three hundred organizations, 65 percent agreed with the statement that

> organizations in our society tend to encourage their members to behave unethically, dishonestly and inhumanely in relationship to one another. Businesses, elementary and high schools, colleges and universities, government agencies, families, hospitals, police departments, churches, professional associations, athletic teams, political parties, and communities —*all were identified as ethically deficient by a significant percentage of those completing the questionnaire and with government agencies and business coming off worse and families coming off slightly better.* [italics added][6]

The finding has affinity to Jean-Jacques Rousseau's eighteenth-century view that people are born noble only to be corrupted by society.

Perhaps symbolic of today's organizational problems is Silicon Valley, often portrayed as the paradigm for the nation's future. Leaders of the electronics industry are folk heroes—smart, sleek, and sophisticated. But not all measure up to the standards set by its pacesetter, Hewlett-Packard. Reporting on a sting carried out by his undercover agents, San Jose police chief Joseph McNamara stated that, in many cases, top management was either asleep at the switch or, worse still, part of the corruption. Some examples:

- Inventory control was often nonexistent. In one company, assembly workers stole computers that were never reported missing.
- Some security and management personnel were involved in thefts and drug dealing.
- Management drug use was so ostentatious that a top executive passed around a sugar jar full of cocaine at a company celebration.
- In one company with 400 employees, almost everyone was on drugs.
- In other companies, 60 to 80 percent of employees used drugs.
- Employees believed that drug use and a certain amount of theft were "acceptable" to management.
- Only 2 of 150 companies asked for help after receiving a letter from the police department calling their attention to problems.

After reporting his disillusionment, McNamara made this telling point: *"The climate of the workplace is shaped by management*. Where positive work ethics and values flourish, economic health is preserved. It isn't warmed-over 'humanism' to protect employees from corporate deviants responsible for drug and theft rings. It is hard-nosed business sense! [italics added]"[7] Business concerns have no monopoly in the "organizational deviance" category. Even the established professions have encountered hard times. Doctors have tumbled from their pinnacles in public esteem; lawyers are bitterly divided because "there is plain greed on the part of too many";[8] and historian Max Lerner said professions are a disgrace because "the bottom line is what counts, whatever the means used. *It is the cancer of the professions* [italics added]."[9] Every manager rejoices when health is seen in his or her organization; every manager who is told a cancer is eating away at the organization hopes nonetheless that the tumor is benign. Signs of either health or illness are given on ratings managers make of one another.

Who Rates—and Why?

Fortune magazine has attempted to provide data for making judgments. To get a "fix" on a corporation's character, respondents from each of twenty industries were asked to rank companies in their own industries on the basis of eight attributes: quality of management; quality of product or service; innovativeness; value as a long-term investment; financial soundness; ability to attract, develop, and keep talented people; community and environmental responsibilities; and use of corporate assets. In 1984 IBM and Hewlett-Packard emerged as winners with average scores of 8.26 out of a possible 10.[10] Striking, however, are the shifts reported in *Fortune*'s 1985 results. Only four maintained their place in the top ten, and of the four, one (Hewlett-Packard) dropped from second to fifth, and Eastman-Kodak and Merck dropped from fourth and fifth to ninth and tenth, respectively. To examine *Fortune*'s list is to be reminded that corporate reputation is earned, not bestowed. What, then, makes for organizational excellence?

The question intrigued Thomas J. Peters and Robert H. Waterman, Jr., who answered that "soft is hard, and [that] all the stuff managers have been dismissing for so long as intractable, irrational, intuitive, and informal can be managed. Clearly, it has as much or more to do with the way things work (or don't) around the organization as the formal structures and strategies do."[11] What the pair sought to do was to marry the hardware of strategy and structure to the software of style, systems, staff, skills, and shared values. Their message became an overnight sensation not only among business executives but among leaders of nonbusiness organizations. Harold Kolenbrander, provost of Central College in Iowa, said that the findings "might equally well have resulted from a study of successful colleges, hospitals, law and accounting firms, and the like."[12] Excellence flowed from the character of organizations whose success turned out to be "brilliance on the basics." Tools were no substitute for thought; intellect did not overpower wisdom; analysis did not impede action; and hunger for quick success did not sacrifice shared values. Leaders of successful organizations worked hard to keep things simple in a complex world, insisted on top quality, diligently served their customers, listened to their employees, allowed disorder when it brought results, and encouraged experimentation.

Organizational success meant shared values. Every enterprise, large or small, profit or nonprofit, old or new, has a history that reveals how its decisions are made, its resources used, its values determined, and its character formed. Taken together with an original founding purpose, an articulation of mission, and a set of driving principles, these historical choices shape a distinctive character that becomes an integrating feature of the organization's identity. This character provides the locus, or center, from which actions and behaviors receive coherence, purpose, and direction. These historical choices are, noted Peters and Waterman, commitments about values that form the core of the popular McKinsey model called the Seven Sisters. (See Figure 8-1.)

Figure 8-1. The Seven Sisters

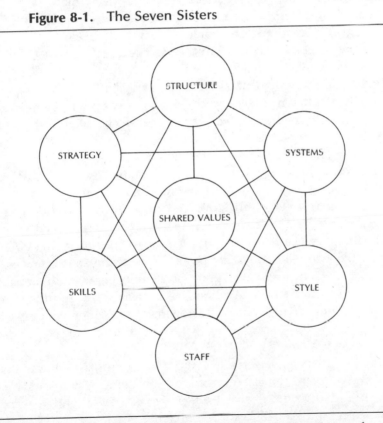

Source: "McKinsey 7-S Framework" from *In Search of Excellence: Lessons from America's Best-Run Companies* by Thomas J. Peters and Robert H. Waterman, Jr. Copyright © 1982 by Thomas J. Peters and Robert H. Waterman, Jr. Reprinted by permission of Harper & Row, Publishers, Inc.

The Leader's Impact

What constitutes the character of an organization is its brain (which stipulates rules whereby the organization survives) and its heart (which pumps the vitality essential to success). Positive results come only when both are brought together and given purpose.[13] Purpose comes through (1) adaptation to the larger culture in which the organization finds its home and (2) founders who have lived long enough to be able to impress their own moral stamp on the organization, wise enough to institutionalize those values, and smart enough to attract successors who will maintain them. What, therefore, may have been seen superficially as overweening pride on the part of the leaders of organizations was actually an act of great simplicity, namely, conviction that their enterprises could and should reflect, more fully and more lengthily, the personal character they had developed for themselves. They recognized how American values influenced them and how they, in turn, influenced others.

The formula was elementary: in every case the leader felt he or she could make a difference. Lee Iacocca's name became a household word when he transformed Chrysler's lackadaisical character into a high-powered engine; Thomas Murphy has been the wizard of Capital City Corporations; and Anthony O'Reilly brought a new spark to the H.J. Heinz Company. The manager is always, and simultaneously, the master and servant of power.[14] Charisma is not enough. For example, the leading performer of all American firms in the past decade has been American Home Products (AHP), which has averaged a return on investment of nearly 30 percent. Although customers know AHP's products (Anacin, Chef Boyardee pasta, Guldin's mustard), few people know its leaders because the corporation's CEO, James Culligan, shuns the limelight. Yet Culligan's honor is untarnished. It follows that while the character of an organization reveals itself in diverse ways, it is the individual at the top who has greatest impact on the organization.[15]

Many insist that character has the decisive impact on success or failure and point to the classic story of Montgomery Ward and Sears, Roebuck and their respective leaders, Sewell Avery and Robert E. Wood. Avery and Wood headed companies that, to outward appearances, had much in common. Both were combinations of mail-order plants and nationwide systems of retail stores; both were headquartered in Chicago; both men were contemporaries. But there the resemblances ended. Avery was one of the most autocratic businessmen of this century, and Wood one of the most democratic. Under Avery, Ward was tightly centralized and rigidly controlled; under Wood, Sears was highly decentralized and permissive to a degree unique in large-scale organizations. Ward's fortunes sagged; Sears's fortunes prospered. Had Wood, who worked five years for Montgomery Ward, assumed the company's presidency, Ward would have been a vastly different enterprise.[16] The incident suggests the inaccuracy of one philosopher's view that when managers think they have significant influence, all that has happened "is the same kind of sequence as when a clergyman is fortunate enough to pray for rain just before the unpredicted end of a drought."[17] More reliable is the comment of television producer Norman Lear, who said that "values trickle down from leadership— and especially from business leadership— almost instantly in today's electronic communications environment.[18]

Bureaucracy: The Good and the Bad

It is, nevertheless, well to recognize the constraints managers face when they try to shape—or reshape—the character of an organization. Unless they are owners of the enterprise, executives are, in a sense, owned by it. Each organization has its own dynamism, its own rhythm, and its own goals, which together constitute a sort of symphony, with executives serving more often like conductors, not composers. Tensions arise in every organization, and to keep them at tolerable levels, managers do the usual things: they organize, they delegate, and they control—in short, they bureaucratize.

Bureaucracy is greatly maligned and greatly needed.[19] By providing established routines, bureaucracies promote stability because they do not base the organization's success on the heroism, virtue, or extraordinary skill of any of its members. Jobs are defined and relationships among them established. Bureaucracy may work hardships, but it is difficult to imagine successful organizations whose members gather each morning to discuss at length these questions: What shall we do today? Who shall do it? How shall it be done?

So accustomed are managers and workers to bureaucracy that its novelty in business is frequently overlooked. A century and a half ago, production processes were handled mainly by foremen, inside contractors, and skilled craftsmen whose superior knowledge placed the capitalist who supplied the money at a distinct disadvantage; even unskilled workers could slow production when they felt that increased productivity would lower their piecework rates. Since large organizations promised economies of scale, capitalists were attracted to the corporate form of organization as a way to limit liability, raise equity capital, and restore power to the owners.[20]

The other side of the coin is that bureaucracies can stifle when emphasis on stopping "bad guy" behavior puts tight controls on the good guy as well.[21] More importantly from moral perspectives, bureaucracies encourage individuals to transfer responsibility from themselves to the system and, by so doing, erode the base on which personal character is built. Pleasing the boss becomes an obsession, and the lively conversational topics among managers "up and down the line is speculation about their respective CEO's plans, intentions, strategies, actions, styles, and public image."[22] A selective morality develops, saying that ethics is doing what the boss wants and that the best ethic is making sure that the boss gets what she or he wants. One of the century's most distinguished theologians, Reinhold Niebuhr, decried the "increasing tendency among modern men to imagine themselves ethical because they have delegated their vices to larger and larger groups."[23]

To break bureaucracy's iron grip, collateral organizations have been designed to operate alongside the formal structure on a relatively permanent basis. Because they provide opportunities for interaction among large numbers of different people working on different projects, they enhance employee mastery over their work environment.[24] An important value shift occurs when workers become persons, not puppets, responsible for their work-related activities. In addition, managers have tried to break bureaucratic shackles by what is called Ethical Participative Management (EPM), which sees in the decision-sharing process something more than the goal of increased efficiency. EPM becomes a means whereby people move from powerlessness and isolation to responsibility and integration—a moral ingredient that harmonizes organizational values with societal values. Control over one's own life, for example, is a value not found in East Asian cultures, which stress submission to external forces and harmony with nature.[25] Obviously, then, collateralism and EPM reflect that Western political value which asserts the right to participate. In democracies, leaders may make decisions, but voters decide on leaders; in nonpolitical organizations, boards, workers' councils, management-employee planning groups, and the like are instruments designed to make individuals accountable and participative.[26] For managers the implications are clear: participation expands freedom, and accountability ensures freedom's responsible use.

Some analysts have even suggested that organizational citizenship be extended to include procedural and substantive rights due to individuals by virtue of their membership in organizations less inclusive than the nation-state.[27] Behind such suggestions is one fundamental moral objective: to turn the alien (employee) into the citizen (co-worker) who matures through participative membership in the group.[28] When these lines of thinking are synthesized, they point out ways to build a very different kind of organization from that common in business today.[29] This represents a healthy evolution because if organizations respond only to material incentives, the only hope for the future is a series of "survivable small shocks or minor catastrophes" —a pathetic way to meet an obvious need.[30] Through this entire process of organizing people into a cohesive and productive group, managers reveal their own character. While the force of their example is powerful, it needs reinforcement that comes through a carefully considered organizational philosophy.

THE ORGANIZATIONAL PHILOSOPHY

The Need

A wise and seasoned Chicago consultant, Michael O'Connor, pointed out how organizational success is tied to an explicit organizational philosophy and how its absence preceded disaster. O'Connor wrote:

- In the third century before Christ, Alexander the Great managed a force of some 80,000 soldiers and supply personnel. He conquered an area more than twice the size of Europe and he did it without electronics, the internal combustion engine or even a Xerox machine.
- The Romans conquered most of the Mediterranean, Europe and the British Isles and, under the management genius of Caesar Augustus, maintained peace in Europe for a hundred years.[31]

Alexander and Augustus are but a small sample of leaders of big and powerful organizations who have existed through the years. But today there is no Alexandrian Empire and there is no Roman Empire. In view of their power and their organizational efficiencies, how can such failures be explained? A significant element in every answer is the fact that each of these great empires lacked a strong guiding philosophy to define its mission.[32] In some cases today, organizations are repeating past errors—a point that led philosopher Michael Hoffman to write: "I am convinced that a major reason why we have witnessed outbreaks of corporate wrongdoing, recently as well as in the past, is not that business people are less ethical than others, but rather that business gives so little thought to developing a moral corporate culture within which individuals can act ethically."[33] Relevant is the insight of Viktor Frankl: "Man is never driven to moral behavior; in each instance he decides to behave morally. Man does not do so in order to satisfy a moral drive or to have a good conscience; he does so for the sake of a cause to which he commits himself."[34]

Founders of successful organizations provide causes when they commit their enterprises to a philosophy of producing and marketing quality goods and services, and of providing fair treatment of workers and stockholders, and when their successors never forget the same philosophic commitment. Such commitments mean a constant interplay between the character of the individual and the character of the institution—one reason that experts talk less of organizational climate and more of organizational character.[35] Character, then, is a distinctive tone that, permeating the entity, embodies the "veiled truth" of the organization's nature. From the type of moral person comes the type of moral organization.[36] To have something special and to do something special are consequences, not causes, of a dominating idea expressed in the organization's philosophy.[37]

A dominating idea can, of course, be a bad idea. If, for example, the dominating idea is growth at all costs, mergermania may result; if it is increased market shares, product quality may suffer; if primary emphasis is on technical innovation, R&D personnel may experience intense emotional stress; if it is board harmony, constructive dissent may vanish. Every organization needs a philosophy, and business is no exception. Without one, executives will place goods and services to "whatever ends people may have: in short, power without defined purpose."[38] A reputable publishing house will provide pornographic books; a manufacturer of rifles for hunters will sell Saturday night specials; and a pharmaceutical firm will distribute crack. Defining purpose is senior management's first obligation.

Meeting the Need

Leaders who have successfully articulated corporate philosophies are many. Because he was one of the first, and because he expressed his beliefs with eloquent simplicity, IBM's Thomas Watson, Jr., is identified as one who lifted the issue of organizational philosophy from relative obscurity to singular preeminence. His words, widely quoted, bear repetition:

> I firmly believe that any organization in order to survive and achieve success must have a sound set of beliefs on which it premises all of its policies and actions. Next, I believe that the most important single factor in corporate success is strict adherence to those beliefs. And finally, I believe that if an organization is to meet the challenges of a changing world, it must be prepared to change everything about itself except those beliefs as it moves through corporate life.
>
> In other words, the basic philosophy, spirit and drive of an organization have far more to do with its relative achievements than do technology or economic resources, organization structures, innovation and timing. All of these things weigh heavily in success but they are, I think, transcended by how strongly managers in the organization believe in its basic precepts and how faithfully they carry them out.[39]

The credo consisted of three doctrines: respect for the individual, the best possible consumer service, and a commitment to excellence. The creed is short in words and long in meaning. And because employees want to know their organization's belief system, organizations profit by writing down their values in a code and monitoring it just like any other business matter. Rites, rituals, and symbols help to make the philosophy meaningful.[40] Chester Barnard put it simply more than a quarter-century ago: "The ethical ideal upon which cooperation depends requires the general diffusion of a willingness to subordinate immediate personal interest for both ultimate personal interest and the general good, together with a capacity to exercise individual responsibility."[41]

Basic Paradigms

An organization's philosophy may be viewed conceptually from two sets of contrasting paradigms: (1) the civility versus the systems ethic and (2) the contract versus the covenant ethic.

Civility Versus Systems Ethic.   The civility ethic stresses operating efficiency where equity is addressed primarily in quantitative terms (good wages, satisfactory retirement benefits, adequate vacation time) and in procedural terms (due process, grievance hearings, and the like). While these elements are important, the procedures tend to be so mechanistic and complex that the organization's needs and the individual's needs exist in uneasy tension. The systems ethic, on the other hand, is less prevalent, even though its expositor, Mary Parker Follett, is an old-timer in organizational theory. To Follett, no large system rests solely on abstract principles, neat organization charts, or precise job descriptions. Both organizations and individuals grow; growth means change; and change is for the better.[42]

The similarities of the civility ethic to Douglas McGregor's Theory X and of the systems ethic to his Theory Y are quite pronounced. In Theory X, managers base their policies on the following premises:

1.   Most people dislike work and avoid it when they can.
2.   Employees must therefore be pressured and tightly controlled if efficient work is to be done.
3.   The average worker accepts controls because it relieves him or her from a responsibility not wanted in the first place.
4.   The primary life goal for most people is security.

By contrast, Theory Y rests on the following beliefs:

1.   The expenditure of physical and mental effort is as natural in work as in play or in rest.
2.   Control and punishment are not the only means for bringing about effort toward a company's ends.
3.   Commitment to objectives is a function of the rewards associated with their achievement, and the most important of such rewards is satisfaction of ego.
4.   The average person can learn not only to accept but to seek responsibility.
5.   The capacity for imagination, ingenuity, and creativity in solving organizational problems is widely distributed.[43]

These theories about organizations have old philosophic roots. The assumptions about human nature in Theory X are not markedly different from the theological ones of Saint Augustine and John Calvin or the philosophic premises of Thomas Hobbes and Machiavelli. Theory Y, on the other hand, reflects more the views of Thomas Aquinas and Jean-Jacques Rousseau. The different assumptions recall the previously noted dilemma that confronted the framers of the American Constitution; their belief in representative government revealed a Theory Y approach, whereas their ingenious system of checks and balances reflected Theory X. What corporate leaders confront today is, in its essential detail, not that much different from what America's early political leaders confronted, namely, the construction of a system that blends a maximum of individual freedoms with a necessary minimum of organizational disciplines.[44] At this point, inductive reasoning helps executives to work from a priori principle to eventually testable conclusions.

Contract Versus Covenant Ethic.   Another way to consider an organization's philosophy is to contrast the contract and covenant ethics. Since both have been discussed previously, it need only be recalled that legally preferred is the contract model, which, in rather simplistic terms, holds that because investors first put the money into a venture, they should be first to get their money out; higher risks require higher rewards. The contract model has been supported by economic theory and by public law, which inclines toward stockholder primacy. The covenant model, by contrast, draws much of its inspiration from religion and places people above pockets: to belong to a community is to have claims upon it.

While the covenant approach appears to be more morally acceptable, certain caveats have to be noted. To define the covenant model as humanitarian and the contract model as narrowly economic is misplaced. Contractualists are also interested in humans. What they say is that the fruits of organized efforts should be allocated strictly on the basis of contributions and since one normally cannot hire workers without first securing capital, providers of capital come first. Furthermore, in today's world and particularly in large organizations, principals often come out a poor second. Agents can and do negotiate deals with substantial, if not total, indifference toward the principals: doctors use hospitals for their own practice; professors exploit institutional prestige to secure lucrative consulting assignments; and managers run fantastic aerial displays with golden parachutes. When concern for principals is minimized, injustices occur.

The advantage of the covenant model, however, is that it invites leaders to take a large view of their responsibilities because, under it, corporations are seen as much as moral organizations as they are as money-making machines. As Catholic University president William Byron noted:

> God made his covenant relationships with people, not with private persons. . . . It is curious indeed that we use the same vocabulary in corporate capitalism but evacuate from it all vestiges of social responsibility. We tend to relate to others inside the body of the corporation in measured, individualistic, sometimes cooperative but often competitive ways. The corporation, in turn, refers to other corporations as "the enemy," to individuals as potential consumers of product or suppliers of labor, and to future generations as distant possibilities unaffected by today's corporate decisions and with no rights to lodge property claims for wise use, care and conservation on today's corporate decision-maker."[45]

A keen sense of the larger community's needs challenges tunnel vision and gives to the covenant ethic its great appeal. If, therefore, the contract ethic emphasizes stockholder claims, the covenant ethic speaks of stakeholders, among whom customers and workers are ranked first. Such prioritizing understandably aggravates stockholders, who feel they are already low on the totem pole. The rankings reveal the values, and the values, in turn, largely determine how companies respond to crises.

First Assessments

It appears, then, that the covenant model provides the basic elements for a good organizational philosophy because it:

- enlarges the contract model based exclusively on duty to stockholders into the idea of duties to stakeholders (customers, employees, suppliers, and so forth)
- ties an organization's private good to the common good
- places primary emphasis on obligations to customer, client, and employee

Companies with that "something extra" have an esprit whereby people relate comfortably to one another. While power struggles exist, the attitude toward them is healthy, and the dominant idea is reflected in procurement, pricing, and investment policies; the nature and place of chartering; and employee compensation, rights, and immunities.

Adequate response to these various demands determines the quality of a good organization, and each solution to each problem is in accord with the prevailing ethic. Richard Eells, who worked for General Electric and taught at Columbia, put the matter of corporate philosophy in these practical terms:

> An organization meets high moral standards when attention is given systematically to the entire span of policy. This means more than *ad hoc* disposition of issues as they arise in the ordinary course of business; it means that, in each functional field, studied effort is given to the selection of salient and persistent issues in that field, and to their resolution according to written policy documents. The purpose of this procedure is to clarify the common purposes to be served in recurrent conflicts of diverse claims, to specify courses of action and to provide ways and means for enforcing the stated policy.[46]

CHARACTER IN ACTION

The Vital Signs

Aside from theory, people ask: Are there specific clues to an organization's real character? If so, what are they? Bowen McCoy of Morgan Stanley Realty has given a comprehensive answer to both questions through *objective* and *subjective* activities.[47] The former involves an examination of:

- the chair's or president's message in the last five annual reports
- senior officers' public speech files
- statements of corporate purposes, goals, and codes of behavior
- printed employee evaluation forms for salary reviews and promotions
- files on current and recent litigation and regulatory compliance

Subjective clues, on the other hand, are found less in statements and more in questions, the most important of which are these:

- How does the organization obtain and hold new clients or customers?
- What criteria lead executives to turn down business? to reject consumer or client demands?
- What criteria are employed in projecting employees' promotion opportunities?

- To what extent are those criteria consistent with employee evaluation forms, organizational goals, and codes of conduct?
- To what degree do younger employees believe in the basic fairness of the performance, evaluation, and feedback systems?
- Is there a formalized program of upward feedback?
- Is there evidence to support a general atmosphere of openness?
- Does the organization tolerate internal conflicts?
- To what degree does the system respect a sincere inquiry from junior employees regarding the rightness or wrongness of a particular organizational action or policy?
- What evidence is there of capacity for growth, change of goals, and preservation and/or change of values?
- What are the basic attitudes and styles of chief administrators toward the government and, particularly, toward regulatory agencies?
- How close to the ethical line is the game played?
- In informal bull sessions, who are the heroes?
- For what values are they admired?
- To what extent are the traditional values maintained and supported when the corporation is under stress?

Perhaps the most valid indicator is the way the organization handles performance appraisals, because this process shows how corporate values are interpreted and inculcated.

If individual performance is appraised fairly within the organization, organizational performance will be appraised fairly by outsiders. The values-in-place syndrome is evident in the process McCoy described at Morgan Stanley. Character, whether in the individual or the institution, means development. Like all development, it involves process—never to be finished and never to be ignored. Addressing the issue systematically brings values into place, and the placement means, in turn, a healthy and well-tempered organization. Ignoring character development ensures a neurotic organization.[48]

Other attempts to provide internal criteria have been paralleled by efforts to establish norms for judging the corporation's external performance. The Council on Economic Priorities offers criteria that are implicit in the five questions it suggests be asked of corporations:

1. Does the company invest in South Africa, and, if so, has it complied with the Sullivan principles on fair labor practices?
2. How much of its annual earnings does the company contribute to charity?

3. Does the company have women or minorities on its board of directors or among its officers?
4. Does the company have contracts related to conventional or nuclear weapons?
5. Is the company willing to provide facts and figures on its social programs?[49]

One of the most valuable aspects of the council's approach is acceptance of the fact that an enterprise is unlikely to score perfectly on every criterion. It may, for example, be engaged in the production of nuclear power and yet have a highly reputable philanthropic program; it may have superior management and yet have little minority representation. The goal, however, is to provide criteria that enable corporations to improve in all aspects of their operations—to develop, in short, a near perfect organizational character. But proof is still in the pudding.

Testing the Philosophy

The actions of Firestone, Johnson and Johnson, and Migros in Switzerland demonstrate the point. Despite evidence that its steel-belted 500 tire was defective, Firestone tended to stonewall critics; particularly reprehensible was the fact that the manufacturer had discovered serious problems with its 500 in 1975 when tires awaiting shipment to General Motors failed more than half the time to meet a government high-speed performance standard. Instead of accepting responsibility, the company assured consumers that "there is no safety-related reason for the public to be concerned about continuing to use Firestone steel-belted radial 500s or any other properly maintained Firestone tire."[50] Much happened between July and October of 1975 to discount the claims, and eventually, under government pressure, Firestone recalled about 10 million tires, even though continuing to maintain that the tires had no safety defects. Firestone lost more than money through its tactics.

Johnson and Johnson took a totally different approach, even though there was no question about the safety of Tylenol, the product that precipitated the crisis. James Burke, Johnson and Johnson's chief, received grim news on September 20, 1982, that three persons in Chicago had died after taking Tylenol capsules. When it was discovered that the company's most successful over-the-counter pain reliever had been laced with lethal doses of cyanide, the great helper became overnight the great killer. Although sales approximating $500 million were jeopardized, Johnson and Johnson recalled some 31 million bottles of Extra Strength Tylenol to protect lives. Organizational philosophy literally directed the decision, in that the company's board had prioritized claimants this way: (1) customers, (2) employees, (3) the community, and (4) stockholders. Existence of this philosophy made the decision a foregone conclusion because company executives acted within a well-established and understood philosophy. There was no need to go back to square one. Clearly stated in the company's credo as a first priority was the idea that "our first responsibility is to the doctors, nurses and patients, to mothers and all others who use our products and services."[51] No time wasted on what stockholder reaction might be because Johnson and Johnson's philosophy clearly stated that *the stockholder is best served if consumers, employees, and community come first.*

The third case involved a Swiss supermarket chain called Migros. A Zurich housewife had purchased sausage and kept it for some time without refrigeration, despite clear instructions that, without it, the meat would go bad. When she later fed the cooked sausage to her son, he became violently ill and died. Reporters who swooped down upon Migros were referred to Dr. Hans Blumenthal, the Migros quality-control executive. After he pointed out how the woman had ignored cooking and storage instructions, a reporter asked if it was possible to produce sausage in a way that guaranteed no dangerous bacteria would ever reach the public. When Blumenthal conceded that such a process was possible, he was asked, "Why then didn't you make your sausage so pure that no one could die even if they failed to read or follow directions?" The answer was straightforward: producing it would be so expensive that only the rich could afford it, and this countered the Migros philosophy, which was to serve all the Swiss people with wholesome food at reasonable prices. The response meant that, under the Migros philosophy, the company could not afford zero-defect products. But Blumenthal went on to show how Migros was first to introduce open-code dating, first to provide detailed customer instructions, first to publish a complete ingredient list, and the like. Migros today, with nearly 30 percent of the Swiss market, attributes its success to a dominating idea expressed in a philosophy the Swiss people understand and accept.

In healthy organizations, therefore, the "people" element (customers, employees, managers) is prioritized on Mary Parker Follet's premise that companies grow only when people grow. Concern for customers is motivated by concern for workers in a sound organization, a concern that expresses itself in myriad ways. The Herman Miller Company of Zeeland, Michigan, for instance, is a prime example of positive attention to the physical setting for employees. It adheres faithfully to the three-pronged philosophy of company founder D.J. DePree: product innovation, customer service, and employee involvement. Its facilities showcase its philosophy. A once splendid summer estate has become a conference center where discussions on research, development, and customer services move the philosophy to reality; talking with company executives is more like "discussing philosophy than the future of business—but then that is the big reason why Herman Miller is such an attractive place to work."[52] A *Fortune* reporter spoke with awe and incredulity when he wrote that "annual meetings begin with a prayer; alcohol is neither served at company functions nor allowed on expense accounts; top executives refer to their stewardship of products and their covenant with their employees; employees speak regularly of 'joining' rather than working for the firm."[53] It was smart symbolism to allocate half of the company's 1983 annual report to employee interviews because management thereby affirmed publicly its conviction that healthy financial conditions come only through healthy working conditions.

People-sensitive organizations like Hewlett-Packard and IBM have been joined by others, like Frito-Lay and McDonalds, who practice what the McKinsey consulting firm called the "touchie-feelie" approach. Although the approach has been criticized for alleged deficiencies in analytic sophistication, results suggest that it pays off. Wall Mart, the fourth ranking retailer in the country, is led by Sam Walton, who is known to employees as Mr. Sam. Convinced that the best ideas come from clerks and stock boys, Walton visits them frequently. Employees proudly wear buttons proclaiming: "We care about people!" The $2 billion enterprise is a "caring" enterprise.

A final example of a character company is found in the Cressona story. When Alcoa abandoned one of its plants along the Schuylkill River in 1978 (after it had been shut down during a labor dispute), a former Alcoa executive, James Steine, gathered a few backers to buy the company and christened it Cressona. Within five years, the company had racked up a list of successes difficult to match by any other factory in smokestack America. When the Big Three (Alcoa, Reynolds, and Kaiser) closed plants and reduced work forces, Cressona refused to lay off employees, even during the dark days of the 1982 recession. The 1981 efforts of the Aluminum Workers International Union to organize the plant were defeated by well over a two-to-one margin. What explains the "infant's" story that differs so much from the Big Three adults'? Several factors: employees are given raises every May; work flexibility has enabled the company to produce at about a two-to-one effectiveness rate over Alcoa; no time clocks are placed in the plant; managers and employees work on teams; and the company has become a good citizen, contributing money for construction of a community dam and a Little League baseball field. Under its covenant ethic, another "caring" enterprise has become an economically successful one.[54]

CONCLUSION

Few who work for organizations step back often enough to assess their own character and the character of their workplace. The assessments, properly and objectively made, could be revealing. Does the assessment reveal match or misfit? If the latter, who is the odd partner—the organization or the individual? What action should be taken to preserve a proper "fit"? When and how? The analysis is probably the most serious exercise career people will ever make. And the pulse-taking is part of an ongoing process of the moral manager's work.

POSTSCRIPT

In an "afterword" on his own brilliant career as professor of law, Karl Llewelyn raised a question—and a hope—that closely describes this writer's mood as the inquiry comes to a close. Llewelyn wrote:

> What would it look like if I were doing it over? And it is a bit disheartening to realize that what it would come to would be pretty much a shifting of emphasis and arrangement: a fuller development of matters mentioned and passed over; a correction and rounding out of things dealt with too largely in the flat or in a light that hid or twisted some portion of their meaning; a surer, sharper drawing of some line that had earlier been ventured vaguely as a guess; while even what might seem "new" would prove on more careful thinking to be stuff already adumbrated in thought and present in flavor. In one way, it is disheartening. One set of ideas seems to be about all any ordinary man can manage in one lifetime, and the time and labor needed to work them into use seem so often to accompany their obsolescence.[1]

Despite disappointments, however, there lives the hope that a word or phrase may clarify an issue, provide a touchstone to serve managers well in moments of doubt, or help students on those "little things" that, according to Llewelyn, take a "long life-time to learn, those little things which make us US, make us worthwhile to our people and to ourselves."[2] Efforts in "little things" to help managers and would-be managers become more worthwhile to themselves and to others are, even when inadequate, appropriate— and perhaps never more so than now, when fears grow that a no-fault psychology has moved from such seemingly remote things as driver insurance to such immediate things as drug abuse for workers and role abuse by managers. Carried to an extreme, no-fault means no responsibility. And no responsibility means no freedom. Managing freedom creatively is the ultimate way to manage enterprises efficiently.

There is, therefore, more than a business interest at stake when managers review their own development plan and design it for others. Virtues that make people good are needed to make institutions great. This is because, in the configuration of social relationships that is an organization, transactions always go on. The transactions are normally viewed as allocations of resources (the science of economics) and allocations of power (the science of politics), but both are subject to the practical science of ethics. Administration is a practical art that builds on practical sciences.

While, as repeatedly stressed, it has not been a primary goal of this inquiry to develop sharp and precise connections between principle and practice, a valedictory that (1) summarizes some of the major points of the analysis and (2) offers a few ways to develop working connections between the two is appropriate.

SUMMARY POINTS

- Because people need other people to fulfill themselves, those who provide the conditions for such fulfillment are engaged in one of society's most essential tasks.
- The more critical are the needs to be served, the more honorable is the assignment. Providing goods, services, and jobs obviously responds to a vital need, and encouraging the work of the providers are the managers.
- Honorable work requires honorable people.
- To the traditional management task of dispensing justice to a variety of market claimants has been added a new assignment, participating in the revolution for social justice. The task involves greater business involvement in public policy issues.
- If people are an organization's most precious assets, knowing what makes them tick is a must for those who lead. At this point, what biologists, brain researchers, and sociobiologists are reporting from their research is so startling that environmental scanning must go beyond the market. For example, sociobiologists now claim the ability to define the remaining mysteries of life—its origins, its workings, and its goals. Since their claims, even if not completely validated, have consequences for education, personnel policies, and the like, their conclusions and their findings require the critical attention of managers.

- "What is a human being" and "what is being human" are related but independent questions. Answers to the first question come largely from science; answers to the second come largely from philosophy. The practical impact of this conclusion is that social scientists and philosophers are as necessary to understanding management development as are the physical scientists.
- Managers require virtue, an old-fashioned word with ongoing durability.
- Not false pride but a sense of obligation drives executives to demand the best from themselves and, at least, the "better" from subordinates—a point requiring early and frequent statement in the organization's philosophy and through reiteration of its code of ethics.
- As character comes before charisma, so, too, does virtue come before versatility. To understand what virtue is and to live by what virtue demands are two related, but different, things.
- Example is the best teacher, embodying those qualities that constitute virtue—prudence, fairness, fortitude, and temperance—enhances the manager's teaching role.
- While all virtues are values, not all societal values are virtues.
- Since the values of the "elders" are challenged by each new generation, management's understanding and reexamination of the regnant culture are ongoing tasks.
- Understanding values begins first with the culture's core because it is this "lived ethic" that has:
  (a) withstood the tests of time
  (b) existed prior to philosphic analysis and validation
  (c) enabled individuals to live with one another in relative peace
  (d) provided criteria that legitimize institutions and roles
- In a global economy, comprehension by executives of their own culture is a necessity, and appreciation of other cultures a highly desirable auxiliary.
- Every culture rests on traditions, some of which (slavery, subordination of women, hostility to certain ethnic groups or religions) have defied moral principles.
- It follows from the above that imperfections in the culture require purging, and people of power (as business leaders surely are) are necessarily involved.
- Reconciling a national culture to universal norms is sometimes made difficult by ideologues who, taking certain values of the culture, tend to make their preferred parts the whole of the culture.

- Ideologues do serve a constructive purpose in bringing to the surface contradictions in the culture so that more relevant syntheses of values can be made. Since, in the synthesizing process, managers play a significant role, business school curricula and in-house development programs cannot ignore the ingredients that go into the synthesis. Among these ingredients are ethical and moral values.
- Managers are best circumstanced to meet the challenges involved in social change when they understand those fundamental norms which emerge from ethical analysis, apply the norms in a logically consistent way, and have good reasons to justify their actions when exceptions are made.
- Humane leadership depends on respect for equality and justice, truth and freedom. Turning respect into reality takes into account the many meanings that each concept may have, as well as the possibility of contradictions among meanings. Illustrations of conflicts include the following:

  (a) Since representative governments and market systems depend for survival on trust, truth telling by those in whom trust has been placed (government officials, corporate executives, union presidents, lawyers, and accountants) is a necessity. However, when the culture legitimizes departure from the norm because of the role a person holds, the person who makes the departure should (1) be excused but not praised and (2) make a public act or gesture to express remorse over a necessity to place obligations to role above obligation to truth. Cyrus Vance's resignation as Secretary of State—after his role led him to deceive America's allies during the Iranian hostage crisis—is a good example. Vance left public life with only one medal: his honor.

  (b) Freedom is a process toward individual self-fulfillment, and each person has primary responsibility for developing the internal discipline that makes such progress possible. What adult employees lack, executives can rarely supply, and attempts to do so invite unwarranted forms of paternalism.

  (c) Certain types of paternalism are, on the other hand, legitimate when intervention helps the individual and the organization. Provisions for career counseling and health care facilities are examples.

  (d) In exercising freedom, people are expected to behave rationally. It is no violation of freedom to block irrational behavior, but in such instances the burden of proof for the action falls on the interventionist.

(e) Seeking to advance the ideal of equality can lead to certain forms of injustice (quota systems) against those not responsible for creating equalities in the first place. Like exceptions in truth telling, exceptions in dispensing justice must be logically defensible, and the burden of defense again falls on authorities.

- A manager without justice is a manager without mind. An executive without compassion is an executive without heart. Compassion, however, cannot be extended if its effect is to harm others in the organization. Seniority, past contribution, and job-related pressures are among the factors that help define the need for justice and the extent of what might loosely be called organizational compassion.

PRACTICAL STEPS

Achieving one or more of the goals suggested by one or more of the foregoing propositions is helped when practical steps are taken by each individual according to his or her own resources and needs. Steps common to all (executives, midmanagers, professors, and students) could include the following:

- Maintain a journal (not a diary) of significant ethical problems that have arisen either in or outside the organization. Necessary, of course, is the writer's own reaction to, and proposed solution of, the problem.
- Share with a few trusted and critical "others" your way of ethical reasoning and invite challenges. If, for example, you are a utilitarian, how much "rule breaking" or "exception taking" will you tolerate in yourself? by others? Where is the line finally drawn? Why?
- Write a description of someone you most admire and refer to it periodically. If the description starts to lose appeal, ask why.
- Prepare (or have prepared) a small reading list of significant articles or books that deal with moral issues in the organization and allocate

time for reading and in-depth discussion with colleagues on the subject covered.

- Participate in annual "retreats" devoted primarily to moral issues related to the organization.
- Use quarterly (or, at least, annual) moral audits to assess your own development.
- Apply results of the moral audit to determine (1) the "fit" between the organization and you and (2) improvements that could be made in the relationship, including checkpoints to signal when a separation is warranted.

THE EXECUTIVES

Beyond the need common to all are certain things that executives themselves are best able to consider and, if appropriate, implement. Among the further suggestions are the following:

- Send a "president's message" regularly through in-house media to explain the organization's expectations for employees' on-the-job as well as off-the-job behavior in public places.
- Feature stories on employees who have behaved with singular moral conviction when faced by an ethical problem that arose in the organization.
- Provide incentives and rewards for employees who have helped the organization to become more efficient and more ethical.
- Provide for regular review of the enterprise's code of ethics by representatives from management and workers, and share the reviewers' assessments with other employees.
- Share the fruits of such reviews with scholars so that the latest insights into the manager's/organization's moral problems can be studied by teachers and incorporated as case studies into curricula.
- Given the probable expansion of executive duties in the public realm, reconsider job descriptions for the president and board chairman with a view of separating the two roles while at the same time providing for effective interactions.
- Schedule regular luncheons for managers to engage in dialogue with experts in the fields of moral development, history, philosophy, intellectual thought, and the like. Ideas, not problems, should be the agenda.
- Since executives seek to "manage" their contacts with ideologues

in ways designed to preserve and promote their organization's well-being, their public relations departments need the best, not second-best, talent. Such talent should have regular and consistent access to the CEO even as it is regularly and consistently accessed by the "boss."

- Management of intricate external relationships with ideologues is harmed if (1) ideologues are dismissed out of hand as irritants or (2) only probusiness ideologues are embraced. At times "friends" may be no better than foes. Those who, for example, seek to "theologize" the corporation may bring solace through sanctification but, in the long run, may be no more useful than the hostile elites. Objectivity, not selectivity, is the guide when executives pick their "friends" and confront their "enemies."

- Establish managerial "sabbaticals"—an off-the-job time for reflection that leads, hopefully, to better people for better organizations.

THE NEED FOR MODELS

One significant step the business fraternity (broadly defined to include practitioner, professor, and student) might consider is seemingly self-serving. But if management is indeed an honorable profession, if it is composed mainly of honorable people, if such honorable people provide examples to subordinates, and if, finally, example is the best teacher, two questions need to be asked: Why restrict the manager's teaching function to his or her own organization? Why ignore the need of every honorable fraternity to singularly honor its singular members? It is an interesting commentary on American society that honor is paid mainly to actors and athletes—Emmy awards in television, Oscars in movies, Heismans in football, Hall-of-Famers in baseball—who are more widely known than Pulitzer and Nobel designees.

All this is by way of preface to a suggestion whose first critics will be found, not among the hostile elites but within the business community itself. Despite this fact, there is need for a Business Hall of Fame, an institution whose membership reflects the best that the business world has—or had—to offer. Models of admiration (even contempt) have largely vanished, and the void reflects widespread indifference to morality. But students need life-enhancing models, and universities have failed to provide them.

The institution might be limited to current CEOs; it could be a group of elder statesmen elected from the ranks of retirees; or it might be composed of those who have died—people like Robert Wood and Ted Houser from retailing, Milton Perlmutter and Robert Cullom from the food industry, Owen Young and Thomas Watson from manufacturing, J. Edwin Matz and Roger Hull from life insurance, and so on. The organizing agent could be one of many institutions: a prestigious business school; the American Assembly of Collegiate Schools of Business, which includes the deans of all major business schools; the Academy of Management, which is composed of well-known practitioners and management scholars; a think tank; or the Business Roundtable. The mechanism is secondary. In its early years the institution may be ignored or lampooned, but the wisdom of philosopher Alfred North Whitehead calls for dramatic restatement through people's lives, not philosophers' words:

> Now it is to be observed that it is the successful who are the important people to get at, the men with business connections all over the world. . . . The conduct of business now requires intellectual imagination of the same type as that which in former times had mainly passed into those other professions.[3]

Managers owe to society in general and to students in particular—even more than to themselves—an institution that honors those who, by their intellectual imagination and moral behavior, not only took their organizations forward but upward.[4] Perhaps the most appropriate valediction is the words of Johnson and Johnson's CEO James Burke: "I know of no other human activity that provides for a more full and rewarding life than business."[5] Why not recognize that fact?

NOTES

INTRODUCTION

1. John F. Budd, Jr., "Corporate Ethics and Credibility" (remarks made at the spring meeting of the Public Affairs Council of the Machinery and Allied Products Institute, May 9, 1986).
2. Address to the Business Ethics Workshop at DePaul University in Chicago, July 8, 1985.
3. Quoted in *World Insurance Outlook*, ed. Michael Hogue and Douglas Olson (Philadelphia: Corporation for the Philadelphia World Insurance Congress, 1982), 681.
4. Victoria Sackett, "Everyday Ethics and Ann Landers," *Public Opinion* 9 (November–December 1986): 9.
5. *New York Times*, October 28, 1985, p. D4.
6. Chester Barnard, *The Function of the Executive* (Cambridge: Harvard University Press, 1938), esp. Chap. 13.
7. Herbert Simon, *Administrative Behavior* (New York: The Free Press, 1947), 47.
8. Ann Crittenden, "The Age of Me-First Management," *New York Times*, August 19, 1984.
9. Terence Mitchell and William Scott, "The Barnard-Simon Contribution: A Vanished Legacy" (manuscript, University of Washington), 21. See also their provocative article "The Universal Barnard: His Micro Theories of Organizational Behavior," *Public Administration Review* 45 (Fall 1985): 239–57. Robert Reich cautions against painting corporate executives too darkly in his *Tales of a New America* (New York: Times Books, 1987), 250–52.
10. Michael Slote, *Good and Virtue* (Oxford: Clarendon Press, 1984), esp. Chap. 4.
11. Bernard Williams, *Moral Luck* (Cambridge: Cambridge University Press, 1981), 23.
12. Allan Bloom, *The Closing of the American Mind: How Higher Education*

Has Failed Democracy and Impoverished the Souls of Today's Students (New York: Simon and Schuster, 1987), 14.

13. Alexander W. Astin and Kenneth G. Green, *The American Freshman: Twenty-Year Trends, 1966–1985* (Los Angeles: Higher Education Research Institute/University of California, 1986), 18.

14. John Wauck et al., "Glimpses of the Harvard Past," *American Scholar* (Summer 1987): 431–32.

15. Quoted by Joseph Ferrillo, "The Ethics Industry," *New Age*, August 1985, 23.

16. Edmund Pincoffs, "Quandary Ethics," in *Revisions*, ed. Stanley Hauerwas and Alasdair MacIntryre (Notre Dame, Ind.: Notre Dame University Press, 1983), 93.

17. Value ethics has long been recognized as the ethic of a divinity. So far as Christian ethics is concerned, there has been a split between those who have pledged allegiance to the use of formal prescriptive principles, on the one hand, and those representing the cause of more existential responses to a particular situation, on the other. It is a debate that has divided Catholic and Protestant moralists, and one that has occurred as fiercely in Europe as in the United States. James M. Gustafson, "Context versus Principles: A Misplaced Debate in Christian Ethics," *Harvard Theological Review* 58 (April 1965): 171–202. See also Professor Dennis P. McCann, "Theology Approaches Business Ethics: Where Do We Go from Here?" (unpublished paper, DePaul University Business School, n.d.).

18. *Running Out of Time: Reversing America's Declining Competitiveness* (New York: The American Assembly Report, November 1987), 11.

CHAPTER 1: GATEWAY TO THE MANAGERIAL WORLD

1. Chester Barnard, *The Functions of the Executive* (Cambridge: Harvard University Press, 1938; reprinted in 1968), 273–74.

2. A.M. Hocart, *Kingship* (New York: Oxford University Press, 1927), 46.

3. *Leaders Magazine* (July/August/September 1978): 6.

4. Perceptive studies of the time-trap problem include R. Alec MacKenzie, *The Time Trap* (New York: Amacom, 1972), and Alan Lakein, *How to Get Control of Your Time and Your Life* (New York: P.H. Wyden, 1973).

5. Ross A. Webber, *Time and Management* (New York: Van Nostrand Reinhold, 1972), and Robert C. Solomon and Kristine Hanson, *It's Good Business* (New York: Atheneum Publishers, 1985).

6. Warren G. Bennis, *The Unconscious Conspiracy: Why Leaders Can't Lead* (New York: American Management Associations, 1976), 28.

7. Henry Mintzberg, *The Nature of Managerial Work* (New York: Harper and Row, 1973). See the study completed a decade later by Lance C. Kurke and Howard E. Aldrich, "Mintzberg Was Right: A Replication and Extension of the Nature of Managerial Work," *Management Science* 29 (August 1983): 975–84.

8. Robert Stein, *Media Power* (Boston: Houghton Mifflin, 1972), 260. An equally hard-hitting critique is the book by Tom Goldstein, *The News at Any Cost: How Journalists Compromise Their Ethics to Shape the News* (New York: Simon and Schuster, 1985).

9. Ann Crittenden, "The Age of 'Me-First' Management," *New York Times*, August 19, 1984, business section. See also *Time*, June 10, 1985, 56.

10. Peter Baida, "M.B.A.," *American Scholar* 54 (Winter 1984–85): 24.

11. Charles T. Munger, vice chairman of Berkshire Hathaway Inc., Omaha, in testimony May 1984 before a congressional subcommittee investigating corporate takeovers.

12. Irving S. Shapiro (with Carl B. Kaufmann), *America's Third Revolution: Public Interest and the Private Role* (New York: Harper and Row, 1984), 6, 10.

13. "The Chemistry of Charisma," *Science Digest* 91 (October 1983): 77.

14. See Howard Gardner, *Frames of Mind: The Theory of Multiple Intelligences* (New York: Basic Books, 1983).

15. Richard Boyatzis, *The Competent Manager* (New York: Wiley-Interscience, 1982). A good summary of this material may be found in Daniel Goleman, "Successful Executives Rely on Own Kind of Intelligence," *New York Times*, July 31, 1984.

16. G.C. Wigglesworth, "The Training Whirl (and How to Keep It from Sucking You Under)," *Training* (May 1984): 74. See also M. Black, "Irrationality at the Top," *Science Digest* 92 (September 1984): 14.

17. Quoted in Graham Hough, *The Romantic Poets* (New York: W.W. Norton, 1964), 170. See also James L. McKenney and Peter G.W. Keen, "How Managers' Minds Work," *Harvard Business Review on Human Relations* (New York: Harper and Row, 1979), Chap. 3.

18. Jacob Burckhardt, *Force and Freedom: Reflections on History* (New York: Panthcon Books, 1943), 339–42.

19. Diane Rothbard Margolis, *The Managers: Corporate Life in America* (New York: William Morrow, 1979), 143.

20. *Washington Post Weekly Review*, September 9, 1985.

21. James Jenks and John Kelly, "When a Manager Is Duty-Bound Not to Pass the Buck," *Wall Street Journal*, July 1, 1985. See the book by Jenks and Kelly, *Don't Do, Delegate!* (New York: Franklin Watts, 1985).

22. Stuart Taylor, Jr., "Ethics and the Law: A Case History," *New York Times Magazine*, January 9, 1983. See also J. Blackman's comment in the *Philadelphia Inquirer*, January 16, 1983.
23. *Philadelphia Inquirer*, August 7, 1984, pp. 1A, 12A.
24. *Summa Theologica*, Part 1 of Part 2, question 19, article 9.
25. F. O'Keefe, Jr., and Marc H. Shapiro, "Personal Criminal Liability Under the Federal Food, Drug and Cosmetic Act: The Dotterweich Doctrine," *Food-Drug-Cosmetic Law Journal* 30 (January 1975): 5–78.
26. Alan N. Salpeter and Richard A. Salomon, "Discovery Rule Changes End Open Season on CEOs," *National Law Journal* (May 13, 1975): 15, 17.
27. Francis Bowes Sayre, "Criminal Responsibility for Acts of Another," *Harvard Law Review* 43 (March 1980): 689–723.
28. Peter F. Drucker, "The New Meaning of Corporate Social Responsibility," *California Management Review*, 26 (Winter 1984): pp. 53–63.

CHAPTER 2: THE NATURE AND POWER OF THE CULTURE

1. Octavio Paz, "Mexico and the United States: Ideology and Reality," *Time*, December 20, 1982, 42. The classic analysis of Mexico in terms understandable to foreigners is Paz's book *The Labyrinth of Solitude* (New York: Grove Press, 1962).
2. James Gruenbaum, "Women in Politics," *The Political Science Quarterly* 34 (1981): 104–20.
3. Harvey Weitz, "Ergonomics Experts as Witnesses," *National Law Journal* (August 29, 1983): 15–17.
4. Lawrence M. Friedman, *Total Justice* (New York: Russell Sage Foundation, 1965), 38–43.
5. William Broyles, Jr., "Promise of America," *U.S. News and World Report*, July 7, 1986, 25–26.
6. British Institute of Management, *Management in a Changing Society* (London: British Institute of Management, 1974), Foreword.
7. Richard Ruch and Ronald Goodman, *Image at the Top* (New York: Free Press/Macmillan, 1983). Quoted in "The Best of Business," *Harvard Business Review* 5 (Fall 1983): 44.
8. P.L. Bernstein and T.H. Silbert, "Are Economic Forecasters Worth Listening To?" *Harvard Business Review* 62 (September–October 1984): 32–40.
9. Michael J. O'Connor, "Why Do Some Organizations Do Better and Last Longer Than Others?" *Arthur Anderson Company Review* (Spring 1984): 14.

10. Miriam Beard, *A History of the Businessman* (New York: Macmillan, 1983), 716.

11. Edmund Burke, *Reflections on the Revolution in France* (New York: Penguin Books, 1976), 194–95.

12. John Nef, *The Conquest of the Material World* (Chicago: University of Chicago Press, 1964), 363.

13. J.G.A. Pocock, *Virtue, Commerce, and History: Essays on Political Thought and History, Chiefly in the Eighteenth Century* (New York: Cambridge University Press, 1985), 198.

14. Elvin Hatch, *Culture and Morality* (New York: Columbia University Press, 1983). See also his *Theories of Man and Culture* (New York: Columbia University Press, 1973). Others, notably Jose Ortega y Gasset, saw twentieth-century totalitarian governments using technology to subdue the freedoms that in the nineteenth-century made civilization possible. *The Revolt of the Masses*, trans. Anthony Kerrigone, ed. Kenneth Moore (Notre Dame, Ind.: Notre Dame University Press, 1985).

15. Alexis de Tocqueville, *Democracy in America*, ed. J.P. Mayer (Garden City, N.Y.: Doubleday/Anchor, 1969), Chap. 4.

16. Franz Boas, *Race, Language and Culture* (Chicago: University of Chicago Press, 1982).

17. William C. Frederick, *Embedded Values: Prelude to Ethical Analysis*, Working Paper Series (Pittsburgh: University of Pittsburgh, Graduate School of Business, 1982). See also Neal W. Chamberlain, *Enterprise and Environment* (New York: McGraw-Hill, 1968), esp. Chap. 4; Peter Berger, *The Sacred Canopy: Elements of a Sociological Theory of Religion* (Garden City, N.Y.: Doubleday, 1967), Chap. 5; George W. England, *A Manager and His Values* (Cambridge: Ballinger, 1975); and Richard Means, *The Ethical Imperative: The Crisis in American Values* (Garden City, N.Y.: Doubleday, 1969), Chap. 5.

18. Edgar H. Schein, *Organizational Cultures and Leadership* (San Francisco: Jossey-Bass, 1985), 1–22.

19. Annette Baier, "Dialogue on Applied Ethics," *Humanities* 2 (April 1981): 15.

20. Walter J. Ong, *Orality and Literacy: The Technologising of the Word* (London/New York: Methuen, 1982).

21. *The Connecticut Mutual Life Report on American Values in the 1980s* (Hartford: Connecticut Mutual Life Insurance Co., 1981), 17.

22. Warren I. Susman, *Culture as History: The Transformation of American Society in the Twentieth Century* (New York: Pantheon Books, 1984).

23. Robert A. Nisbet, *Twilight of Authority* (New York: Oxford University Press, 1975).

24. See Anant R. Negandhi, "Management of the Third World," *Asia Pacific Journal of Management* (September 1983): 15–19.

25. Geert Hofstede, *Culture's Consequences: International Differences in Work-Related Values* (Beverly Hills, Calif.: Sage Publications, 1980).

26. John W. Hunt, "Applying American Behavioral Science Abroad," and Leonard Goodstein, "American Business Values and Cultural Imperialism," *Organizational Dynamics* (Summer 1981): 55–62 and 49–54, respectively.

27. Alonzo L. McDonald, "Of the Floating Factories and Mating Dinosaurs," *Harvard Business Review* 64 (November–December 1986): 82–86.

28. Shortly after this essay was completed, the author read—and highly recommends—the article by Steven Prokesch, "Remaking the American CEO," *New York Times*, January 25, 1987, pp. 1F, 8F.

29. David A. Heenan, *The Re-United States of America* (Reading, Mass.: Addison-Wesley, 1983). See also the studies by Alan Dawley, *Class and Community* (Cambridge: Harvard University Press, 1976); Leon Fink, *Workingmen's Democracy* (Urbana: University of Illinois Press, 1983); and Lawrence Goodwyn, *Democratic Promise* (New York: Oxford University Press, 1976).

30. Richard John Neuhaus, "Religion, Secularism and the American Experiment," *This World* (Spring/Summer 1985): 36.

31. Alexis de Tocqueville, *Democracy in America*, and John Dos Passos, *U.S.A.* (Boston: Houghton Mifflin, 1963).

32. Peter K. Francese, "Demographic Trends Reshaping Retirement Security" (paper delivered to the 1985 Economic Security Symposium sponsored by the Pension Research Council of the Wharton School and the Boettner Research Institute of the American College, Bryn Mawr, Pennsylvania, November 6, 1985). Estimates of zero population growth may be altered by illegal immigrations, according to Nathan Glazer, ed., *Clamor at the Gates* (San Francisco: Institute for Contemporary Studies Press, 1980). Relevant is the study by John Naisbitt, *Megatrends: Ten New Directions Transforming Our Lives* (New York: Warner Books, 1982).

33. Quoted by Marvin D. Jensen, "Access to Higher Education Through Distant-Learning," *Contemporary Education* 51 (Winter 1980): 71.

34. Oscar Handlin, ed., *American Immigration Collection*, 42 volumes (Salem, N.H.: Ayer Publishers, 1969).

35. Wilbur J. Cash, *The Mind of the South* (New York: Alfred A. Knopf, 1941), x. Another scholar argued forcefully that three themes have directed the course not only of southern regional development but also of southern urbanization: the predominance of staple crop agriculture,

a biracial society, and subservience to the national economy. The cumulative effect of these forces has been that farmers and their values have remained at the center of southern civilization, and that the region's urbanization and prosperity have consequently suffered. David R. Goldfield, *Urban Growth in the Age of Sectionalism* (Baton Rouge: Louisiana State University Press, 1977). See also his *Cotton Fields and Skyscrapers* (Baton Rouge: Louisiana State University Press, 1982).

36. "Individualism Comes of Age," *Fortune* 43 (February 1951): 176. The key essays were edited by Russell Davenport in a book called *USA: The Permanent Revolution* (Westport, Conn.: Greenwood Press, 1980).

37. Steven Lukes, "Types of Individualism," in *Dictionary of the History of Ideas*, vol. 2 (New York: Charles Scribner's Sons, 1973), 594–604. American writers have also expressed disdain for individualism, and the study by Robert Bellah and his associates depicts individualism in terms not too far removed from those of de Maistre and Durkheim. Robert Bellah et al., *Habits of the Heart: Individualism and Commitment in American Life* (Berkeley: University of California Press, 1985).

38. Stephen Whicher, ed., *Selections from Ralph Waldo Emerson* (Boston: Houghton Mifflin, 1957), 139. Helpful are John William Ward's essays "Individualism Today," *Yale Review*, 49 (spring 1960): 380–92, and "The Ideal of Individualism and the Reality of Organization," in *The Business Establishment*, ed. Earl F. Cheit (New York: John Wiley and Sons, 1964), Chap. 2. See also Francis L.K. Hsu, *Rugged Individualism Reconsidered: Essays in Psychological Anthropology* (Knoxville: University of Tennessee Press, 1983).

39. "American Movies and the American Character," *Center Magazine*, 15 (May/June 1982): 47–56.

40. Georg Wilhelm Friedrich Hegel, *Philosophy of History* (New York: John Wiley, 1944). See the excellent analysis by L.S. Stepelevich, "The Dialectic of Value Change," in *Dynamics of Value Change: Proceedings of the Eleventh Conference on Value Inquiry*, ed. Ervin Laszlo and James B. Wilbur (Geneseo, N.Y.: State University of New York at Geneseo, 1978), 77–90.

41. Quoted by Katharine Byrne, "George Orwell and the American Character," *Commonweal*, April 12, 1974, 135.

42. Raymond Sokolor, "Junket of the Year: Les Intellos," *Wall Street Journal*, February 15, 1983; and Lori Granger, "Television a la American? Non! Non!" *Advertising Age* (December 20, 1982): M-19. When Lang visited America in November 1984, he said he had made a mistake in his 1982 speech by terming American culture's influence

on France *imperialism*; it also had a "positive" influence. *New York Times*, November 16, 1984, p. C-26.

43. Justin Kaplan, *Walt Whitman: A Life* (New York: Simon and Schuster, 1980).

44. Arthur M. Schlesinger, Jr., *The Cycles of American History* (New York: Houghton Mifflin, 1986). See esp. the chapter "Foreign Policy and the American Character."

45. *San Jose Mercury News*, January 23, 1985.

46. John P. Diggins, *The Lost Soul of American Politics: Virtue, Self-Interest, and the Foundations of Liberalism* (New York: Basic Books, 1984). Diggins challenged the view of the influential historian J.G.A. Pocock, who argued that American thought emerged from a renaissance type of "civic humanism" in which virtue always conquers vice. *The Machievellian Moment: Florentine Political Thought and the Atlantic Republican Tradition* (Princeton, N.J.: Princeton University Press, 1975).

47. Frank Rossi, "Ugly Past," *The Philadelphia Inquirer*, May 18, 1984.

48. *Washington Post National Weekly Edition*, June 4, 1984, p. 37. A well-written defense of reasons to maintain a high optimism in America is Ben J. Wattenberg, *The Good News Is the Bad News Is Wrong* (New York: Simon and Schuster, 1985), especially Part I. Part III, incidentally, is less valuable because its data base and its generalizations are open to serious challenge.

49. Seymour Martin Lipset, "Feeling Better: Measuring the Nation's Confidence," *Public Opinion* 8 (April–May 1985): 6–9.

50. James Bryce, *The American Commonwealth* (New York: Putnam, 1959).

51. Robert N. Bellah et al., *Habits of the Heart: Individualism and Commitment in American Life* (Berkeley: University of California Press, 1985).

52. John Stuart Mill, *Utilitarianism* (Indianapolis, Ind.: Bobbs-Merrill, 1971).

53. John F. Wilson, *Public Religion in American Culture* (Philadelphia: Temple University Press, 1979). See also George Marsden, ed., *Evangelicalism and Modern America* (Grand Rapids, Mich.: Eerdmanns, 1985).

54. Richard John Neuhaus, *The Naked Public Square: Religion and Democracy in America* (Grand Rapids, Mich.: Eerdmans, 1984).

55. Harvey C. Mansfield, Jr., "Hobbes and the Science of Indirect Government," *American Political Science Review* 65 (1971): 97–110.

56. From the classical age of Athens, democracy was viewed as a door to mob rule; it was Jean-Jacques Rousseau who transformed it from a dirty word to a virtuous ideal. James Miller, *Rousseau: Dreamer of Democracy* (New Haven: Yale University Press, 1984).

57. Ellis Sandoz, "Power and Spirit in the Founding Fathers," *This World* (Fall 1984): 72.

58. Morris Janowitz, *The Reconstruction of Patriotism* (Chicago: University of Chicago Press, 1983).

59. Richard H. Viola, *Organizations in a Changing Society: Administration and Human Values* (Philadelphia: W.B. Saunders, 1977), 131.

60. Marvin Minsky, ed., *Robotics* (New York: Anchor/Doubleday, 1984). See also Harley Shaiken, *Work Transformed: Automation and Labor in the Computer Age* (New York: Holt, Rinehart and Winston, 1985).

61. Relevant are the articles by Fariborz Damanpour and William M. Evan, "Organizational Innovation and Performance: The Problem of Organizational Lag," *Administrative Science Quarterly* 29 (1984): 392–409, and Linsu Kim, "Organizational Innovation and Structure," *Journal of Business Research* 8 (1980): 225–45.

62. Paul C. Gianelli, "The Admissability of Novel Scientific Evidence: *Frye* v. *United States*, a Half-Century Later," *Columbia Law Review* 80 (1980): 1200–1250.

63. Jacques Ellul, *The Technological System* (New York: Continuum Publishers, 1980), 44–45.

64. Norman Lear, "Short-Term Thinking and the Decline of Values," *New Oxford Review* 53 (September 1986): 13–18.

65. Adam Smith, *Inquiry into the Nature and Causes of the Wealth of Nations* (New York: Modern Library, 1937), 114.

66. The chart was developed by Professor James Kuhn of the Columbia Graduate School of Business.

CHAPTER 3: IDEOLOGIES, IDEOLOGUES, AND ORGANIZATIONS

1. Karl Mannheim, *Ideology and Utopia*, trans. Louis Worth and Edward Shils (New York: Harcourt, Brace, 1936). Mannheim's work is still considered a classic on the meanings, nuances, evolution, and power of the term.

2. Paul F. Lazarsfeld, William H. Sewell, and Harold L. Wilensky, eds., *The Uses of Sociology* (New York: Basic Books, 1967), 63. These careful scholars were quite skeptical of ideology's analytical usefulness. For a somewhat different view, see Thomas Sowell, *A Conflict of Visions: Ideological Origins of Political Struggle* (New York: William Morrow, 1987).

3. Gerald Cavanaugh, *American Business Values in Transition* (Englewood Cliffs, N.J.: Prentice Hall, 1976), 1, 13.

4. Alpheus Mason, *Brandeis and the Modern State* (Princeton: Princeton University press, 1933), 30.

5. Clarence C. Walton, ed., *The Ethics of Corporate Conduct* (Englewood Cliffs, N.J.: Prentice Hall, 1977), 17.

6. Peter Navarro, *The Policy Game: How Special Interests and Ideologies Are Stealing America* (New York: John Wiley and Son, 1984), esp. Chap. 7, "The Logic of Ideology."

7. See Murray J. Edelman, *Political Language: Words That Succeed and Politics That Fail* (New York: Academic Press, 1977), and Roger Harrison, "Understanding Your Organization's Character," *Harvard Business Review* 50 (May–June 1972): 119–28, for comments that bear on this point.

8. George Cabot Lodge, "Managerial Implications of Ideological Change," in *The Ethics of Corporate Conduct*, ed. Clarence C. Walton (Englewood Cliffs, N.J.: Prentice Hall, 1977), Chap. 2.

9. Neil McKendrick, John Brewer, and J.H. Plumb, *The Birth of a Consumer Society: The Commercialization of 18th Century England* (Bloomington: University of Indiana Press, 1982).

10. Will Morrisey, "Culture in the Commercial Republic," *Book Forum* 6 (Spring 1982): 118.

11. Francis X. Sutton et al., *The American Business Creed* (Cambridge: Harvard University Press, 1956). The new pattern is outlined by George Cabot Lodge, *The New American Ideology* (New York: New York University Press, 1986).

12. Adolf Berle and Gardiner Means, *The Modern Corporation and Private Property* (New York: Macmillan, 1932). See also Kenneth Boulding, *The Organizational Revolution* (Chicago: Quadrangle Books, 1968).

13. Rowland Berthoff, *An Unsettled People: Social Order and Disorder in American History* (New York: Harper and Row, 1971).

14. William G. Scott, "Organicism: The Moral Anesthetic of Management," *Academy of Management Review* 4 (January 1979): 21. See also Daniel Bell's brilliant insights in *The Cultural Contraditions of Capitalism* (New York: Basic Books, 1976), esp. Chaps. 1, 4, and 5.

15. Ralph Dahrendorf, "The Intellectual and Society: The Social Function of the 'Fool' in the Twentieth Century," in *On Intellectuals: Theoretical Studies, Case Histories* ed. Philip Rief (Garden City, N.Y.: Doubleday, 1969). See also Paul A. Bore, *Intellectuals in Power* (New York: Columbia University Press, 1986), and Aleksander Gella, ed., *The Intelligentsia and the Intellectuals: Theory, Method and Case Study* (Beverly Hills, Calif.: Sage Publications, 1976). Such intellectuals often cluster at key institutions—universities like Harvard and Stanford, newspapers like the *New York Times* and the *Washington Post*, foundations like the Ford Foundation, and think tanks like the Council for Foreign Relations and Brookings. See Leonard Silk and Mark Silk, *The American Establishment* (New York: Basic Books, 1980). These institutions are

said to control America, but a contrary theme (that business conglomerates control institutions) has been made by David Halberstram, *The Powers That Be* (New York: Vintage Books, 1979).

16. A selective use of statistics is evident when we are told that in 1977 the U.S. military spent $46.00 for every $100.00 of new producers' fixed capital formation. The comparable figure for Japan was $3.70, and for West Germany, $18.90. Yet Russia, not the two nations cited, provides the relevant comparison. As an example, see Seymour Melman, *Profits Without Production* (New York: Alfred A. Knopf, 1983).

17. Robert R. Reich, "The Next American Frontier," *Atlantic Monthly*, 251 (March 1983): 43–58. See also Mancur Olson, *The Rise and Fall of Nations: Economic Growth, Stagflation, and Social Rigidities* (New Haven: Yale University Press, 1982), and Simon Ramo, "The U.S. Technology: A New Political Issue," in *The Economy and the President: 1980 and Beyond*, ed. Walter E. Hoadley (Englewood Cliffs, N.J.: Prentice Hall, 1980), 156–76.

18. Lester Thurow, "Revitalizing American Industry: Managing in a Competitive World Economy," *California Management Review* 27 (Fall 1984): 15.

19. Wassily Leontief, "The Choice of Technology," *Scientific American* (June 1985): 37–45.

20. *Wall Street Journal*, September 5, 1985.

21. Jack Givens, "Automobile Industry, Heal Thyself," *Advertising Age*, September 29, 1980, 5, 32–33. Mr. Givens is a Chrysler executive. See Philip Mattera, *Off the Banks: The Rise of the Underground Economy* (New York: St. Martin's Press, 1985).

22. Felix Rohaytn, "American Roulette," *New York Review of Books* (March 29, 1984): 11–16.

23. Robert Wiebe, *The Search for Order, 1877–1920* (New York: Hill and Wang, 1967).

24. Alan Trachtenberg, *The Incorporation of America: Culture and Society in the Gilded Age* (New York: Hill and Wang, 1982), 231.

25. James Oliver Robertson, *America's Business* (New York: Hill and Wang, 1985).

26. Edward S. Herman, *Corporate Control, Corporate Power* (Cambridge: Cambridge University Press, 1981), 301.

27. Michael Harrington, "The Virtues and Limitations of Liberal Democracy," *Center Magazine* 14 (March-April 1981): 52. See his book, *Decades of Decision* (New York: Simon and Schuster, 1980), for a detailed development of his position.

28. Robert A. Dahl, *Dilemmas of Pluralist Democracy: Autonomy vs. Control* (New Haven: Yale University Press, 1982), 194.

29. J.G.A. Pocock, *The Machiavellian Moment: Florentine Political Thought in the Atlantic Republican Tradition* (Princeton: Princeton University Press, 1975), 69–70.

30. Robert A. Brady, *Business as a System of Power* (New York: Columbia University Press, 1943). The criticisms from the left have been gathered and expressed cogently by Douglas F. Dowd in *The Twisted Dream: Capitalist Development in the United States Since 1776* (Cambridge: Winthrop Publishers, 1974).

31. Erich Fromm, *Marx's Concept of Man* (New York: Frederick Ungar, 1961), 93–100. For a balanced and sophisticated treatment of socialism's strengths and weaknesses, the reader will find very helpful Robert L. Heilbroner, *Marxism: For and Against* (New York: W.W. Norton, 1980). See also Robert Paul Wolff, *Understanding Marx: A Reconstruction and Critique of Capital* (Princeton: Princeton University Press, 1985).

32. Karl Polanyi, *The Great Transformation* (Boston: Beacon Press, 1957), 145, 148.

33. Joseph Schumpeter, *Capitalism, Socialism and Democracy* (New York: Harper and Row, 1942), 139–42. For fine summaries of Schumpeter's views, see Herbert Kisch, "Joseph Alois Schumpeter," *Journal of Economic Issues* 13 (March 1979): 141–57, and Martin Kessler, "The Synthetic Vision of Joseph Schumpeter," *Review of Politics* 23 (July 1961): 334–55.

34. Gerald Cavanaugh, "Free Enterprise Values," *Review of Social Economy* 40 (December 1982): 330–39. Barry Schwartz has extended the critique of self-interest philosophers by pointing out how a basic fallacy gains ideological respectability when certain "schools of thought" converge—as they do in neoclassical economics, evolutionary biology (Wilson), and psychological behaviorism (Skinner). *The Battle for Human Nature* (New York: W.W. Norton, 1986).

35. From Chesteron's essay "The Well on the Shallows." See Alzini Stone Dale, *The Outline of Sanity: A Biography of G.K. Chesterton* (Grand Rapids, Mich.: Eerdmans, 1982). Two contemporary authors have argued from a different perspective to a parallel conclusion, namely, that once the burden of capitalism is lifted from a person's shoulders, human nature will change for the better. Samuel Bowles and Herbert Ginkis, *Democracy and Capitalism: Property, Community and the Contradictions of Modern Social Thought* (New York: Basic Books, 1986).

36. Rudolf J. Siebert, "Hans Kung: Toward a Negative Theology?" *Ecumenist* 17 (January–February 1979): 17. R.H. Tawney had put it more bluntly when he argued that capitalism was not so much un-Christian as anti-Christian. *The Acquisitive Society* (New York: Macmillan, 1920). For an excellent review of Tawney, see Ross Terrill,

R.H. Tawney and His Times (Cambridge: Harvard University Press, 1973).

37.   Robert Heilbroner, *The Nature and Logic of Capitalism* (New York: W.W. Norton, 1985).

38.   Dennis P. McCann, "Political Ideologies and Practical Theology: Is There a Difference?" *Union Seminary Quarterly Review* 36 (Summer 1981), 243–57. At the end of his perceptive analysis, McCann concludes that, while often blurred, the differences are real.

39.   National Conference of Catholic Bishops, "First Draft: Catholic Social Teaching and the U.S. Economy," *Origins* 14 (November 15, 1984):. See also Donal Dorr, *Options for the Poor: A Hundred Years of Vatican Social Teaching* (New York: Orbis, 1983). The prelates soon recognized the enormity of the problem they had tackled. Archbishop Rembert Weakland, chairman of the task force, confessed that, as the committee began hearing from different economic experts, he found himself nearly in agreement with contradictory views: "We went in one day, in six hours, from what one would call extreme right neoclassicism to a socialist position! You can see why, at the end of that day, we sat there and kind of shook our heads and said, 'Lord, what did they get us into here?' " It should be noted that their second draft (October 7, 1985) was modified to take into account not only the needs of the poor but of the lower middle class. And individuals who resist church intervention in economic affairs will find a useful corrective in the essays by two Jesuits, William Byron and Avery Dulles, "The Responsibility of National Conferences of Bishops to Address Issues in Today's Church," in *Theological Awareness and Temporal Responsibilities* (Washington, D.C.: Catholic University of America, 1985), chaps. 1 and 2. See also the series of short articles in *Business and Society Review* (Summer 1985): 4–44. Finally, for a balanced view of church attitudes toward capitalism, see the superb essay by Thomas M. Gannon, "Religion and the Economy: Alliance or Conflict?" *This World* 7 (Winter 1984): 66–82.

40.   Thomas Donaldson, "What Justice Demands," *Review of Social Economy* 40 (December 1982): 301–10.

41.   Brent Bozell, "Capitalist Self-Seeking, or Christian Self-Denial?" *Oxford Review* (October 1986): 18–23. One of the more interesting critiques of the Catholic Church's position has come from Franciscan theologian Joseph Chinnici, who argues that the Church itself has swallowed the business ideology in many of its most critical elements. *Spiritual Capitalism and the Culture of American Catholicism* (unpublished paper, Franciscan School of Theology, Berkeley, California, 1985).

42.   Clarence C. Walton, "Commentary," in *Free Enterprise*, ed. Bert Elwert (Chicago: College of Business Administration, University of Illinois

at Chicago, 1983), 73–81. The current catch-22 scenario sharply contrasts with nineteenth-century views in which "religious faith, national tradition and a moderate nationalism provided validity and certainty to [America's] ideals." Edward Purcell, *The Crisis of Democratic Theory* (Lexington: University of Kentucky Press, 1973), 5.

43. Peter Berger, "Ethics and the New Class," *Worldview* 12 (April 1978): 6–11.

44. Irving Kristol, "The Adversary Culture of Intellectuals," *Encounter* 53 (October 1979): 5–14. See also M. Bruce Johnson, ed., *The Attack on Corporate America* (New York: McGraw-Hill, 1978).

45. George Gilder, *The Spirit of Enterprise* (New York: Simon and Schuster, 1984).

46. Thomas M. Gannon, "Religion and the Economy: Alliance or Conflict?" *This World* 7 (Winter 1984): 68.

47. Milton Friedman, *Capitalism and Freedom* (Chicago: University of Chicago Press, 1962), 15.

48. John Fayerweather, "Nineteenth Century Ideology and Twentieth Century Reality," in *World Business: Promise and Problems*, ed. Courtney C. Brown (New York: Macmillan, 1970), 85–98.

49. Alfred C. Neal, *Business Power in Public Policy* (New York: Praeger, 1981), 157.

50. Edwin M. Epstein, *The Corporation and American Politics* (Englewood Cliffs, N.J.: Prentice Hall, 1969), 189.

51. On this point of government-corporate interlocks, see William H. Becker, *The Dynamics of Business-Government Relations: Industry and Exports, 1893–1921* (Chicago: University of Chicago Press, 1982), and Theodore P. Kovaleff, *Business and Government During the Eisenhower Administration: A Study of the Anti-Trust Policy of the Anti-Trust Division of the Justice Department* (Athens, Ohio: Ohio University Press, 1980).

52. *Wall Street Journal*, September 9, 1983.

53. *Wall Street Journal*, August 4, 1983.

54. Max Green, "Labor's Bad Bargain: The AFL-CIO Veers Left," *Policy Review* (Fall 1984): 20–24. After the Mondale defeat, the unions launched an aggressive "buy American" advertising campaign to combat job losses due to foreign competition. Taking the lead was the United Food and Commercial Workers Union, whose 1.3 million members from grocery workers, retail clerks, insurance, financial and health care employees make it one of the largest AFL-CIO affiliates. Nell Henderson, "Mama Knows Best," *Washington Post National Weekly*, September 9, 1985, p. 20.

55. Even in foreign affairs, special interest groups have been active, and the power of the Israeli lobby has been remarked upon frequently. Robert Keyser said that Washington reporters and politicians "share

cynical understanding that Israel and its American friends constitute probably the single most effective lobbying force in the country; they take its victories for granted." *Washington Post National Weekly Edition*, June 11, 1984.

56. Don Gevirtz, *Business Plan for America* (New York: Putnam, 1984).

57. Irving Shapiro, *America's Third Revolution* (New York: Harper and Row, 1984).

58. Edwin M. Epstein, *PACs and the Modern Political Process* (paper presented to the conference sponsored by the Center for Law and Economic Studies, Columbia University School of Law, November 12–13, 1982). From a moral perspective, campaigns have two values: (1) as channels of communication on public issues and political candidates and (2) to alert voters who will have to live under rules promulgated by the victors. Unduly influencing the elective process is, consequently, immoral. Charles Beitz, "Political Finance in the United States: A Survey of Research," *Ethics* 95 (October 1984): 144. There has always been such concern about the power of the corporate purse that it is impossible to acknowledge the voluminous amount of literature. This author found helpful Jeffrey Pfeffer, *Power and Organizations* (Marshfield, Mass.: Pitman, 1981), Arthur S. Miller, *The Modern Corporate State: Private Governments and the American Constitution* (Westport, Conn.: Greenwood Press, 1976), and Edward S. Herman, *Corporate Control and Corporate Power* (Cambridge: Cambridge University Press, 1981). For excellent articles, see Edwin M. Epstein, "Dimensions of Corporate Power," *California Management Review* 16 (Winter 1973): 9–23; and Frank J. Sorauf, "Political Parties and Political Action Committees: Two Life Cycles," *Arizona Law Review* 22 (October 1980): 445–63. Finally, for a rather comprehensive perspective critical of PAC-like activities, see Jeffrey Berry, *The Interest Group Society* (Boston: Little, Brown, 1984).

59. *Wall Street Journal*, September 5, 1984.

60. *Wall Street Journal*, August 18, 1982.

61. Amaitai Etzioni, *Capital Corruption: The New Attack on American Democracy* (New York: Harcourt, Brace, Jovanovich, 1984).

62. A.S. Prakash Sethi and Nobuaki Namiki, *Public Perceptions of and Attitudes Toward Political Action Committees (PACs)* (Dallas: University of Texas at Dallas, School of Management, Center for Research and Business and Social Policy, Special Report, 1982), 7–8.

63. Clarence J. Brown, "The Servility of Business" in Robert Hessen, ed., *Does Big Business Rule America?* (Washington: Ethics and Public Policy Center, 1981), 50–54.

64. Gaston D. Rimlinger, "Capitalism and Human Rights," *Daedalus* 112 (Fall 1983): 51–52.

65. Norman Podhoretz, *The Bloody Crossroads: Where Literature and Politics Meet* (New York: Simon and Schuster, 1986). See esp. the essay "The Adversary Culture and the New Class."

66. Michael Novak, *Toward a Theology of the Corporation* (Washington: American Enterprise Institute for Public Policy Research, 1981). See also Michael Novak and John W. Cooper, eds., *The Corporation: A Theological Inquiry* (Washington: American Enterprise Institute for Public Research, 1981). Compare Novak's views to the opposing views of theologian Richard John Neuhaus in "Religion, Secularism and the American Experiment" and of George Marsden in "Secularism and the Public Square," *This World* 11 (Spring/Summer 1985): 36–62.

67. George F. Gilder, *Wealth and Poverty* (New York: Basic Books, 1980).

68. George Dennis O'Brien, "The Christian Assault on Capitalism," *Fortune*, December 8, 1986, 183. See O'Brien's book *God and the New Haven Railway: And Why Neither Is Doing Very Well* (Boston: Beacon Press, 1987).

69. André Delbecq, *Reflections* (Santa Clara, Calif.: School of Business, University of Santa Clara, 1980), 4, 7.

70. *Fortune*, December 26, 1983. Writing in *Forbes* magazine on April 23, 1984, Michael Cieply asks why religious people of many faiths were finding fault with business. The answer was suggested years ago in Karl Polanyi's thesis that the market system values all life only in terms of money. *The Great Transformation* (New York: Rinehart and Co., 1957).

71. *New York Times*, November 7, 1984. Also relevant are the observations of Douglas S. Sherwin, a businessman with over forty years of practical experience, in his article "The Ethical Roots of the Business System," *Harvard Business Review* 61 (November–December 1983): 183–92. Sherwin advanced the same view as Brown: the value of business's social good must be seen "in relation to that of the many other social goods recognized—equality, justice, health, and the quality of life" (p. 185).

72. George Cabot Lodge, "Managerial Implications of Ideological Changes," in Walton, *The Ethics of Corporate Conduct*, Chap. 2, 79–105.

73. The "choice" may be not a choice but a necessity if the poll reported in 1975 by the *Harvard Business Review* (November–December 1975) turns out to be correct: 1,844 executives in the upper ranks of American corporations indicated an overwhelming preference for the traditional ideology, but 73 percent thought that by 1985 the communitarian philosophy would prevail. Since answers had not come clearly by 1985, the ideological debates will continue, according to Herbert McClosky and John Zoller, *The American Ethos: Public Attitudes Toward Capitalism and Democracy* (Cambridge: Harvard University Press, 1984). These

authors noted that "in their formative years, capitalism and democracy were for the most part allied in the struggle to throw off the countless restrictions on human conduct that had grown up over centuries of feudalism and aristocratic rule. Yet . . . since the mid-19th century, events in both Europe and the United States have frequently pitted them against each other" (p. 161).

CHAPTER 4: FROM PERSON TO PRINCIPLE

1. Quoted in Garret L. Bergen and William V. Haney, *Organizational Relations and Management Action* (New York: McGraw-Hill, 1966), 3.
2. *California Management Review* 27 (Fall 1984): 157.
3. George Homans, *Social Behavior: Its Elementary Forms* (New York: Harcourt Brace and World, 1961).
4. Carl Madden, "Forces Which Influence Ethical Behavior," in *The Ethics of Corporate Conduct*, ed. Clarence C. Walton (Englewood Cliffs, N.J.: Prentice Hall, 1977), 33.
5. Sigmund Freud, *The Future of an Illusion* (London: Hogarth Press, 1928).
6. Vance Packard, *The Hidden Persuaders* (New York: D. McKay, 1957).
7. Kurt Lewin, "Frontiers in Group Dynamics: Concept, Method and Reality in Social Science," *Human Relations* 1 (1947): 5–41, and Edgar H. Schein, "Management Development as a Process of Influence," *Industrial Management Review* 2 (May 1961): 59–77.
8. Richard Bandler and John Grinder studied the unusual methods of Milton Erickson, a Phoenix psychiatrist who had developed a technique for hypnosis called indirect induction. Avoiding the usual dangling of watch fobs and the like, Erickson matched his tone of voice, breathing rate, eye movements, posture, and muscle tension to those of the subject. Richard Bandler and John Grinder, *Frogs into Princes* (Moab, Utah: Real People Press, 1979). See also Eric H. Marcus, "Neurolinguistic Programming," *Personnel Journal* 62 (December 1983): 972–78.
9. Paul Berg et al., "Potential Biohazards of Recombinant DNA Molecules," *Science* 185 (July 26, 1974): 303.
10. John Naisbitt, *Megatrends* (New York: Warner Books, 1982), 73.
11. The decision was a response to a patent application filed in 1972 by Ananda M. Chakrabarty, a General Electric microbiologist. "Court Rules, 5-4 US Patent Law Covers New Life," *Higher Education and National Affairs* 29 (June 20, 1980): 3.
12. How brain research has leaped forward comes through simple figures. From 1980 to 1983, the National Institute of Mental Health increased

its grants for basic research in the brain sciences by more than 150 percent—up to $30.5 million for the 1983 fiscal year. On the corporate front, Merck and Company has contributed $43.5 million for a brain research center.

13. "Is Free Will a Fraud?" *Science Digest* 91 (October 1983): 55. Dr. Restak, a specialist in forensic neurology, has elaborated this view in his books *The Brain: The Last Frontier* (Garden City, N.Y.: Doubleday, 1979) and *Pre-Meditated Man* (New York: Penguin Books, 1977).

14. Peter van Inwagen, *An Essay on Free Will* (Oxford: Clarendon Press, 1983).

15. Edward O. Wilson, *Sociobiology: The New Synthesis* (Cambridge: The Belknap Press of Harvard University Press, 1975) and *On Human Nature* (New York: Bantam Books, 1979).

16. This point has been carefully examined by Frank Elliott in "Biological Roots of Violence," *Proceedings of the American Philosophical Society* 127 (1983): 84–94. See also Janet Raloff, "Locks: A Key to Violence?" *Science News* 124 (August 20, 1985): 122–25, and "Biochemical Aggression: The Legal Dimensions," *Science News* 124 (September 10, 1983): 173. More comprehensive studies have come from Richard Dawkins, *The Selfish Gene* (New York: Oxford University Press, 1976); George Pugh, *The Biological Origins of Human Values* (New York: Basic Books, 1977), esp. pp. 397–400; and Eric Fromm, *The Anatomy of Human Destructiveness* (Greenwich, Conn.: Fawcett Publications, 1975).

17. B.F. Skinner, *The Behavior of Organisms* (New York: Appleton-Century, 1938). See also William Dowling, "Are Workers Pigeons?" *Across the Board* 15 (November 1978): 24–32.

18. C. Ray Gullett and Robert Reisen, "Behavior Modification: A Contingency Approach to Employee Performance," *Personnel Journal* 54 (April 1975): 206–11.

19. Fred Luthans and Robert Kreitner, *Organizational Behavior Modification* (Glenview, Ill.: Scott, Foresman, 1975), 26. See the earlier studies by Kurt Lewin, "Frontiers in Group Dynamics: Concept, Method, and Reality in Social Science," *Human Relations* 1 (Spring 1947): 5–41, and Edgar H. Schein, "Management Development as a Process of Influence," *Industrial Management Review* 2 (May 1961): 62–63.

20. Quoted in Dowling, "Are Workers Pigeons?" p. 30. See also Walter Nord, "Beyond the Teaching Machine: The Neglected Area of Operant Conditioning in the Theory and Practice of Management," *Organization Behavior and Human Performance* 4 (November 1969): 375–40.

21. David A. Nadler and Edward R. Lawler III, "Quality of Work Life: Perspectives and Directions," *Organizational Dynamics* 11 (Winter 1983): 25.

22. B.F. Skinner, *Beyond Freedom and Dignity* (New York: Alfred W. Knopf, 1972), esp. pp. 101–26 and 184–215.

23. "New Tool: Reinforcement for Good Work," *Psychology Today* (April 1972): 68–69.

24. Former British Prime Minister James Callaghan in Alan M. Webber, "James Callaghan: The Statesman as CEO," *Harvard Business Review* 64 (November–December 1986): 112.

25. Kenneth Boulding, *The Organizational Revolution* (Westport, Conn.: Greenwood Press, 1984).

26. Sheldon S. Wolin, "Max Weber: Legitimation, Method, and the Politics of Theory," *Political Theory* 9 (August 1981): 401–24.

27. *Egoism* has sometimes been confused with *emotivism* as defined by G.E. Moore in *Principia Ethica* (Cambridge: Cambridge University Press, 1903).

28. Gilbert Ryle, *The Concept of Mind* (London: Hutchinson, 1949), 81. Other examples of what this tautology meant were outlined by Sir John C. Eccles, "The Self-Conscious Mind and the Meaning and Mystery of Personal Existence," *Teachers College Record* 82 (Spring 1981): 403–26, and David B. Claus, *Toward the Soul: An Inquiry into the Meaning of Psyche Before Plato* (New Haven: Yale University Press, 1981).

29. Andrew Cuschieri, "Socio-Juridic Condition of the Individual in Roman Culture," *The Jurist* 43 (1983): 143. See the excellent surveys by Norman Bowie, "Rights" (unpublished essay, University of Delaware Center on Values, Newark, 1982), and E.A. Goerner, "Letter and Spirit: The Political Ethics of the Rule of Law vs. the Political Ethics of the Rule of the Virtuous," *Review of Politics* 45 (October 1983): 533–75. A more detailed treatment may be found in Carl Wellman, *A Theory of Rights: Persons Under Laws, Institutions, and Morals* (Totowa, N.J.: Rowman and Allanheld, 1985).

30. Fred M. Frohock, "Arithmetic vs. Morality: Liberalism and Collective Choice," *Syracuse Scholar* 6 (Spring 1985): 5–26.

31. A helpful summary of the uses each type of ethics has for business may be found in Kenneth Goodpaster's essay "The Concept of Corporate Social Responsibility" in *Just Business: New Introductory Essays in Business Ethics*, ed. Tom Regan (Philadelphia: Temple University Press, 1983), esp. pp. 295–98.

32. James R. Rest, "A Psychologist Looks at the Teaching of Ethics," *The Hastings Center Report* 12 (February 1982): 29–30. See also Nozick, *Philosophical Explanations*, 473–74 and 498–504. Beyond responsiveness is the further need for compassion, a point stressed by F.A. Jenner in his essay "Psychiatry, Biology and Morals" in *Morality as Biological Phenomenon*, ed. Stent.

33. Richard Delgado and Peter McAllen, "The Moralist as Expert Witness," *Boston University Law Review* 62 (July 1982): 869–926.

34. Charles Taylor, "The Diversity of Goods," in *Utilitarianism and Beyond*,

ed. Amartya Sen and Bernard Williams (New York: Cambridge University Press, 1982), 129.

35.   John Stuart Mill, *Utilitarianism* (Indianapolis: Bobbs-Merrill, 1971).

36.   David Lyons, *Forms and Limits of Utilitarianism* (Oxford: Clarendon Press, 1965), and "Rawls vs. Utilitarianism," *Journal of Philosophy* 69 (October 5, 1972): 535–45.

37.   Charles Fried, *Right and Wrong* (Cambridge: Harvard University Press, 1978), 2. For the master's own views, see Immanuel Kant, *The Metaphysics of Morals*, trans. Mary Gregor (New York: Harper and Row, 1964), 38–42.

38.   Nozick, *Philosophical Explanations*, 495–96.

39.   James Brommer, "The Foreign Corrupt Practices Act and the Dilemma of Applied Ethics," *Business and Professional Ethics* 4 (Fall 1985): 17–42.

40.   W.D. Ross, *The Right and the Good* (Oxford: Oxford University Press, 1930).

41.   A German theologian named Bruno Schuller suggested deonutility when he noted that the ethical norm applied in our dealings with others or to the environment should be viewed "only as a particular application of that moral universal norm: 'The greater good is to be preferred.' " "What Ethical Principles Are Universally Valid?" *Theology Digest* 19 (Spring 1971): 24. Implicit is the argument that the self-evident truths that support deontological reasoning are of such generality that specific actions require consideration of their moral consequences. While certain universal prohibitions may be defended on the basis of religion, they are less defensible on the basis of philosophy.

42.   A Catholic University of America philosopher emphasized the point when he wrote that natural law has more the "character of advice with respect to procedure than a set of conclusions. The advice amounts to this: Proceed with confidence that intelligence can determine in a general way what is good for man." Jude P. Dougherty, "The Determination of Moral Norms," *The Proceedings of the American Catholic Philosophical Society* 52 (Washington: The Catholic University of America, 1978), 42–43. See also Robert Sokolowski, *Moral Action: A Phenomenological Study* (Bloomington: University of Indiana Press, 1986).

43.   See the seminal article by Armen Alchian and Harold Demsetz, "Production Information Costs and Economic Organizations," *The American Economic Review* 62 (December 1972): 777–95. Barry Mitnick of the University of Pittsburgh has been identified as a major expositor of this theory. Of his many papers, this author found two most illuminating: "Agents in the Environment: Managing in Boundary Expanding Roles" (presented at the 1982 meeting of the Academy of Management in New York) and "Agency Problems in Political Insti-

tutions" (presented at the 1984 annual meeting of the Midwest Political Science Association in Chicago).

44. Barry Mitnick, "The Theory of Agency and Organizational Analysis" (paper presented at the 1986 annual meeting of the American Political Science Association, Washington D.C., August 29, 1986).

45. Chester Barnard's old classic, *The Functions of the Executive* (Cambridge: Harvard University Press, 1938), is in this mold.

46. Eric Moreen, "The Economics of Ethics: A New Perspective on Agency Theory" (unpublished article, University of Washington, Seattle, 1986).

47. Kenneth Arrow, "The Economics of Moral Hazard: Further Comment," *American Economic Review* 58 (June 1968): 538. See also Arrow's *The Limits of Organization* (New York: W.W. Norton, 1974), 26–27.

CHAPTER 5: EQUALITY AND JUSTICE

1. Letter from Abraham Lincoln to his friend James Speed, 1855.

2. John Rawls, *A Theory of Justice*, (Cambridge: Harvard University Press, 1972), 3.

3. Robert Nozick, *Chronicle of Higher Education* 32 (April 16, 1986): 8.

4. Remarks by Archbishop Rembert Weakland at a symposium sponsored by the Trinity Church Program on Ethics, New York City, May 30, 1983.

5. Wallace Matson, *"Justice*: A Funeral Oration," *Social Philosophy and Public Policy* 1 (Fall 1984): 113.

6. William Sloan Coffin, *Report of the Committee on Freedom of Expression at Yale* (New Haven: Yale University Press, January 8, 1975), 39.

7. Douglas Rae et al., *Equalities* (Cambridge: Harvard University Press, 1981), 1. See also John Schaar, "Some Ways of Thinking About Equality," *Journal of Politics* 26 (1964): 867–95 and Walter Weisskopf, "Image of Man in Economics," *Social Research* 40 (Autumn 1973): 547–63.

8. Alexis de Tocqueville, *Democracy in America*, trans. J.P. Mayer (New York: Doubleday/Anchor, 1969), 504–5. The same concern by contemporaries was made by Robert A. Nisbet in "The New Despotism," *Commentary* (June 1975): esp. pp. 32–35, and Irving Kristol in "The Poverty of Equality," *Wall Street Journal*, July 12, 1981.

9. Edmund Burke, *Works*, vol. 5 (London: Rivingtons, 1842), 180–81.

10. Lawrence Stone and Jeanne Stone, *An Open Elite: England 1540–1880* (New York: Oxford University Press, 1984).

11. Gregor McClennan, David Held, and Stuart Hall, eds., *Society in Contemporary Britain* (London: Basil Blackwell, 1984). See also David

Cooper's study, *Illusions of Equality* (London: Routledge and Kegan Paul, 1980). Cooper frankly admits preference, "without bashfulness, for the inegalitarian label" (p. 163).

12.   Quoted in Eric F. Goldman, "The Century of the American Dream," *Saturday Review* (December 13, 1975): 28.

13.   Lars Osberg, *Economic Inequality in the United States* (Armonk, N.Y.: M.E. Sharpe, 1984), 4. To illustrate: The "different technical measure of dispersion [the Gini index, the Theil measure, the coefficient of variation, or the Atkinson measure] will give differing degrees of emphasis to inequality among those at the top end of a distribution, among those in the middle of a distribution, or among those at the bottom of a distribution" (p. 257). One possible reason for American acceptance of income disparities is the many ways used to measure wealth. Emphasis on annual income, lifetime income, total wealth, and economic power led to very different concepts of economic inequality, and the very choice of the variables was value laden.

14.   David Brion, *Slavery and Human Progress* (New York: Oxford University Press, 1984).

15.   Douglas Rae, "Two Contradictory Ideas of Political Equality," *Ethics* 91 (April 1981): 451–56. See also George J. Stigler, *The Economist as Preacher and Other Essays* (Chicago: University of Chicago Press, 1982).

16.   Vincent Bary, *Moral Issues in Business* (Belmont, Calif.: Wadsworth, 1979); see his criticism of moral egoism, pp. 39–43. See Benjamin I. Page, *Utilitarian Arguments for Equality* (Madison: University of Wisconsin, Institute for Research on Poverty, 1979).

17.   Page, *Utilitarian Arguments*, Chap. 5.

18.   Rae, *Equalities*, 132–33. How equality has political, legal, social, and economic meanings was discussed by Thomas Nagel in *Moral Questions* (Cambridge: Cambridge University Press, 1979), esp. 106–10.

19.   Ronald Dworkin, *A Matter of Principle* (Cambridge: Harvard University Press, 1985), 201. For a detailed analysis of the connection between philosophical principles and legal reasoning, see Dworkin's *Law's Empire* (Cambridge: Harvard University/Belknap Press, 1985).

20.   Honora O'Neill, "Opportunities, Equalities, and Education," *Theory and Decision* 7 (1976): 275–95. See also John Schaar, "Equality of Opportunity and Beyond" in *Nomos*, vol. 9, ed. J. Roland Pennock and John W. Chapman (New York: Atherton Press, 1969), 227–31.

21.   Peter Weston, "The Empty Idea of Equality," *Harvard Business Review* 95 (1982): 583–96.

22.   Michael Walzer, *Spheres of Justice: The Defense of Pluralism and Equality* (New York: Basic Books, 1983), 252–54.

23.   Arthur Okun, *Equality and Efficiency: The Big Tradeoff* (Washington, D.C.: Brookings Institution, 1975), 66–69. See also Robert Kuttner,

The Haves and the Have Nots (Washington: American Council of Life Insurance, 1983).

24. Amy Guttman, *Liberal Equality* (New York: Cambridge University Press, 1980). Guttman believes that of the two assumptions that control policy decisions—(1) people are equal in pursuing their own self-interest and (2) people are equal in their ability to participate rationally in society's work—the latter is preferable, and this preference leads her to favor the welfare state.

25. George Bernard Shaw, *Man and Superman* (Harmondsworth, England: Penguin Books, 1972), 251.

26. Chester I. Barnard, *The Functions of the Executive* (Cambridge: Harvard University Press, 1938), 280.

27. Ernest Havermann, "On a Great Judge's Death: A Moving Memoir," *Life* (August 25, 1961): 39.

28. William Nelson, "The Very Idea of Pure Procedural Justice," *Ethics* 90 (July 1980): 502–11.

29. Felix Cohen, "Transcendental Nonsense and the Functional Approach," *Columbia Law Review* 35 (1935): 809.

30. Lawrence M. Friedman, *Total Justice* (New York: Russell Sage Foundation, 1985), Chap. 5. Plato's three meanings of justice, often taken as a base for today's discussions, have been analyzed by Otto Bird in "The Idea of Justice," *The Great Books, 1974* (Chicago: Encyclopaedia Brittanica, 1974), 166–209. The three are (1) justice as an instrument of the ruling class, (2) justice as a social contract, and (3) justice as giving others their due by virtue of their humanity.

31. R.H. Tawney, *Equality* (London: Unwin Books, 1964).

32. Jennifer L. Hochschild, *What's Fair?* (Cambridge: Harvard University Press, 1981), 336.

33. Rawls, *Theory of Justice*, p. 1. See also his essay "Social Unity and Primary Goods" in *Utilitarianism and Beyond*, ed. Amartya Sen and Bernard Williams (Cambridge: Cambridge University Press, 1982), Chap. 8.

34. Charles Fried, *Right and Wrong* (Cambridge: Harvard University Press, 1978), 160–63. Fried himself did not agree with Rawls's overall conclusions.

35. Martin Golding, "The Primacy of Welfare Rights," *Social Philosophy and Public Affairs* 1 (Autumn 1983): 119–27.

36. Robert Nozick, *Anarchy, State and Utopia* (New York: Basic Books, 1974).

37. Ebenezer Elliott, *The New Oxford Book of Light Verse* (Oxford: Oxford University Press, 1978), 51.

38. Rawls has been sharply criticized for his veil-of-ignorance theory on grounds that it is only *after* the veil is lifted that reflection on choice

is meaningful and that his insistence that our natures are antecedently given—literally fixed in concrete—is misplaced because it ignores what changes experience brings. Michael Sandel, *Liberalism and the Limits of Justice* (Cambridge: Cambridge University Press, 1982), 160–61, 179. Sandel makes this interesting point:

> *If all parties to the original position are similarly situated by virtue of the veil of ignorance, there should be no need for bargaining. The veil of ignorance allows the parties to come to a unanimous choice, but a choice between what? If the parties are similarly situated, is there truly a plurality of individuals involved, or are the participants so unified that the distinctness between their nature has collapsed? Now not only do we not know what the choices are chosen from, but we are not sure that more than one distinct individual is available to make the choice. (90–91, 101)*

39. Barry Clark and Herbert Gintis, "Rawlsian Justice and Economic Systems," *Philosophy and Public Affairs* 7 (Fall 1978): 324–25.

40. Walzer, *Spheres of Justice*, p. 17. See also Harry Eckstein, "On the 'Science' of the State," *Daedalus* 108 (Fall 1979): 1–20.

41. Dworkin, *A Matter of Principle*, p. 220.

42. Ronald Dworkin, *Taking Rights Seriously* (Cambridge: Harvard University Press, 1977), 285. Glimpses into the sharp differences which divorce Walzer and Dworkin may be found in the exchange reported in the *New York Review of Books* (July 21, 1983): 43–46. Perceptive comments have been written by Tom L. Beauchamp, "The Ethical Foundations of Economic Justice," and Thomas Donaldson, "What Justice Demands," in *Review of Social Economy* 40 (December 1982): 291–300 and 301–10, respectively. Their emphasis on distributive justice elicited sharp criticism from Arnold F. McKee, who said that "surely a just economy encompasses much more than distribution; if the intention is to view our participation in the economy entirely from the angle of what is received, this is misleading." Arnold F. McKee, "Beauchamp and Donaldson on Economic Justice," *Review of Social Economy* 42 (April 1984): 63. Very helpful is Lester Thurow's "Toward a Definition of Economics Justice," *Public Interest* 31 (Spring 1973): 56–80. Scott Gordon, in *Welfare, Justice and Freedom* (New York: Columbia University Press, 1981), mounted a vigorous attack on all theorists who make a monistic principle the all-encompassing way of philosophic analysis.

43. Bruce A. Ackerman, *Social Justice and the Liberal State* (New Haven: Yale University Press, 1982).

44. Michael Tooley, *Abortion and Infanticide* (New York: Oxford University Press, 1984).

45. Some philosophers prefer to use the word *claims*, rather than *rights* or

claims and of the machinery for their mutual accommodation . . . in cases of conflict." Nicholas Rescher, *Distributive Justice: A Constructive Critique of the Utilitarian Theory of Distribution* (Indianapolis, Ind.: Bobbs-Merrill, 1967), 82.

46. James P. Sterba, *The Demands of Justice* (Notre Dame, Ind.: University of Notre Dame Press, 1980), esp. Chap. 2. See also the perceptive essay by A.F. McKee, "From a Theory of Economic Justice to Its Implementation," *Review of Social Economy*, 79 (1979): 63–78.

47. The worker, for example, who gets less than he or she deserves while another worker performing the same task equally well is paid more is the victim of a double injustice: he or she is exploited and is paid less than another. A.D. Woozley, "Injustice," *American Philosophical Quarterly* 7 (1973): 115–16.

48. Very helpful are these three works: Norman E. Bowie, *Towards a New Theory of Distributive Justice* (Amherst: University of Massachusetts Press, 1971); Paul Freund, *On Law and Justice* (Cambridge: Harvard University Press, 1973); and Richard B. Brandt, *Social Justice* (Englewood Cliffs, N.J.: Prentice Hall, 1962).

49. This particular interpretation was defined as "personalism" by Emmanuel Mounier (1905–50), a French philosopher and a Resistance hero during World War II. In the United States, personalism meant entitlement, and no one can discuss entitlement in the American context without recalling Daniel Bell's seminal article, "The Revolution of Rising Entitlement," *Fortune* (April 1975): 170–85.

50. See M. Lutz and K. Lux, *The Challenge of Humanistic Economics* (Palo Alto, Calif.: Benjamin Cummings, 1979), and Robert Dahl, "On Removing Certain Impediments to Democracy in the United States," *Political Science Quarterly* 92 (Spring 1977): 7–8.

51. Smith, *Wealth of Nations*, vol. 2, p. 654.

52. Francis Edgeworth, *The Pure Theory of Taxation in Collected Works Relating to Political Economy*, vol. 1 (London: Macmillan, 1925), 11–14 For a contemporary view, readers should consult Philip Greene, *The Pursuit of Inequality* (New York: Pantheon Books, 1980).

53. Joel Feinberg, *Rights, Justice and the Bounds of Liberty: Essay in Social Philosophy* (Princeton: Princeton University Press, 1980), 265–85.

54. Josef Solterer, "The Social Economy: An Analogue of Piaget's Development," *Review of Social Economy* 40 (October 1982): 175.

55. The relationship of compassion to justice was explored by a Catholic University professor whose views, it was said, influenced President Roosevelt and his New Deal. John Ryan, *Distributive Justice* (New York: Macmillan, 1916). A superb exposition of the concept of proportional justice is found in William Galston, *Justice and the Human Good* (Chicago: University of Chicago Press, 1980).

56. Harry Eckstein, "Civic Inclusion: The Political Aspect," in *Working*

Papers on Authority Relations (Irvine, Calif.: University of California at Irvine, February 1983).

57.   Tom Peters and Nancy Austin, "MBWA (Managing by Walking Around)," *California Management Review* 28 (Fall 1985): 11. Extracted from their book *A Passion for Excellence* (New York: Random House, 1985).

CHAPTER 6: TRUTH AND FREEDOM

1.   *The Forbes Scrapbook of Thoughts on the Business of Life*, 228.

2.   For a superb survey of Russian philosophical thought (which, incidentally, emphasizes salvation over syllogism), see Frederick C. Copleston, *Philosophy in Russia: From Herzen to Lenin and Berdyaez* (Notre Dame, Ind.: University of Notre Dame Press, 1986).

3.   Quoted by Clifford Geertz in "Ideology as a Cultural System," in *Ideology and Discontent*, ed. David Apter (New York: Free Press, 1964), 65.

4.   Joel Feinberg, "Wollaston and His Critics," in *Rights, Justice and the Bounds of Liberty: Essays in Social Philosophy* (Princeton: Princeton University Press, 1980).

5.   David Rockefeller is chairman of Chase Manhattan. Quoted from "Is Dishonesty Good for Business?" *Business and Society Review* no. 30 (Summer 1979): 16.

6.   *Idem* Rockefeller, "Is Dishonesty Good for Business?"

7.   John Dewey, *Democracy and Education* (New York: Macmillan, 1916), 4.

8.   Albert Dondeyne, *Truth and Freedom: A Philosophical Study* (Pittsburgh: Duquesne University Press, 1964), 29.

9.   Gerhard O. Forde, "Bound to Be Freed: Luther on the Gospel of Human Freedom," *Bulletin* 57 (Winter 1977): 3.

10.   This idea of truth is a derivative of Alfred Tarski's definition of absolute truth, which Karl Popper analyzed in his essay "Truth, Rationality, and the Growth of Scientific Knowledge," in *Conjectures and Refutations* (New York: Harper and Row, 1968), 224–25.

11.   Daniel Coleman, *Vital Lies, Simple Truths* (New York: Simon and Schuster, 1985).

12.   Sissela Bok, *Lying: Moral Choice in Public and Private Life* (New York: Pantheon Books, 1978).

13.   Catherine Cookson, *The Lord and Mary Ann* (New York: Bantam Books, 1972), 151

14.   Extracted and modified from a true story reported by James Childress,

"Paternalism in Health Care," in *Medical Responsibility*, ed. Wade L. Robison and Michael S. Pritchard (Clifton, N.J.: Humana Press, 1979), 15–27.

15. Based on the story by the Pulitzer prize–winning journalist J.A. Livingston in the *Philadelphia Inquirer*, March 18, 1984, p. 16D.

16. By an interesting twist of fate, Burger was chief justice of the Supreme Court when, by a 9–0 vote, the lower court's ruling was reversed. But when the chief justice wrote a lengthy commentary denouncing those who would in any way tolerate lying by their clients, Justice Brennan wrote:

This court has no constitutional authority to establish rules of ethical conduct for lawyers practicing in the state courts. Nor does the court enjoy any statutory grant of jurisdiction over legal ethics. . . . The court's essay regarding what constitutes the correct response to criminal client's suggestion that he will perjure himself is pure discourse without force of law. Lawyers, judges, bar associations, students and others should understand that the problem has not now been "decided."

In a separate concurring opinion, Justice Harry Blackmun wrote: "Except in the rarest of cases, attorneys who adopt 'the role of the judge or jury to determine the facts,' pose a danger of depriving their clients of the zealous and loyal advocacy required by the Sixth Amendment." As for Professor Freedman: "I don't think any lawyer's actions will be changed by this decision," he said, "We'll just go back to the mythology" of lawyer's pretending not to know. Quoted in the *National Law Journal* (March 10, 1986): 37. See the editorial "Clients and Perjury," *Washington Post National Weekly Edition*, March 17, 1986, p. 27.

17. William Safire, "Lying in State," *New York Times*, May 1, 1980, p. 31.

18. Alan Vickery, "Breach of Confidence: An Emerging Tort," *Columbia Law Review* 82 (November 1983): 1424–68. Vickery quoted the law commission's proposed reformulation of an action in tort: "Obligation of confidence should come into existence where the recipient has expressly given an indication to the giver of the information to keep confidential that information . . . or where such an undertaking is . . . to be inferred from the relationship of the giver and the recipient or from the latter's conduct" (1457).

19. Quoted in Roderick M. Chisholm and Thomas D. Feehan, "The Intent to Deceive," *Journal of Philosophy* 74 (March 1977): 143–59.

20. Richard Posner, *The Economics of Justice* (Cambridge: Harvard University Press, 1983).

21. Robin West, "Authority, Autonomy and Choice: The Role of Consent in the Moral and Political Views of Franz Kafka and Richard Posner," *Harvard Law Review* 99 (December 1985): 384–428.

22. Lynne Belaief, *Freedom Beyond Tragedy* (Hamden, Conn.: Quinnipiac College, 1985), 16–23.

23. Times of crisis (depression and war) have forced Americans to institutionalize their freedom. Nicholas Murray Butler, *Why War?* (New York: Scribners, 1940), 138.

24. Norman F. Cantor, *The English: A History of Politics and Society to 1760* (New York: Simon and Schuster, 1967), 434.

25. Cecelia Kenyon, "The Declaration of Independence: Philosophy of Government in a Free Society," in *Aspects of American Liberty*, ed. George W. Corner (Philadelphia: American Philosophical Society, 1977), 114–15.

26. James MacGregor Burns, *The Vineyard of Liberty* (New York: Alfred Knopf, 1980).

27. Christopher Lasch, *The Culture of Narcissism: American Life in an Age of Diminishing Expectations* (New York: W.W Norton, 1981). Lasch was the first to document this trend.

28. David Riesman, "Egocentrism," *Encounter* (August-September 1980): 21.

29. Dr. Christian Barnard, "Freedom—I'm Against It," *Leaders* (Spring 1979): 8–10.

30. In 1885, after *The Adventures of Huckleberry Finn* was published, the public library in Concord, birthplace of American freedom, banned the book on the grounds that it "is of very low grade of morality." A century later, some black leaders wanted it banned from libraries, saying it was "racist trash." Freedom to write and to read collided with freedom to denounce. *Time*, June 10, 1986.

31. These questions were addressed by Herbert McClosky and Alida Brill in *Dimensions of Tolerance: What Americans Believe About Civil Liberties* (New York: Russell Sage Foundation, 1983). Early investigations into possible answers were given in McClosky's famous mid-1960 articles: "Consensus and Ideology in American Politics," *American Political Science Review* 58 (1964): 361–82, and, with John H. Schaar, "Psychological Dimensions of Anomie," *American Sociological Review* 30 (1965): 14–40. For a sharp criticism of McClosky's hypothesis, see Jennifer L. Hochschild, "Dimensions of Liberal Self-Satisfaction: Civil Liberties, Liberal Theory, and Elite-Mass Differences," *Ethics* 96 (January 1986): 386–99. Hochschild accused McClosky and Brill of mixing facts and values in problematic ways:

Conflicting interpretations of the same evidence require us to consider how elites come to be elites. If, as McClosky and Brill sometimes imply, they achieve their status (and tolerance) because they are smarter, more self-confident, and more enlightened than the masses, then we could not hope to transfer tolerance downward even if we did transfer power. In that case, we should thank our lucky stars that merit rises to the top. If, however, the alternative theory that McClosky and Brill ignore is the case—that elites (and masses) achieve their status through birthright, race, sex, or sheer blind luck—and if the theory of social learning is correct, then we have no reason to believe that tolerance cannot be transferred downward, and every reason to transfer power (and therefore tolerance) to the masses." (p. 393)

32.   Herbert Marcuse, "Repressive Tolerance," in Robert Wolff, Barrington Moore, Jr., and Herbert Marcuse, *Pure Tolerance* (Boston: Beacon Press, 1969), 88.

33.   Charles Van Doren, "The Idea of Freedom," *The Great Ideas of Today: Great Ideas of Books of the Western World 1973*, Part II (Chicago: Encyclopaedia Brittanica, 1973), 296. The country's bicentennial sparked a number of symposia. Two scholarly studies were those produced under the auspices of the American Philosophical Society, *Aspects of American Liberty: Philosophical, Historical and Political* (Philadelphia: Independence Square, 1977), and the *Proceedings of the American Catholic Philosophical Association*, vol. 50, ed. George McLean, OMI (Washington: Catholic University of America, 1976),

34   Jacques Maritain, *Freedom in the Modern World*, trans. R.O'Sullivan (New York: Charles Scribners Sons, 1936), 31. Maritain's insights have been enlarged by H. Richard Niebuhr in his brilliant book, *The Responsible Self* (New York: Harper, and Row, 1963).

35.   John Dewey, *Philosophy in Civilization* (New York: Minton, Balch, 1931), 291.

36.   For example, circumstantial freedom does not normally impose honesty, "the beginning point of ethics," but it can create an environment in which dishonesty is sharply discouraged. Ivan Hill, *The Ethical Basis of Freedom* (Chapel Hill, N.C.: The American Viewpoint Inc., 1978), 9.

37.   A.J. Ayer, "Freedom and Necessity," in *Philosophical Essays* (London: Macmillan, 1954), 280.

38.   John Gray, in *Hayek on Liberty* (New York: Basil Blackwell, 1984), provides a brilliant analysis of Hayek, who believes that there is much knowledge in peoples that government social engineers can never capture. Policymakers should, therefore, leave people as much alone as possible—laissez faire.

39.   Avery Dulles, "The Meaning of Freedom in the Church," *Bulletin* 57 (February 1977): 31.

40.   D. Robert Yarnall, Jr., *Can Managers Handle Freedom?* (Henry Robinson Towne Lecture to the American Society of Mechanical Engineers, New York, N.Y. December 15, 1978).

41.   Ronald Dworkin, *Taking Rights Seriously* (Cambridge: Harvard Uni-

versity Press, 1977), 180. See also Henry Shue, *Basic Rights* (Princeton: Princeton University Press, 1980), esp. pp. 13–18.

42. Kenneth C. Davis, *Discretionary Justice: A Preliminary Inquiry* (Baton Rouge, La.: Louisiana State University, 1969), 37. See also his later book, *Discretionary Justice in Europe and America* (Urbana, Ill.: University of Illinois Press, 1976).

43. Glen Robinson, "The Making of Administrative Policy: Another Look at Rulemaking and Adjudication and Administrative Procedure Reform," *University of Pennsylvania Law Review* 118 (1970): 485–539.

44. John Stuart Mill, *On Liberty*, ed. Albert Castell (New York: Appleton-Century-Crofts, 1947), 9. There have been a number of recent useful discussions, including Gerald Dworkin, "Paternalism" in *Morality and the Law*, ed. Richard A. Wasserstrom (Belmont, Calif.: Wadsworth, 1971), 107–26; Joel Feinberg, "Legal Paternalism," *Canadian Journal of Philosophy* 1 (1971): 105–24; N. Fotion, "Paternalism," *Ethics* 89 (1979): 191–98; and Bernard Gert and Charles M. Culver, "Paternalistic Behavior," *Philosophy and Public Affairs* 6 (1976): 45–58.

45. Gerard Elfstrom, "On Dilemmas of Intervention," *Ethics* 93 (July 1983): 709–25.

46. A.T. Nuyen, "Paternalism and Liberty," *Journal of Applied Philosophy* 1 (Spring 1983): 27–37. See also David Miller, "Constraints on Freedom," *Ethics* 94 (October 1983): 66–86; Gerald Dworkin, "Paternalism," *The Monist* 56 (1972): 64–84; and Rosemary Carter, "Justifying Paternalism," *Canadian Journal of Philosophy* 7 (1977): 133–45.

47. Feinberg, *Rights, Justice and the Bounds of Liberty*, 69–70.

48. Daniel Callahan wrote a splendid essay on this point: "Minimalized Ethics," *The Hastings Center Report* (October 1981): 19–25. See also Frithjof Bergmann, *On Being Free* (Notre Dame, Ind.: Notre Dame University Press, 1977), esp. Chap. 2, "Theory of Freedom."

49. *People v. Film Recovery Systems*, 5th Cir. Ct., Cork County, Illinois, June 14, 1985.

CHAPTER 7: THE PERSONAL DIMENSION

1. Committee for Economic Development, *Investing in Our Children: Business and the Public Schools* (New York: CED, 1985), 20.

2. Harvey C. Mansfield, Jr., ed., *Selected Letters of Edmund Burke* (Chicago: University of Chicago Press, 1983). Quoted by Robert Nisbet in "In Love with Politics," *American Scholar* 54 (Winter 1984): 122.

3. Address to the Cosmos Club, Washington, D.C., October 4, 1983.

4. Robert K. Fullinwider, "Civic Education and Traditional Values," *Philosophy and Public Policy* 6 (Summer 1986): 6.

5.   Charles W. Power and David Vogel, *Ethics in the Education of Business Managers* (Hastings-on-Hudson: The Hastings Center, 1981).

6.   Harold J. Leavitt, *Corporate Pathfinders* (Homewood, Ill., Dow Jones–Irwin, 1986), 222–23.

7.   The survey was conducted by Professor William Frederick and James Weber of the University of Pittsburgh and Marilynn Cash Matthews of Washington State University.

8.   L.A. Kosman, "Being Properly Affective: Virtues and Feelings in Aristotle's Ethic," in *Essays on Aristotle's Ethics*, Ed. Amelie Okesenberg Rorty (Berkeley: University of California Press, 1980), 103–16. See also Troels Engberg-Pedersen, *Aristotle's Theory of Moral Insight* (Oxford: Clarendon Press, 1983).

9.   Richard V. Scacchetti, "The Professionalization of Management," *Fairleigh Dickinson Business Review* 6 (Summer 1966): 5.

10.   Warren G. Bennis, "Revisionist Theory of Leadership," *Harvard Business Review* 39 (January-February 1961): 148. See also his *Changing Organizations* (New York: McGraw-Hill, 1966).

11.   Mark T. Lilla, "Ethos, Ethics, and Public Service," *The Public Interest* 63 (Spring 1981): 14. See also Robert Johann, "A Matter of Character," *America* 116 (January 21, 1967): 95.

12.   Christina Hoff Sommers, ed., *Vice and Virtue in Everyday Life* (San Diego: Harcourt Brace Jovanovich, 1985).

13.   Christina Hoff Sommers, "Ethics Without Virtue: Moral Education in America," *American Scholar* 53 (Summer 1984): 382, 387.

14.   Edmund Pincoffs, "Quandary Ethics," *Mind* 80 (1971): 552–71.

15.   Lord Hailsham, "Reflections on a Remark by Cicero: Laws, Ethics and Authority," *Encounter* 56 (February-March 1981): 43.

16.   *Washington Post National Weekly*, May 21, 1984, 25.

17.   Robert Sam Anson, *Exile: The Unquiet Oblivion of Richard M. Nixon* (New York: Simon and Schuster, 1984).

18.   Warren H. Schmidt and Barry Z. Posner, *Managerial Values and Expectations: The Silent Power in Personal and Organizational Life* (New York: American Management Associations, 1982), 55.

19.   This point was emphasized by columnist George Will, who said that virtue is "self-control, respect for other's rights and concern for distant consequences." *Newsweek*, November 11, 1984, 92.

20.   Quoted by M.F. Burnyeat, "Aristotle on Learning to Be Good," in *Essays on Aristotle's Ethics*, ed. Rorty, p. 75.

21.   Ian Buruma, *Behind the Mask* (New York: Pantheon, 1984).

22.   Alasdair MacIntyre, *After Virtue: A Study in Moral Theory* (Notre Dame, Ind.: University of Notre Dame Press, 1981), chap. 14.

23.   Barbara Tuchman, "The March of Folly from Troy to Vietnam" (the Twentieth Cosmos Club Award Address, Washington, D.C., October 4, 1983), 17.

24. *The Autobiography of Benjamin Franklin* (New York: Basic Books, n.d.), 102–3.

25. John S. Gillis, *Too Tall, Too Small* (Champaign, Ill.: Institute for Personality and Ability Testing Inc., 1982).

26. Stanley Hauerwas, *Vision and Virtue: Essays on Christian Ethical Reflections* (Notre Dame, Ind.: University of Notre Dame Press, 1981), 69.

27. Thomas De Quincey, "On Murder Considered as One of the Fine Arts," in Edward Bulwer-Lytton and Thomas De Quincey, *The Arts of Cheating, Swindling and Murder* (Westport, Conn.: Hyperion Press, 1975), 141.

28. Judith N. Shklar, *Ordinary Vices* (Cambridge: Harvard University Press, 1984).

29. Will Durant, *The Mansions of Philosophy* (New York: Simon and Schuster, 1929), 264–65.

30. W.B. Yeats, *Autobiographies* (London: Macmillan, 1955), 11–12.

31. Stanley Hauerwas, *Vision and Virtue*, 62.

32. Maimonides, "Laws Concerning Character Traits," in *Ethical Writings of Maimonides*, ed. Raymond L. Weiss (New York: Dover Publications, 1973), 46–7.

33. Josef Pieper, *The Four Cardinal Virtues* (New York: Harcourt, Brace and World, 1965), 3.

34. Goetz Briefs, "The Ethos Problem in the Present Pluralistic Society," *Review of Social Economy* 41 (December 1983): 275.

35. *New York Review of Books*, November 24, 1983, p. 14. See also Rosemary Radford Ruether, "Courage Is a Christian Virtue," *Cross Currents* 32 (Spring 1983): 8–16.

36. Author's conversation with Stanley Teele in the summer of 1955.

37. Harold Leavitt, *Corporate Pathfinders* (Homewood, Ill.: Dow Jones–Irwin, 1986), 95.

38. Ira Goldberg, "Temperance and Economic Assumptions," *The Forum for Social Economics* (Fall 1983): 35–50. See also Joan Robinson, *Economic Heresies: Some Old-Fashioned Questions in Economic Theory* (London: Macmillan, 1971).

39. Alan Donagan, *The Theory of Morality* (Chicago: University of Chicago Press, 1977), 6.

40. C.E. Huber, *The Promise and Perils of Business Ethics* (Washington, D.C.: Association of American Colleges, 1979), 1. John Edward Sullivan, O.P., said that among philosophical subjects "religion is surely the most controversial." *The Great Ideas Today, 1977* (Chicago: Encyclopaedia Brittanica, 1978), 206.

41. Jakob J. Petuchowski, "The Dialectics of Reason and Revelation" in *Rediscovering Judaism*, ed. Arnold Jacob Wolf (Chicago: Quadrangle Books, 1965), 30–37.

42. Ephraim E. Urbach, *The Sages* (Jerusalem: Magnes Press of the Hebrew

University, 1975). Since human life revealed all sorts of strange vicissitudes and inconsistencies, it is not surprising that the Talmud, at times, reflects such inconsistencies. One Jewish scholar said, "Whatever the faults of the rabbis were, consistency was not one of them." Solomon Schechter, *Aspects of Rabbinic Theology* (New York: Schocken Books, 1961), 64.

43.   Maimonides, "Laws Concerning Character Traits," 46.

44.   National Conference of Catholic Bishops, Washington, D.C., *Origins* 14 (November 15, 1984): 338–39.

45.   Compare Thomas E. Legere, *Thoughts on the Run* (Minneapolis, Minn.: Winston Press, 1983), with Abraham Maslow, *Religions, Values, and Peak Experiences* (Columbus: Ohio State University Press, 1964), 54.

46.   Garth L. Hallett, *Christian Moral Reasoning: An Analytic Guide* (Notre Dame, Ind.: University of Notre Dame, 1982), 221. One of this author's theories is that humans must recognize that they live in two intimately related yet distinct worlds (spiritual and secular) and therefore must participate in both. Striking a similar theme is Louis Lavelle, "L'existence des Deux Mondes," *Revue Philosophique de Louvain*, 81 (February 1983): 5–36.

47.   James Gustafson, *Say Something Theological* (Chicago: University of Chicago Press, 1981).

48.   Stanley Hauerwas, *A Community of Character: Toward a Constructive Christian Social Ethic* (Notre Dame, Ind.: University of Notre Dame Press, 1981), esp. pp. 145–150.

49.   James M. Gustafson, *Can Ethics Be Christian?* (Chicago: University of Chicago Press, 1975), Chap. 4. See also Donagan, *The Theory of Morality*, Chap. 2.

50.   E.F. Schumacher, *A Guide for the Perplexed* (New York: Harper and Row, 1977), 51.

51.   Parker J. Palmer, *To Know as We Are Known: A Spirituality of Education* (New York: Harper and Row, 1983), xi.

52.   James M. Gustafson, *Ethics from a Theocentric Perspective*, vol. 1 of *Theology and Ethics* (Chicago: University of Chicago Press, 1981).

53.   John C. Haughey, S.J., *The Holy Uses of Money: Personal Finance in the Light of Christian Faith* (New York: Doubleday, 1986).

54.   Gustafson, *Can Ethics Be Christian?* pp. 100–101.

55.   T.R. Martin, ed., *Stewardship: The Corporation and the Individual* (New York: KCG Productions, 1983), esp. chaps. 1, 7, and 8.

56.   Gustafson, *Can Ethics Be Christian?* p. 106.

57.   Max L. Stackhouse, "An Ecumenist's Plea for a Public Theology," *This World* (Spring-Summer 1984): 64.

58.   Charles S. McCoy, *Management of Values: The Ethical Differences in Corporate Policy and Performance* (Boston: Pitman, 1985), 223–26.

59.   John Roth, ed., *The Philosophy of Josiah Royce* (New York: Thomas Y.

Crowell, 1971), 278–79. Kenneth Goodpaster made Royce's point on loyalty a central theme in his brief analysis of business ethics: "Loyalty: Separating the Selfish from the Morally Mature," *Dallas Morning News*, June 21, 1981, p. 4D.

60. Hallett, *Christian Moral Reasoning*, 109. See esp. the excellent Chap. 6, "Christian Criteria of Right and Wrong."

61. Ralph Henry Gabriel, *The Course of American Democratic Thought: An Intellectual History Since 1815* (New York: Ronald Press, 1940), v. It is this need to relate religious reasoning to other forms of reasoning that has intrigued David Tracy in his brilliant and controversial book, *Blessed Rage for Order: The New Pluralism in Theology* (New York: Seabury Press, 1975). For an effective summary of Tracy's position (and its critics), see Jesse Nash, "Tracy's Revisionist Project: Some Fundamental Issues," *American Benedictine Review* 34 (September 1983): 240–67.

62. A. Ohmann, "Skyhooks: With Special Implications for Monday Through Friday." Originally published in 1955, the article has been given continued circulation in *The Harvard Business Review: On Human Relations* (New York: Harper and Row, 1979), Chap. 26.

63. James C. Worthy, *Shaping an American Institution: Robert E. Wood and Sears Roebuck* (Urbana: University of Illinois Press, 1984).

64. James C. Worthy, "Religion and Its Role in the World of Business," *Journal of Business of the University of Chicago* 31 (October 1959): 293–303. The point was made more specific by Steven S. Schwarzchild, who wrote: "Ethics means that there are values and standards beyond man. . . . If we are lucky, the atheists, like Marx and Camus, will create their own values which largely coincide with those of authentic biblical religion. But if we are unlucky—and that is at least equally possible—the atheists like de Sade, Alfred Rosenberg, Stalin, etc., will create ethical monstrosities." Steven S. Schwarzchild, "A Little Bit of Revolution," in *The Secular City Debate*, ed. Daniel Callahan (New York: Macmillan, 1966), 152.

65. Donald Siebert, "Time to Revive a Commitment to Ethics," *New York Times*, December 25, 1983.

66. Lincoln Electric Company annual report 1966, p. 88.

67. J. Irwin Miller, "How Religious Commitments Shape Corporate Decisions," *Harvard Divinity Bulletin* (February-March 1984): 4–7.

68. Dale D. Simmons, *Personal Valuing* (Chicago: Nelson-Hall, 1982), esp. Chap. 3, "Content and Organization of Value Systems."

69. George Herbert Mead, *Mind, Self and Society* (Chicago: University of Chicago Press, 1934), and Jean Piaget, *The Moral Judgment of the Child* (New York: Free Press, 1932). Piaget's views have been carefully presented by Margaret A. Boden in her fine introduction, *Piaget* (Brighton, England: Harvester Press, 1983).

70. Among Kohlberg's many contributions are the following: "Moral Development," in *International Encyclopedia of Social Sciences* (New York: Crowell, Collier, Macmillan, 1968); "Education for Justice: A Modern Statement of the Platonic View," in *Moral Education*, ed. R. Mosher (Cambridge: Harvard University Press, 1969); "From Is to Ought: How to Commit the Naturalistic Fallacy and Get Away with It in the Study of Moral Development," in *Cognitive Development and Epistemology*, ed. T. Mischel (New York: Academic Press, 1971), 151–235; "Stages of Moral Development as a Basis for Moral Education," in *Moral Education: Interdisciplinary Approaches,* ed. C.M. Beck, B.S. Crittenden, and E.V. Sullivan (Toronto: University of Toronto Press, 1971), 23–92; and *Collected Papers on Moral Development and Moral Education* (Cambridge: Center for Moral Education, Harvard University, 1973).

71. For a detailed analysis of Kohlberg's and, to a lesser degree, Piaget's approach, see Hugh Rosen, *The Development of Sociomoral Knowledge: A Cognitive-Structural Approach* (New York: Columbia University Press, 1980).

72. Michael S. Pritchard, "Stages of Moral Development: A Critique of Kohlberg" (unpublished essay, Western Michigan University, Kalamazoo, 1982). See also John Benson, "Who Is the Autonomous Man?" *Journal of the Philosophy of Religion* 58 (January 1983): 1–13. Two fine in-depth studies are those by Robert Kegan, *The Evolving Self: Problem and Process in Human Development* (Cambridge: Harvard University Press, 1982), and Gilbert C. Meilaender, Jr., *The Theory and Practice of Virtue* (Notre Dame, Ind.: University of Notre Dame Press, 1984). Meilaender, incidentally, offers one of the best analyses of the opportunities and risks inherent in all efforts to teach virtue.

73. On this point, see the perceptive assessment by Kenneth Goodpaster, "Kohlbergian Theory: The Philosophical Counter-Invitation," *Ethics* (April 1982): 491–98.

74. Nicholas Emler, Stanley Renwick, and Bernadette Malone, "The Relationship Between Moral Reasoning and Political Orientation," *Journal of Personality and Social Psychology* 5 (November 1983): 1073–80.

75. James Fowler, ed., *Toward Moral and Religious Maturity: First International Conference on Moral and Religious Development* (Morristown, N.J.: Silver Burdett, 1980), 61. See also Gerald Dworkin, "Moral Autonomy," in *Morals, Science and Sociality,* ed. H. Tristram Engelhardt and Daniel Callahan (Hastings-on-Hudson: The Hastings Center, 1978), 156–71. Dworkin says that "it is only through a more adequate understanding of notions such as tradition, authority, commitment, and loyalty, and of the forms of human community in which these have their roots, that we shall be able to develop a conception of autonomy free from paradox and worthy of admiration" (170). But

the force of modernity makes the individual "a law unto himself" and thus free from history.

76.   Robert S. Michaelsen, *The American Search for Soul* (Baton Rouge: Louisiana State University Press, 1975), 107.

77.   Sommers, *Vice and Virtue*, p. 385.

78.   *Ethics Resource Center Report* (Washington, D.C.) 2 (summer 1985): 1, 4–5. Efforts by various professors and organizations to develop better ethical understanding of organizational problems have been traced by Ivan Hill, ed., *The Ethical Bases of Economic Freedom* (Chapel Hill, N.C.: American Viewpoint Inc., 1976), esp. parts 2 and 3.

79.   See Sigmund Freud's 1925 paper, "Some Psychical Consequences of the Anatomical Distinction Between the Sexes," *The Standard Edition of the Complete Works of Freud*, ed. James Strachey (London: Hogarth Press, 1961) 19: 248–51, 257–58. Rounded pictures of Freud's approach are found in Frank J. Sulloway, *Freud: Biologist of the Mind* (New York: Basic Books, 1979); Paul Roazen, *Freud: Political and Social Thought* (New York: Alfred A. Knopf, 1968); and in the short piece by Robert R. Holt, "Freud's Impact on Modern Morality," *Hastings Center Report* 10 (April 1980): 38–45.

80.   Quoted in William F. Whyte, "Culture and Work," in *Culture and Management: Text and Readings in Comparative Management*, ed. Ross Webber (Homewood, Ill.: Richard D. Irwin, 1969), 31. The "effective manager" is expected to remove all behavioral traits that are associated with the "feminine" in American culture, according to R. Loring and T. Wells in *Breakthrough: Women in Management* (New York: Van Nostrand Reinhold, 1972), 92.

81.   Georgia Sassen, "Success Anxiety in Women: A Constructivist Interpretation of Its Source and Its Significance," *Harvard Educational Review* 50 (1980): 13–24. Sassen suggests that women have a heightened perception of the emotional and moral costs of success as defined in male terms. Relevant is the article by K.I. Spenner and D.L. Featherman, "Achievement Ambitions," *Annual Review of Sociology* 4 (1978): 373–420, which provides a marvelous review of the literature from sociological perspectives.

82.   In another important study, male managers were found to perceive (1) the presence of women in the organization as creating difficult social interactions, (2) that women were less able to cope with crises than men, and (3) that other men and women would prefer to have male supervisors and would be uncomfortable with a woman superior. Bernard M. Bass, Judith Crusell, and Ralph A. Alexander, "Male Managers' Attitudes Toward Working Women," *American Behavioral Scientist* 15 (November-December 1971): 221–36, and Debra Kaufmann and Michael Fetters, "The Executive Suite: Are Women Per-

ceived as Ready for the Managerial Climb?" *Journal of Business* 11 (1983): 211.

83. Carol Gilligan, *In Different Voice* (Cambridge: Harvard University Press, 1982), 174–75. Her first insights were presented many years ago in an essay, "The Adolescent as a Philosopher: The Discovery of Self in a Postconventional World," *Daedalus* (Fall 1971): 1051–84. Christopher Lasch concluded his study by noting how "caring capacity" as expressed in gratitude, remorse, and forgiveness enables individuals to transcend their selfishness and thereby grow morally. Christopher Lasch, *The Minimal Self: Psychic Survival in Troubled Times* (New York: W.W. Norton, 1984).

84. Carol Coston, "Circles in the Water: Style and Spirit of Feminine Leadership," *New Catholic World* (March-April 1985): 90. This contrasts sharply with the findings of the Schmidt-Posner survey for the American Management Associations, wherein, among personal qualities generally admired in the workplace, caring and forgiveness ranked near the bottom of the scale. *Managerial Values*, p. 34.

85. Richard S. Ruch and Ronald Goodman, *Image at the Top: Crisis and Renaissance in Corporate Leadership* (New York: Free Press/Macmillan, 1983), 58.

86. Unpublished paper presented to the Trinity Church Center/American Management Associations Conference on Ethics, New York City, March 29, 1984.

87. Donagan, *The Theory of Morality*, pp. 131–41. See also Ronald M. Green, *Religious Reason: The Rational and Moral Basis of Religious Belief* (New York: Oxford University Press, 1978), Chap. 6. One female theologian brought the argument full circle by writing that the "unconditional claims that go beyond the external force of sanctions to the internal force of conscience . . . is where morality is found." Monika Hellwig, *Understanding Catholicism* (New York: Paulist Press, 1981), 186.

88. Louis C. Gawthrop, *Public Sector Management, Systems and Ethics* (Bloomington: University of Indiana Press, 1984), 161 et seq.

CHAPTER 8: THE ORGANIZATIONAL DIMENSION

1. P. Ranganath Nayak and John M. Ketteringhiam, *Break-Throughs* (New York: Rawson Associates, 1986), 233.

2. See Niklas Luchman, *Trust and Power* (New York: John Wiley, 1980), and Bernard Barber, *The Logic and Limits of Trust* (New Brunswick, N.J.: Rutgers University Press, 1983).

3. Compare Clarence C. Walton, *Corporate Social Responsibilities* (Belmont, Calif.: Wadsworth, 1968), and Archie B. Carroll, *Business and Society: Managing Corporate Social Performance* (Boston: Little, Brown, 1981), Chap. 2.

4. Albert D. Chandler, Jr., *The Visible Hand* (Cambridge, Mass.: Harvard University/Belknap Press, 1977).

5. A.A. Berle, Jr., and Gardiner Means, *The Modern Corporation and Private Property* (New York: Macmillan, 1932), esp. Book II. For fifty years a debate has raged over whether diffusion of ownership does, in fact, adversely affect the drive to profit maximization, and one of the latest empirical studies suggests that this may not be the case. Harold Demetz and Kenneth Lehn, "The Structure of Corporate Ownership: Causes and Consequences," *Journal of Political Economy* 93 (December 1985): 1155–77. The authors conclude that "catering to amenity potential *is* maximizing owner *utility* if not owner profit. Such maximization hardly constitutes evidence of a separation between ownership and control" (p. 1176).

6. Robert F. Allen, "The Ik in the Office—and in Our Schools, Factories, Hospitals, Churches, Government Agencies and Communities" (unpublished paper), 10–11. Cleveland, OH.: Robert F. Allen Associates Inc. Italics added. See also Charles T. Hutchinson's thoughtful essay, "Prospectives for Corporate Leadership," *Business Horizons* 26 (November–December 1983): 32–36.

7. *San Jose Business Journal*, January 21, 1985, p. 5.

8. Peter Megargee Brown, "A Lawyer Criticizes Lawyers," *New York Times*, January 7, 1984.

9. *Saturday Review*, November 11, 1975, 10–12.

10. Claire Makin, "Ranking Corporate Reputations," *Fortune*, January 10, 1983, 34–51. IBM's right to those laurels has been sharply challenged by Richard T. De Lamater in *Big Blue: IBM's Use and Abuse of Power* (New York: Dodd, Mead, 1986).

11. Thomas J. Peters and Robert H. Waterman, Jr., *In Search of Excellence: Lessons from America's Best-Run Companies* (New York: Harper and Row, 1982), 11–13.

12. *Council of Independent Colleges Report* (May 1984): 5. Relevant to the issue of value orientations in nonprofits is the essay by James A. Donahue, "Religious Institutions and Moral Agents: Toward an Ethics of Organizational Character" in *Labor Management Dialogue: Church Perspectives*, ed. Adam J. Maida (St. Louis: The Catholic Health Associations of the United States, 1982), 147.

13. Stafford Beer, *The Heart of the Enterprise* (New York: John Wiley and Sons, 1980), xii, 3, 309.

14. Fernando Bartolome and Andre Laurent "The Manager: Master and

Servant of Power," *Harvard Business Review* 64 (November–December 1986): 77–81.

15. Tom Zito, "The Bang Behind the Bucks and the Life Behind the Style," *Newsweek*, special issue, Fall 1984, 24.

16. James C. Worthy, *Shaping an American Institution: Robert E. Wood and Sears Roebuck* (Urbana: University of Illinois Press, 1984), xiv.

17. Alasdair C. MacIntyre, *After Virtue: The Study of Moral Theory* (Notre Dame, Ind.: University of Notre Dame Press, 1981), 72. Originally published in London by Duckworth, c. 1981.

18. Norman Lear, "Short-Term Thinking and the Decline in Values," *New Oxford Review* (September 1986): 18.

19. Max Weber felt that organizations, to be efficient, must have a hierarchal structure based on legal and formal authority that would then guide all employees to behave according to a set of rational rules and regulations. *Economy and Society* (New York: Bedminster Press, 1968). See also Frederick Taylor, *The Principles of Scientific Management* (New York: Harper Bros., 1911), and Henry Fayol, *General and Industrial Management*, trans. Constance Storrs (London: Pitman and Sons, 1949).

20. David Nelson, *Managers and Workers: Origins of the Factory System in the United States, 1880–1920* (Madison: University of Wisconsin Press, 1975), 34–46. For a good review of bureaucracy's origins, see Douglas E. Booth, "The Problems of Corporate Bureaucracy and the Producer Cooperative as an Alternative," *Review of Social Economy* 43 (December 1980): 298–324.

21. Robert A. Frosch, "Improving American Innovation," *Technological Innovation in the Eighties: The American Assembly* (Englewood Cliffs, N.J.: Prentice Hall, 1983), Chap. 3, and J.A. Waters, "Catch 20.5: Corporate Morality as an Organization Phenomenon," *Organizational Dynamics* (Spring 1981): 219.

22. Robert Jackall, "Moral Mazes: Bureaucracy and Managerial Work," *Harvard Business Review* 61 (September–October 1983): 121. Economist William Dugger has argued that while the corporation is an efficient organization, it is driven to build large bureaucracies whose maintenance deprives investors of a fair return and consumers of a fair price. Bureaucracy also has the pernicious effect of encouraging "homosocial reproduction," that is, promoting only those who fit the bureaucratic mode. William M. Dugger, *An Alternative to Economic Retrenchment* (New York: Petrocelli Books, 1984), Part II, "Reforming the Corporation." That bureaucracy works to destroy people in their psychological growth is a thesis advanced by Robert Howard in *Brave New Workplace* (New York: Viking Press, 1985), 118–30.

23. Reinhold Niebuhr, "A Critique of Pacificism," *Atlantic Monthly* 139 (May 1927): 639.

24.   David Rubenstein and Richard W. Woodman, "Spiderman and the Burma Raiders: Collateral Organization Theory in Action," *Journal of Applied Behavioral Sciences* 20 (1984): 1–16.

25.   Giorgio Inzerilli and Michael Rosen, "Culture and Organization Control," *Journal of Business Research* 11 (1983): 286. The authors provide an excellent summary of the literature on organizational cultures. Also relevant is Marshall Sashkin, "Participative Management Is an Ethical Imperative," *Organizational Dynamics* (Spring 1984): 16–17.

26.   T.H. Marshall, *Citizenship and Social Class* (Cambridge: Cambridge University Press, 1950), 28–29.

27.   William M. Evan, *Organization Theory: Structure Systems and Environments* (New York: John Wiley and Son, 1976).

28.   This theme is persuasively argued by Michael Walzer in *Spheres of Justice* (New York: Basic Books, 1983).

29.   Jay W. Forrester, "A New Corporate Design," *Industrial Management Review* 7 (Fall 1965): 5.

30.   Edward S. Herman, *Corporate Control, Corporate Power* (Cambridge: Cambridge University Press, 1981), 301.

31.   Michael O'Connor, "The Importance of an Organziational Philosophy," *Arthur Andersen Review* 1 (Spring 1984): 13–14.

32.   Ibid.

33.   W. Michael Hoffman, "Developing the Ethical Corporation," *Bell Atlantic Review* 3 (Spring 1986): 33.

34.   Viktor Frankl, *Man's Search for Meaning* (New York: Washington Square Press, 1963), 158.

35.   Elizabeth M. Fowler, "Exploring Corporate Culture," *New York Times*, February 8, 1984.

36.   Allan Cox, *The Cox Report on the American Corporation* (New York: Delacorte Press, 1982). See also the pattern followed at Procter and Gamble.

37.   Terence E. Deal and Allan A. Kennedy, *Corporate Cultures: The Rites and Rituals of Corporate Life* (Reading, Mass.: Addison-Wesley, 1982), 27.

38.   John Maurice Clark, *Economic Institutions and Human Welfare* (New York: Alfred A. Knopf, 1957), 33.

39.   Thomas J. Watson, Jr., *A Business and Its Beliefs* (New York: McGraw-Hill, 1963), 5–6.

40.   W. Harvey Hegarty and Henry P. Sims, Jr., "Organizational Philosophy, Policies and Objectives Related to Unethical Decision Behavior: A Laboratory Experiment," *Journal of Applied Psychology* 64 (1979): 331–38.

41.   Chester Barnard, *The Functions of the Executive* (Cambridge: Harvard University Press, 1960), 293.

42. Mary Parker Follett, *Creative Experience* (Boston: Longmans, Green and Company, 1924), 63.

43. Douglas McGregor, *The Human Side of Enterprise* (New York: McGraw-Hill, 1985, anniversary edition).

44. Rensis Likert, *Human Organization: Its Management and Value* (New York: McGraw-Hill, 1967). See the results of the experiment reported by Ross A. Webber in *Management: Basic Elements of Managing Organizations* (Homewood, Ill.: Richard D. Irwin, 1975), Chap. 9.

45. William J. Byron, "Christianity and Capitalism: Three Concepts from the Tradition, Three Challenges to the System," *Review of Social Economy* 11 (December 1982): 316.

46. Richard Eells, *The Government of Corporation* (New York: Free Press/Macmillan, 1962), 231–32.

47. Bowen McCoy, "Saddhu Revisited" (paper presented at a symposium sponsored by the Trinity Center on Ethics and Corporate Policy, New York City, March 1984).

48. Manfred Kets de Vries and Danny Miller, *The Neurotic Organization: Diagnosing Changing Counter-Productive Styles of Management* (San Francisco: Jossey-Bass Publishers, 1984).

49. Council on Economic Priorities, *Rating America's Corporate Conscience* (New York: Council on Economic Priorities, 1987).

50. *New York Times*, July 8, 1970.

51. Johnson and Johnson, *Our Credo*, n.d.

52. Pilar Dilidas, "Profiting by Good Design," *Interiors* (March 1981): 112.

53. *Fortune*, June 15, 1981.

54. *Philadelphia Inquirer*, April 20, 1984, p. 11C.

POSTSCRIPT

1. Karl Llewelyn, *Bramble Bush: On Law and Its Study* (Dobbs Ferry, N.Y.: Oceana Publications, 1960). Ralph Waldo Emerson put a different and less favorable interpretation on theorists when he wrote:

An intellectual man discusses ethical and philanthropic questions with great coolness from hour to hour and from year to year; the process is very pleasant to him; he is not tired, for he is flattered alike by your opposition, which he can presently vanquish, and by our silence which is a secret compliment to his power. Everybody is tired but him; and why should he be weary, since his presence is a perpetual victory? (A. W. Plumstead and Harrison Hayford, eds., *The Journals and Miscellaneous Notebooks of Ralph Waldo Emerson* [Cambridge: Harvard University/Belknap Press, 1969], 473.)

2. Llewelyn, *Bramble Bush*.
3. Alfred North Whitehead, *The Aims of Education and Other Essays* (London: Williams and Norgate, 1932), 53, 95.
4. Richard Levering et al., *The Best 100 Companies in America to Work For* (Reading, Mass.: Addison-Wesley, 1984). The best seek to promote virtue in every employee (p. x).
5. Quoted by Thomas Horton, president of the American Management Association, in *What Works for Me: Sixteen CEOs Talk About Their Careers and Commitments* (New York: Random House, 1986), 35.

INDEX

ABOUT THE AUTHOR

Clarence C. Walton is widely recognized as a pioneer in the field of business ethics. His first book, in 1964, *Ethos and the Executive*, was awarded the James Hamilton prize for excellence and his *Conceptual Foundations of Business*, written with Richard Eells, won a McKinsey prize. Since that time he has continued to write highly regarded books and articles on corporate morality. Walton's scholarship has been enriched by managerial experiences as Associate Dean of Columbia's School of General Studies and the Philip Young Professor. In 1969 he became president of the Catholic University of America in Washington where he served until 1978 before resuming teaching and research. He recently retired from his position as C. Lamont Post Distinguished Professor at The American College.

Dr. Walton has conducted seminars in ethics for many large corporations, served as a director on five corporate boards and a trustee of many nonprofit organizations. He chaired panels on nonpublic education for the federal government and on fair housing for the Commonwealth of Pennsylvania. His academic awards include fifteen honorary degrees, the Beta Gamma Sigma designation for outstanding contributions to the study of business, the Sumner Marcus medal for scholarly contributions to the field of business and society, and the Solomon Huebner gold medal for his work in the area of ethics for financial services.